PSYCHOLOGY
AND TORTURE

THE SERIES IN CLINICAL AND COMMUNITY PSYCHOLOGY

CONSULTING EDITORS
Charles D. Spielberger and Irwin G. Sarason

Auerbach and Stolberg Crisis Intervention with Children and Families
Burchfield Stress: Psychological and Physiological Interactions
Burstein and Loucks Rorschach's Test: Scoring and Interpretation
Cohen and Ross Handbook of Clinical Psychobiology and Pathology, volume 1
Cohen and Ross Handbook of Clinical Psychobiology and Pathology, volume 2
Diamant Male and Female Homosexuality: Psychological Approaches
Froehlich, Smith, Draguns, and Hentschel Psychological Processes in Cognition and Personality
Hobfoll Stress, Social Support, and Women
Janisse Pupillometry: The Psychology of the Pupillary Response
Krohne and Laux Achievement, Stress, and Anxiety
London Personality: A New Look at Metatheories
London The Modes and Morals of Psychotherapy, Second Edition
Manschreck and Kleinman Renewal in Psychiatry: A Critical Rational Perspective
Morris Extraversion and Introversion: An Interactional Perspective
Muñoz Depression Prevention: Research Directions
Olweus Aggression in the Schools: Bullies and Whipping Boys
Reitan and Davison Clinical Neuropsychology: Current Status and Applications
Rickel, Gerrard, and Iscoe Social and Psychological Problems of Women: Prevention and Crisis Intervention
Rofé Repression and Fear: A New Approach to the Crisis in Psychotherapy
Smoll and Smith Psychological Perspectives in Youth Sports
Spielberger and Diaz-Guerrero Cross-Cultural Anxiety, volume 1
Spielberger and Diaz-Guerrero Cross-Cultural Anxiety, volume 2
Spielberger and Diaz-Guerrero Cross-Cultural Anxiety, volume 3
Spielberger and Sarason Stress and Anxiety, volume 1
Sarason and Spielberger Stress and Anxiety, volume 2
Sarason and Spielberger Stress and Anxiety, volume 3
Spielberger and Sarason Stress and Anxiety, volume 4
Spielberger and Sarason Stress and Anxiety, volume 5
Sarason and Spielberger Stress and Anxiety, volume 6
Sarason and Spielberger Stress and Anxiety, volume 7
Spielberger, Sarason, and Milgram Stress and Anxiety, volume 8
Spielberger, Sarason, and Defares Stress and Anxiety, volume 9
Spielberger and Sarason Stress and Anxiety, volume 10: A Sourcebook of Theory and Research
Spielberger, Sarason, and Defares Stress and Anxiety, volume 11
Spielberger, Sarason, and Strelau Stress and Anxiety, volume 12
Strelau, Farley, and Gale The Biological Bases of Personality and Behavior, volume 1: Theories, Measurement Techniques, and Development
Strelau, Farley, and Gale The Biological Bases of Personality and Behavior, volume 2: Psychophysiology, Performance, and Applications
Suedfeld Psychology and Torture
Ulmer On the Development of a Token Economy Mental Hospital Treatment Program
Williams and Westermeyer Refugee Mental Health in Resettlement Countries

IN PREPARATION

Diamant Homosexual Issues in the Workplace
Reisman A History of Clinical Psychology
Savin-Williams Gay and Lesbian Youth: Expressions of Identity
Spielberger and Diaz-Guerrero Cross-Cultural Anxiety, volume 4
Spielberger and Vagg The Assessment and Treatment of Test Anxiety

PSYCHOLOGY AND TORTURE

Edited by

Peter Suedfeld
University of British Columbia

⬤HEMISPHERE PUBLISHING CORPORATION
A member of the Taylor & Francis Group
New York   Washington   Philadelphia   London

PSYCHOLOGY AND TORTURE

1 2 3 4 5 6 7 8 9 0   B R B R   8 9 8 7 6 5 4 3 2 1 0 9

This book was set in Times Roman by Hemisphere Publishing Corporation. The editors were Amy Lyles Wilson, Todd W. Baldwin, and Deanna D'Errico; the production supervisor was Peggy M. Rote; and the typesetters were Anahid Alvandian, Bonnie Sciano, and Lori Knoernschild.
Cover design by Debra Eubanks Riffe.
Braun-Brumfield, Inc. was printer and binder.

A CIP catalog record for this book is available from the British Library.

Library of Congress Cataloging-in-Publication Data

Psychology and torture / editor, Peter Suedfeld.
    p.   cm. — (The Series in clinical and community psychology)

    Includes bibliographical references.

    1. Torture—Psychological aspects. 2. Torture victims—Counseling of. I. Suedfeld, Peter, date. II. Series.

HV8593.P79 1990   89-39732
158'.3—dc20   CIP
ISBN 0-89116-976-8
ISSN 0146-0846

The editor dedicates this book to **Raoul Wallenberg** who, during his term as Swedish Consul in Budapest (1944–45), saved tens of thousands of Jews from being exterminated by the German and Hungarian governments. Escaping from Nazi death squads in 1945, he "disappeared" during the Soviet occupation of Hungary. After repeated denials, the government of the USSR finally admitted that he had been held as a political prisoner in that country, but claimed that he had died in 1957. However, eyewitnesses reported that he was still alive and imprisoned as late as 1975. His fate has yet to be disclosed. As a valiant and selfless fighter against one system of torture and death, and tragic victim of another, he stands to the world as a symbol of millions of other resisters and sufferers.

Contents

II
PSYCHOLOGY'S RESPONSE TO TORTURE

The original manuscripts for chapters 1, 2, and 9 form the Report of the American Psychological Association's Subcommittee on Psychological Concerns Related to Torture.

Contributors

JACQUELINE C. BOUHOUTSOS, who received her PhD with highest honors from the University of Innsbruck (Austria), is a professor of clinical psychology at the University of California: Los Angeles and maintains a private clinical practice in Los Angeles. She has chaired the American Psychological Association's Committee on International Relations in Psychology and was instrumental in the establishment of the Division of Media Psychology. Among her other professional interests are psychology-related media activities and the development of ethics procedures and issues. A Fellow of the APA (Division of Clinical Psychology), she is coauthor of *Sexual Intimacy Between Therapists and Patients,* as well as of many book chapters and articles. *Address:* 228 Santa Monica Blvd., Santa Monica, CA 90401.

ENRIQUE BUSTOS, a Chilean by birth, studied political science in that country and became a political refugee in Sweden in 1973. He received his MSc in psychology from the University of Stockholm and has worked in Copenhagen at the International Rehabilitation and Research Center for Torture Victims and the OASIS Center for Treatment and Counseling of Refugees, which he helped establish. At present, he conducts a private practice in Stockholm, acts as consultant to OASIS and other refugee-oriented institutions in Scandinavia, and works part-time at the Refugee Department of the Swedish Red Cross. His major area of publication and conference participation is the treatment of victims of organized violence. *Address:* Fleminggatan 56, 1 tr S-112 45, Stockholm, Sweden.

BARBARA CHESTER has her PhD in behavioral genetics from the University of Minnesota and has served as a teacher, trainer, and consultant in the United States and abroad in universities, prisons, human service organizations, governmental bodies, and corporations. The author of one book and several articles on the issue of individual and social violence, she is currently the Clinical Director of the Center for Victims of Torture in Minneapolis. *Address:* Center for Victims of Torture, 722 Fulton St. SE, Minneapolis, MN 55414.

RAINA E. EBERLY obtained her PhD at the University of Minnesota and is currently a staff psychologist and Director of Internship Training at the Veterans Administration Medical Center in Minneapolis, as well as a clinical assistant professor at the University of Minnesota. Her research activities have focused on adjustment and rehabilitation, most recently of former prisoners of war. *Address:* VA Medical Center, 1 Veterans Dr., Minneapolis, MN 55417.

BRIAN E. ENGDAHL has a PhD in counseling psychology from the University of Minnesota, where he currently serves as a clinical assistant professor of psychology as well as being Chief of the Counseling Psychology Section of the Minneapolis Veterans Administration Medical Center. He is a member of the Treatment Committee at the Center for Victims of Torture. His research interests include the adjustment of former prisoners of war, personality predictors of subsequent disease, and computerized adaptive psychological assessment. *Address:* VA Medical Center, 1 Veterans Dr., Minneapolis, MN 55417.

STEPHEN V. FARAONE, who has a PhD from the University of Iowa, works as a clinical psychologist at the Veterans Administration Medical Center in Brockton, MA. He is also an instructor of psychiatry at the Harvard Medical School and has published in a variety of areas ranging from statistical methods to the etiology of major psychiatric disorders. He has a longstanding interest in mental health issues related to human rights and has been very active with the Amnesty International Health Professional Network. Some of his work on this topic has appeared in *American Psychologist* and the *Journal of the American Medical Association. Address:* Psychology Service (116A), VA Medical Center, Brockton, MA 02401.

JANICE T. GIBSON received an EdD from the University of Virginia and is a professor of developmental psychology and Associate Dean of Academic Affairs and Research in the School of Education at the University of Pittsburgh. She has also been a Fulbright Research Professor in Greece (twice), a National Academy of Sciences Research Exchange Scientist in the Soviet Union and a Visiting Fellow at the Kennan Institute of Advanced Russian Studies in the Woodrow Wilson International Center, Washington, DC. She has published 12 books and numerous research articles in the area of human development. *Address:* Office of the Dean, School of Education, University of Pittsburgh, Pittsburgh, PA 15260.

STEVEN B. KENNEDY was Director of the International Affairs Office at the American Psychological Association until December 1988. From 1980, he coordinated the Association's international human rights efforts. He received his MA in international relations from Yale University. As a principal in a Washington editorial and publication services firm, he now works as a writer, editor, and translator. He is coauthor of *Latin American Psychology: A Guide to Research and Training* (published by the APA in 1987), and of "Psychology and Health: Contributions of Psychology to the Improvement of Health and Health Care" (*Bulletin of the World Health Organization,* 1987). *Address:* 20106 Seabreeze Ct., Germantown, MD 20814.

MICHAEL LEVIN, a professor of philosophy at the City College and Graduate Center of the City University of New York, obtained his PhD at Columbia University. His major books include *Feminism and Freedom* and *Metaphysics and the Mind–Body Problem.* He has published extensively in the philosophy of science and the foundations of logic and mathematics and also writes widely on contemporary social issues both in scholarly journals and in popular publications such as *Fortune* and *Newsweek. Address:* Department of Philosophy, CCNY, 118th St. & Convent Ave., New York, NY 10037.

BARBARA G. MELAMED received her PhD at the University of Wisconsin. She has taught at Case Western Reserve University and is now a professor of clinical psychology at the University of Florida in Gainesville. She has published widely and has also been active as a therapist, particularly in studying and treating the consequences of traumatic experiences. She is a Fellow of the American Psychological Association (Divisions of Clinical Psychology and Health Psychology). *Address:* Department of Clinical Psychology, University of Florida, Gainesville, FL 32610.

JODI L. MELAMED, Barbara Melamed's daughter, is enrolled in the international baccalaureate program at East Side High School in Gainesville, FL. She is a member of Amnesty International. Address: c/o Barbara Melamed.

ERVIN STAUB was educated in Budapest, Vienna, and the United States and earned his PhD at Stanford University. He has taught at Stanford, the University of Hawaii, the London School of Economics and Political Science, and Harvard and is now a professor of psychology at the University of Massachusetts, Amherst. His major research interest has been in the origins and correlates of helping and altruism and, more recently, group violence. He is the author of several publications in the area of torture; his forthcoming book, *The Roots of Evil: The Psychological and Cultural Origins of Genocide,* is also relevant to this topic. He is a Fellow of the American Psychological Association (Divisions of Developmental Psychology, Personality and Social Psychology, and the Society for the Psychological Study of Social Issues). *Address:* Department of Psychology, University of Massachusetts, Amherst, MA 01002.

PETER SUEDFELD was born in Budapest. He received his advanced education in the United States and earned his PhD from Princeton University. He has taught at Princeton and Rutgers and has held visiting positions at the University of Illinois, Yale University, and the University of New South Wales. He is currently a professor of psychology and Dean of the Faculty of Graduate Studies at the University of British Columbia, Vancouver, Canada. His major research interest has been in human adaptation to extreme, unusual, and stressful environments. Among his major publications is *Restricted Environmental Stimulation: Research and Clinical Applications.* He is a Fellow of the Royal Society of Canada, the Academy of Behavioral Medicine Research, and the Canadian and American Psychological Associations. *Address:* Department of Psychology, University of British Columbia, Vancouver, B.C. V6T 1W5, Canada.

Jacqueline C. Bouhoutsos, Barbara G. Melamed, and Peter Suedfeld are members of the Subcommittee on Psychological Concerns Related to Torture, Committee on International Relations in Psychology, American Psychological Association.

Preface

Peter Suedfeld

There is growing evidence that torture is epidemic throughout major parts of the world (and endemic in some countries). It is extremely difficult to obtain valid estimates of the number of victims, there being many reasons for either exaggerating or minimizing the figures, but the fact that torture is certainly not rare has been reflected in autobiographical accounts, historical analyses, studies by national and international bodies, and the mass media. Publication of such reports has led to worldwide revulsion and a determination to stop torture and to first rescue and then treat its victims as needed. This is a transpolitical issue: Torture has been committed by governments and nongovernmental groups that vary widely in political and religious ideology, economic status, geographic location, and ethnic makeup.

As Amnesty International has shown (e.g., 1984), there is no point in trying to assess the degree to which various parties have been guilty of the maltreatment of prisoners. One problem in judging the matter is the unequal availability of information. In some countries, the press and the citizenry are subject to such stringent controls or are in such severe danger from governmental or nongovernmental practitioners of torture that little if any critical reporting reaches the outside world. Other regions of the world may be considered insufficiently important to warrant extensive reporting in Western media. These characteristics, sometimes coupled with political biases that may predispose the mass media to criticize some regimes more assiduously than others and with the desire of some human rights organizations not to appear hostile to particular political ideologies, could well result in a distorted awareness of the prevalence of torture. Above all, and regardless of the accessibility of information, our view is that the need for psychologists to understand and deal with torture is beyond ideology.

Psychologists can be involved in the process of torture in several roles. One is that of victim; another is that of perpetrator. A third role is much more natural to psychologists than either of the others: defending victims by vigorously opposing torture and treating its consequences. The last role is as a provider of knowledge concerning the causes and effects of torture. Psychological research may identify environmental, social, and personality variables that are relevant to torture, predict and explain the effects of various torture procedures, assess situations in which torture has been or is likely to be used, and refine methods for aiding survivors of torture.

Although organized psychology has only recently begun to respond to the prevalence of torture, individual members of the profession have been interested in the topic for a long time. At least since World War II, military and other psychologists have studied the mistreatment of prisoners and tried to ameliorate its adverse effects. Some psychological organizations have become involved in the issue for at least a decade. The Société Française de Psychologie, for example, has been actively investigating cases in which psychologists may have been tortured.

Within its general thrust of supporting human rights (Rosenzweig, 1988), the American Psychological Association (APA) adopted an official policy on investigating and dealing with alleged human rights violations involving psychologists either as victims or as perpetrators (APA Joint Subcommittee, 1984). During the consideration of the APA policy, it became clear that torture was a special case of human rights violations. Not only is it one of the most clear-cut and morally repulsive forms of such violation, but because of its nature and consequences it is particularly relevant to the interests of organized psychology. The APA Committee on International Relations in Psychology therefore initiated two activities. The first was to prepare an APA statement on torture. The outcome of this decision was the APA Resolution Against Torture, which was eventually adopted by the Council of Representatives and has resulted in a joint statement by the American Psychological Association and the American Psychiatric Association (see Table 1).

The second initiative was the establishment of the Subcommittee on the Abuse of Psychological Knowledge for Purposes of Torture, later renamed the Subcommittee on Psychological Concerns Related to Torture, to which I shall refer as the Subcommittee. The Subcommittee's terms of reference were to prepare a report evaluating the evidence as to the role of scientific psychology in the design of torture techniques; the involvement of professional psychologists in developing and administering such techniques; psychological studies of those who inflict torture; the psychological sequelae of torture, whether that torture was itself physical or psychological in nature; and the actual and potential contribution of psychologists in therapeutic intervention with survivors of torture. The APA itself pursued its opposition to torture in various other ways as well, including participation in a fact-finding mission to Chile and several publications in the *APA Monitor* and *Psychology Today*. The help of the organization, particularly through the support of the Committee on International Relations in Psychology and the activities of Steven B. Kennedy, then Director of the APA International Affairs Office, was crucial in completing the task of the Subcommittee.

This volume grew out of the report of the Subcommittee, an early version of which served as the core of a symposium at the 1987 meeting of the APA (Suedfeld, 1987). However, it soon appeared that contributions by experts who were not members of the Subcommittee would enhance the range and value of the original report. Accordingly, several specialists who had previously made notable contributions to the study of torture in one aspect or another were invited to write chapters for this collection.

The first section of the book examines torture itself from several perspectives. It begins with a summary of those techniques that are in wide contemporary use in the mistreatment of prisoners and their historical connections with earlier methods (Suedfeld). Melamed, Melamed, and Bouhoutsos then review our current knowledge about the sequelae of torture in light of what we know about the general topic of posttraumatic stress disorder. Engdahl and Eberly look at the broader context of suffering in severe forms of captivity or imprisonment. Staub then considers social

Table 1   Joint Resolution Against Torture of the American Psychological Association and the American Psychiatric Association

---

WHEREAS, American psychologists are bound by their *Ethical Principles* to "respect the dignity and worth of the individual and strive for the preservation and protection of fundamental human rights," and

WHEREAS, American psychiatrists are bound by their Principles of Medical Ethics with Annotations Especially Applicable to Psychiatry to "provide competent medical service with compassion and respect for human dignity," and

WHEREAS, the existence of state-sponsored torture and other cruel, inhuman, or degrading treatment has been documented in many nations around the world, and

WHEREAS, psychological knowledge and techniques may be used to design and carry out torture, and

WHEREAS, torture victims may suffer from long-term, multiple psychological and physical problems,

BE IT RESOLVED, that the American Psychological Association and the American Psychiatric Association condemn torture wherever it occurs, and

BE IT FURTHER RESOLVED, that the American Psychological Association and the American Psychiatric Association support the U.N. Declaration and Convention Against Torture and Other Cruel, Inhuman, or Degrading Treatment or Punishment and the U.N. Principles of Medical Ethics; as well as the joint Congressional Resolution opposing torture that was signed into law by President Reagan on October 4, 1984.

> Approved by the Council of Representatives
> of the American Psychological Association
> February 1, 1986

> Approved by the Board of Trustees
> of the American Psychiatric Association
> December 6–7, 1985

From "Statement by the Joint Subcommittee on Human Rights," American Psychological Association, *American Psychologist*, 1984, *39*, pp. 676–678. Copyright 1984 by the American Psychological Association. Adapted by permission.

psychological factors in the governmental use of torture, and Gibson provides a detailed look at how torturers are trained. At the end of the section, Levin, a philosopher, analyzes moral objections to and justifications of torture.

The second section concentrates on the role of psychologists in the various aspects of torture. I summarize what is now known about psychologists who have either administered or suffered torture connected with their professional capacity, evaluate the evidence as to whether scientific psychology itself has—wittingly or not—contributed to the development of torture techniques, and comment on what is known about coping strategies in this context. Kennedy analyzes the case of a prominent psychologist who was unfairly accused of contributing to torture and of the reaction of psychological societies to this episode. Bouhoutsos presents guidelines for treating torture victims. Bustos addresses some of the ways in which this work reflects back upon the intrapsychic processes of the therapist and the group processes of the institution. Chester's chapter provides information on centers for the treatment of torture victims and the resources now available to victims and those who are concerned about them. Faraone, who has been deeply involved with the U.S. branch of Amnesty International, deals primarily with the role that scientific and professional organizations, including those of psychology, can play in opposing the use of torture.

It is our hope that this book will not only arouse the interest of our colleagues in the problem of torture and in ameliorating its aftereffects, but also inform others concerned with this problem that they have allies in psychology. The work of combating torture and its consequences is neither as far advanced nor as widespread as torture itself; this imbalance must be reversed. The Subcommittee hopes that its report, in this expanded form, will contribute to that reversal.

REFERENCES

American Psychological Association, Joint Subcommittee on Human Rights. (1984). Statement by the Joint Subcommittee on Human Rights. *American Psychologist, 39*(6), 676–678.

Amnesty International. (1984). *Torture in the eighties.* New York: Author.

Rosenzweig, M. R. (1988). Psychology and the United Nations human rights efforts. *American Psychologist, 43*, 79–86.

Suedfeld, P. (Chair). (1987, August). *Psychology and torture: Report of the Subcommittee on the Abuse of Psychological Knowledge for Purposes of Torture.* Symposium conducted at the meeting of the American Psychological Association, New York, NY.

I

THE NATURE AND EFFECTS
OF TORTURE

1

Torture: A Brief Overview

Peter Suedfeld

It is difficult to formulate a perfect definition of torture (Klayman, 1978). There is agreement that its hallmark is the deliberate infliction of severe pain or discomfort. The central point of the definition used by the United Nations General Assembly (1984) is the intentional infliction by agents of the state of severe physical or mental pain or suffering. A gloss on this definition holds that "although infliction of . . . pain is integral . . . the purpose of torture is to break the will of the victim and ultimately to destroy his or her humanity" (Stover & Nightingale, 1985, p. 5).

In the usage of the APA Subcommittee, the discomfort and pain may be physical or mental, or both; the victim is a prisoner in the power of some group or (less frequently) individual. The captor must intend harm to the prisoner. Situations in which, for example, prisoners receive inadequate diet or medical treatment solely because the captor does not have the necessary resources would not be included. We depart from the United Nations definition by including situations in which the agent of torture represents an entity other than a government. We include revolutionary, terrorist, and criminal groups as well as public officials: There seems to be no justification for omitting from consideration torture committed by the Hizbollah terrorists in Lebanon, the Symbionese Liberation Army in the United States, or narcotics dealers in Mexico, to cite only a few well-publicized examples. In many cases, torture is committed by groups whose connection with a government is a matter of debate—for example, death squads in Central America and the myriad terrorist groups financed and equipped by various countries in the Middle East.

There are two points that must be made about the approach taken by the authors of this book. First, we deliberately refrain from sensationalizing accounts of torture, insofar as that is possible with this topic. Detailed descriptions of the acts of torturers and the sufferings of victims will not be found in this book. Many such descriptions are available in autobiographical accounts, in the mass media, in the publications of Amnesty International, and so on. We set out to examine and document, at a scientific and professional level, the relation between psychology as a discipline and the phenomenon of torture, and we have tried to keep this analysis at a cognitive, rather than an emotional, level. It can be argued that one should not deny or downplay emotion when discussing torture, but we feel that much can be gained by approaching the issue from the point of view of fact and logic without continuously emphasizing (even though feeling) both outrage and compassion.

Second, we are explicitly refraining from selecting one or a few groups or countries for specific criticism. Such selectivity is always at risk of being dictated by the critic's own political agenda (cf. Farer, 1988). People on the political left think that reactionary and counterrevolutionary regimes are the worst offenders; those on the right reserve that distinction for revolutionary or postrevolutionary governments. Still others, determined to be (or at least appear) even-handed, will overlook gross differences in the actual phenomenon—for example, by implicitly equating occasional and unauthorized instances of torture in one political jurisdiction with systematic and widespread policy-based mistreatment in another, so as not to seem to be picking only on the latter. The variables involved in making selections are so complex that they cannot be dealt with in an unbiased fashion. Therefore, although we use specific episodes to illustrate some of the points being made, the reader should not infer that those episodes are the worst, most frequent, or most to be condemned of the many occurrences of torture.

WHY TORTURE?

What do torturers expect to achieve? Common rationales for applying torture may be subsumed under five major headings.

1. *Information.* Torture is used to force the victim to provide factual information concerning criminal, political, or military matters of which he or she is presumed to have knowledge. Perhaps the most common example is in military field intelligence settings.

2. *Incrimination.* The goal is to force the prisoner to identify other individuals engaged in behaviors that the captor considers culpable or to confess to having engaged in such behaviors. This is frequently the goal in the torture of prisoners who are either suspected of being part of a conspiratorial group or are being groomed for public trial.

3. *Indoctrination.* The captor wishes to establish conditions under which the prisoner will abandon previously held beliefs and attitudes and adopt others that are more acceptable to the captor. Torture is a preliminary step in bringing about a change in loyalties, as in brainwashing.

4. *Intimidation.* Torture is used to deter the prisoner and others from behavior considered unacceptable by the captor. In many such cases, the torturer ensures that the mistreatment of the victim is publicly known, as a means of frightening other potential victims. In the case of hostages and kidnap victims, torture may be used to deter attempts at rescue by indicating to the police or the victim's government that any strong action would result in additional suffering for the captive. Intimidation also includes torture as a punishment, for example, flogging or amputation as the legally mandated penalty for some crimes or torture by police and prison authorities when prisoners attempt to escape or violate regulations. Furthermore, a pervasive knowledge that political or other prisoners are subject to torture may be used to intimidate large segments of a polity into submission, whether to the ruling group—in cases such as the Soviet Union under Stalin, Germany under

Hitler, Cambodia under Pol Pot, or Chile under Pinochet—or to a rebel force operating within particular areas, such as the Viet Cong or the Sendero Luminoso.

5. *Isolation.* The goal here is to convince both the captor and the captive that they have nothing in common with the other, not even a common humanity. For the torturer, having the complete power to mistreat the prisoner instills contempt and hatred of the group to which the prisoner belongs and increases the torturer's loyalty by isolating him or her from the victimized group and even from society at large. The person being tortured, in turn, learns that the gap between omnipotent guards and helpless prisoners (and perhaps between prisoners and the world in general) is as the difference between different species. It is also a way to harden recruits (e.g., in the practice of the Japanese Army and the Hitler Youth during World War II of using prisoners of war or concentration camp inmates as live targets).

Obviously, in many cases there are mixed objectives and torture may be perceived as being effective in reaching more than one. Furthermore, we have omitted situations in which torture is merely the expression of personal sadism on the part of the captor, a way to obtain other satisfactions (e.g., revenge or sexual gratification), a reflexive continuation of cultural tradition, and so forth. In such instances, torture may not have any specific pragmatic goal. If we were to add this category to the list of *I*s, *irrational* might describe these episodes.

THE COMPONENT CHARACTERISTICS OF TORTURE

To the five *I*s just listed, which describe the goals of torture, we may add a similar list to describe the major components of torture. The first three have been referred to as the three *D*s (Farber, Harlow, & West, 1957); I have added a fourth component to the list (Suedfeld, 1980).

1. *Debility.* The captor deliberately induces physical and mental weakness. This may be accomplished by hunger, fatigue, lack of medical attention, lack of shelter from the elements, lack of sleep, beatings, electric shock, drugs, and so forth.

2. *Dependency.* The prisoner is brought to believe that his or her fate is entirely within the hands (or the whim) of the captor. The victim is isolated from any other source of information or support, rewards and punishments are applied unpredictably and even randomly, friendships and lines of authority among the prisoners are destroyed, and the prisoner is stripped of status and dignity.

3. *Dread.* The victim is kept in a constant state of fear and anxiety. Among the most frequently used techniques are the use of physical pain, threats against family, mock executions, witnessing the maltreatment and death of other prisoners, keeping the prisoner in doubt as to when if ever he or she will be released, and allowing the prisoner to overhear plans for further torture or execution.

4. *Disorientation.* The object is to arouse a state of confusion, uncertainty, and "lostness." One strategy used by torturers is to change treatment unexpectedly to prevent the victim from developing coping techniques (Benfeldt-Zachrisson, 1985). Other relevant techniques are extended solitary confinement, deliberate violation of diurnal and other cycles, sensory overload, and prolonged blindfolding or hooding.

Both taxonomies assume that the torturer's goal is rational, which may in at least some cases be arguable. Each category under the *I*s and *D*s involves mental effects, although the torture may rely largely upon physical means. Thus, the categories support the view held by the American Psychological Association (APA) that no rational torturer has merely physical objectives. Inducing a prisoner to provide intelligence data, to implicate others, to confess to crimes, to change his or her loyalties, and so on, are psychological goals.

Some cases, in which none of the goals listed is readily discernible, may be viewed as extreme versions of isolation, whereby the prisoner's humanity is meant to be destroyed. The most effective technique to this end is the prolonged and systematic degradation and humiliation of the victim. Although no specific study of this category of torture has been made, it is widespread and damaging enough to deserve special attention. Some of the most striking recent reports have described such treatment in Chile (Bales, 1986) and in Cuba (Valladares, 1986).

CONCEPTUAL ISSUES

There are a number of complex issues related to any discussion of torture. One must consider the distinction between torture on the one hand and techniques of interrogation and persuasion that may use psychological principles but do not involve torture, on the other. There may be areas that are difficult to categorize. For example, police interrogation procedures frequently have the goal of making the suspect feel anxious, isolated, and helpless. Are we to characterize such approaches as torture? We have chosen not to do so in this book. By our criteria, torture must involve intense anguish that goes beyond temporary psychological uneasiness. We would distinguish between casual psychological brutality (e.g., a lack of concern for the prisoner's dignity in arresting him or her in public or using a first-name or derogatory form of address) and systematic degradation and humiliation. The concept of torture is diluted when the word is used indiscriminately.

We also differentiate between physical and psychological torture, although the former frequently if not always has psychological concomitants and consequences. Obviously, physical deprivation may lead to intense fear, learned helplessness, states of confusion, and so forth. The same is true of physical actions such as beatings, electric shocks, and other pain-inducing techniques. Equally obvious, these abuses may be administered with psychological suffering as at least one goal. Still, they are different from procedures whereby the prisoner is given adequate and acceptable physical treatment but is subjected to psychological manipulations designed to overcome resistance to the captors.

It may also be useful to establish the position that psychologists take on the morality of torture. Torture, by definition, contravenes the purpose of our discipline and profession, and of our largest professional organization, the APA, which is to be a means of "promoting human welfare" (APA Bylaws, 1985, Article I, p. xxi). Descriptions of torture techniques and episodes convey its abhorrent nature, and professional contact with survivors only deepens that reaction. Most colleagues probably have personal acquaintances who have been victimized in this way. Some, including several of the contributors to this book, have personal experience with various forms of persecution and mistreatment. As a group, then, psychologists are unlikely to harbor much sympathy for torturers.

Philosophers have raised the issue of whether torture can *ever* be justified on moral grounds (e.g., Crozier, 1975). Borderline cases are most likely to be found in the "information" category of the goals of torture. For example, suppose that a lone terrorist has concealed a timed nuclear device somewhere in a large city. There are no clues as to where the bomb is hidden or how it can be disarmed if found. The police are unable to persuade the prisoner to give this information. Does the right of millions of innocent citizens to life outweigh the right of the terrorist not to be tortured into giving the necessary information?

Many observers, including some of our contributors, argue that no use of torture can be justified. Although the issue leaves us in some quandary, it is to some extent a purely theoretical argument. Pragmatically, there are probably very few torture cases among the many that we examine in which the justification is remotely like that in the example just given. The APA Joint Subcommittee on Human Rights therefore did not feel that this issue needed to be addressed at length. However, we do not reject the potential significance of the debate, and the expanded report presented here does include a detailed consideration of the matter by Michael Levin, a specialist on this topic (chapter 6, this volume).

PSYCHOLOGICAL ASPECTS OF TORTURE: HISTORICAL EXAMPLES

An Early Example

Although by no means universal, the use of torture to extract confessions from suspected criminals has a history that goes back at least to ancient Egypt. In classical Greece and Rome, slaves and, under limited circumstances, other noncitizens, could be subjected to torture (although the range of "torturable" suspects, particularly in treason cases, expanded significantly in the latter centuries of the Roman Empire). The practice was codified during the drastic changes in legal procedure that emerged in the 12th and 13th centuries in Europe (Peters, 1985) and was common until the mid-18th century. In Europe, as in Imperial (and contemporary) China, judicial convictions depended heavily on confession and eyewitness testimony; torture was used primarily to obtain testimony from unwilling suspects and witnesses, and also as part of the penalty for extraordinary crimes (e.g., treason).

Psychological considerations are evident in the very first widely known handbook for torturers, *Malleus Maleficarum* [*The Hammer of Witchcraft*] (Sprenger & Kramer, 1486/1968). In giving guidelines to inquisitors investigating allegations of witchcraft, the authors recommend "keeping the accused in a state of suspense, and continually postponing the day of examination, and frequently using verbal persuasions" (p. 217). If the suspect continues to deny guilt and the judge is convinced that she is lying, the instruments of torture are to be applied. The torturers, however, should appear to be reluctant to do this and, after a while, someone should earnestly request that she be released from the torture while verbal persuasion is tried again. If necessary, the judge

> . . . *should have other engines of torture brought before her, and tell her that she will have to endure these if she does not confess. If then she is not induced by terror to confess, the torture must be continued on the second or third day, but not repeated at that present time unless there should be some fresh indication of its probable success.* (pp. 218–219)

Some of these instructions will seem familiar to anyone who is acquainted with modern torture techniques. Among these are the induction of fear and uncertainty; the intercession of an official designated to be perceived as sympathetic to the prisoner; the demonstration of torture instruments before they are actually applied, to exercise the victim's imagination and increase terror; and the intervals of rest between torture sessions. What is obvious is that torturers even 500 years ago— and probably much longer, since it is doubtful that Sprenger and Kramer themselves invented these principles—were quite aware of techniques that magnified the effects of interrogation and torture. One may question whether there have been any major new insights based on modern psychological theory or research.

Brainwashing

There certainly have been claims of such insights, notably in the period shortly before and after World War II. During the Moscow Purge Trials of the 1930s, apparently unharmed defendants confessed in open court to charges that were quite obviously ridiculous. The possibility that some arcane psychological torture technique had been used to achieve this result was raised, but no evidence was found. Rather, NKVD (Soviet secret police) defectors and other analysts later concluded that the procedures used were standard Russian police methods for eliciting confessions. They included the extensive use of physical coercion, threats and prolonged solitary confinement, frequently in darkness, abruptly alternating with marathon sessions of interrogation, bright lights, sleep deprivation, and beatings. In spite of all this, the percentage of victims who acquiesced sufficiently to be trusted in the "show trials" was very small compared to those who refused to confess or recanted their forced confessions before being tried (e.g., Krivitsky, 1939).

The issue arose again in the late 1940s, when political trials similar to those of the Old Bolsheviks occurred in East European Communist countries. Although many of these involved Party leaders who had lost a factional struggle, some of the victims were not Communists (e.g., Cardinal Mindszenty in Hungary), and their submissive behavior could not be ascribed to Party discipline or loyalty (cf. Koestler, 1940). In the early 1950s, the behavior of captured United Nations soldiers in North Korean and Chinese Prisoner of War (POW) camps gave rise to further speculations about brainwashing. This term (Hunter, 1951) assumed a mysterious set of psychological techniques that subverted the allegiance of many POWs. Authors attributed the impact of the alleged technique to Pavlovian conditioning, neurophysiological arousal induced by overstimulation, the use of psychoactive drugs, the manipulation of group dynamics, sensory deprivation, or hypnosis—it was perhaps the first time that the concepts of scientific psychology had been cited in this context (Group for the Advancement of Psychiatry, 1956, 1957; Lifton, 1961; Sargant, 1957; Schein, 1961). Another aspect of the progress of the social sciences was also mentioned: that because of developments such as permissive child-rearing, relativistic morals, lack of discipline in the schools, and so forth, American soldiers in the Korean War lacked the moral and physical fiber to resist their captors as had their counterparts in previous wars (Kinkead, 1959; Mayer, 1956).

There are fatal flaws in these speculations. One is that the supposedly universal submission and collaboration with the captors is a myth. There were in fact many firm resisters among the prisoners, and most POWs—as probably most prisoner populations throughout history—neither actively resisted nor actively collaborated. Second, to the extent that some prisoners did collaborate, they did so for straightforward reasons, such as the promise of better treatment and the avoidance of the physical mistreatment commonly meted out to resisters. Third, on a statistical basis the behavior of this group of prisoners was at least as good as that of other POW samples in the past. Fourth, the techniques used to elicit compliance were direct offshoots of traditional Chinese judicial procedures, mixed with the practices developed by the Chinese Communist Party and its armies during the long history of their movement, and had no connection with the study of psychological research. To the extent that the Chinese attempted to bring about indoctrination, that is, an actual change in political loyalties, they largely failed. As in most prisoner situations, they were more successful in imposing compliance to camp rules. Although there was considerable evidence of both physical and mental torture, the technique was not very novel, mysterious, or potent (Biderman, 1963; Cunningham, 1970).

Although the Soviet and East European show trials and the experiences of the Korean War POWs most intrigued Western observers, a much more impressive and ominous development was that of Chinese "thought reform" institutions. Whereas in most totalitarian systems those who were perceived as enemies were executed, exiled, imprisoned, or turned to forced labor, after taking power on the mainland, the Chinese government undertook to combine punishment and incapacitation with indoctrination. The procedures, later applied in a much less intense form to the POWs, included humiliation, degradation, uncertainty, fear, physical deprivation, and, uniquely, group pressure including intensive criticism and self-criticism sessions. The victims included foreigners, particularly Westerners, who had long been resident in China—such as missionaries and businessmen—as well as Chinese who had opposed the Communist movement or were suspected of being likely to do so (e.g., officials of the Kuomintang government, officers of the Nationalist Army, businessmen and other "capitalist roaders," people who had extensive contact with Westerners, and the relatives of people in these categories).

Successful conversion of Western prisoners tended to last only until they were released and repatriated, or at most for a short period after that. With native Chinese, the degree of success is impossible to ascertain, although the fact that many of them later escaped to Hong Kong to be interviewed by Western behavioral scientists (Lifton, 1961) indicates limited success. In contrast, during 10 years of imprisonment, the late Panchen Lama was converted to the view that the People's Republic of China is the legitimate ruler of Tibet. A recent report stated that

> The Vatican-appointed bishop of Shanghai, apparently converted to communism after 30 years in jail for treason, kissed the ring of his government-approved successor and promised to lead a "normal religious life," the New China News Agency says. . . . The human rights group Amnesty International said he was jailed because he opposed Communist interference in religious affairs. ("Peking converts," 1985, p. B-5)

Similar accounts have emerged more recently from the re-education institutions of Vietnam (Desbarats & Jackson, 1985; Mollica, Wyshak, & Lavelle, 1987). Although conversion, or at least deterrence from opposition, may have been one goal in these cases, the routine and extensive torture of American POWs during the Vietnam War seems to have had little if any rational purpose.

To sum up the brainwashing aspect of psychological torture, some general conclusions may be reached. There were indeed psychological techniques used, some of which could fairly be described as torture. These included extremes of group pressure; degradation and dehumanization; threats of execution or indefinite captivity; threats against loved ones; and deprivation of psychological comforts such as privacy, mail, and contact with neutral or friendly others. There were also psychological sequelae of physical mistreatment such as prolonged fatigue and sleep deprivation, beatings, malnutrition, exposure to the elements, prolonged constraint in uncomfortable positions, and lack of medical care for wounds or disease. Some accounts describe incredible cruelty. For example, Haralan Popov, a Protestant minister imprisoned in Bulgaria for more than 13 years, early in his captivity was forced to stand erect facing a white wall for two weeks without food, water, sleep, or even a change in position, while interrogators questioned and beat him in relays (Popov, 1970). Such abuse frequently resulted in the prisoner's complying with the captors' wishes. Popov, for example, was among a group of ministers who confessed to espionage. But it did not necessarily bring about real conversion. Within two months of his trial, Popov was "classified as unreformed." He conducted clandestine Bible classes and otherwise engaged in forbidden religious activities. Once his sentence was served, he emigrated to Sweden; since then, he has devoted himself to raising support for secret religious activities in Eastern Europe.

CONTEMPORARY TORTURE TECHNIQUES

In the most recent past, a long list of common techniques has been identified in the torture of political prisoners in many countries. An exhaustive compendium published by Amnesty International (1984) listed 66 countries where state torture in the period 1980–1983 had been proven on solid evidence. Some allegations of torture, but without equal proof, had been made in two dozen other countries. Whether this indicates, as some have claimed, that torture is "a growth industry" or whether it reflects greater concern and sensitivity to the mistreatment of prisoners, is an open question.

The following list of contemporary torture techniques is taken primarily from the book by Stover and Nightingale (1985), from Amnesty International publications (e.g., 1978, 1984), and from many articles and books dealing with specific groups of victims or describing the experiences of individual victims. It is by no means comprehensive—torture techniques reflect the infinite creativity of the human mind—but the most frequently noted methods are included.

Active physical pain. According to Amnesty International's (1984) list, the most common methods of torture (at least 90% of reports) are still those that actively inflict physical pain. These include beatings with fists, boots, clubs, whips, barbed wire, and so forth; breaking limbs or eardrums; blinding; amputation or crushing of limbs and digits; pulling or drilling healthy teeth; the insertion of various objects into bodily orifices or under the nails; electric shocks to various parts of the body (frequently including the genitals) with electrodes wired to telephone sets, electric cattle prods, and so on; and burning, stabbing, or cutting parts of the body. New methods have been added [e.g., a "flexible bed" that can be folded backward with the prisoner inside, used in Iran (News Services, March 4, 1987)]. Even such ancient and bizarre methods as the rack, the *falaqa* (suspending the victim and beating him or her on the soles of the feet), and having the victim's flesh bitten by vicious dogs or gnawed by insects still survive.

Passive infliction of pain. In this category, pain is inflicted by passive means: being tied up, confined, or forced to remain in uncomfortable positions or spaces; forced violent and prolonged physical exertion; exposure to sun, cold, and rain (or a technological version, such as being soaked with cold water and having to stand in the full blast of an air conditioner, reported to have occurred in Singapore); and being tied and suspended by the hands or feet (frequently accompanied by beating). The prolonged use of manacles, chains, and other materials that restrict both blood flow and movement also comes under this heading.

Extreme exhaustion. These techniques involve forcing the prisoner to engage in strenuous physical activity until total exhaustion sets in. The specific methods include running, stationary exercises, lifting heavy weights, and spinning around until dizzy. Driving the prisoner to exhaustion is frequently accompanied by sleep deprivation, beatings, and humiliation, the last focusing on the victim's presumed lack of strength and stamina when the activity can no longer be continued. The combination of poor diet and hard labor, practiced in many penal institutions and camps, should probably not be categorized as torture under our original definition.

Fear induction. Still another category of physical torture is the use of techniques that arouse fear of death: near drowning or suffocation, having large quantities of liquid forced through the nostrils, being forced to drink large quantities of liquid, and the administration of drugs that inhibit breathing or other normal bodily processes. Long periods of food and water deprivation have more complex consequences, but threatening a prisoner's survival is certainly one.

Combined physical and mental torture. Other physical maltreatments have a more salient component of mental anguish. Some examples are putting victims in completely dark or intensely lit cells without change in illumination; sleep deprivation; constant questioning; constant harassment by other prisoners; being deprived of clothing; sexual torture, including rape and the hurting or mutilation of sexual organs; and abrupt alteration from low to high stimulation and back again, resulting in "emergence shock."

Primarily mental torture. Here, physical pain or discomfort are minimal or incidental, the emphasis being on mental effects. Among these are threats of death, mutilation, castration, and indefinite captivity, either to the prisoner or to friends and relatives; forcing the prisoner to watch others being tortured or to overhear their (real or faked) screams inflicting torture on children specifically to subjugate their politically dissident parents (according to Amnesty International, this is done systematically in Iraq); mock executions; humiliation, such as being forced to engage in grotesque acts, eat excrement or drink urine, or be naked during interrogations, line-ups, and the like; being given disorienting drugs or being constantly hooded or blindfolded; intense stimulus bombardment; violation of religious beliefs, such as being forbidden to perform religious exercises or being forced to eat prohibited foods; deprivation of sanitary facilities and supplies; being held incommunicado, solitary, and constantly in one's cell; unpredictable alternations of leniency and severity; unpredictable changes in regulations and conditions of confinement; the writing and rewriting of lengthy autobiographical confessions; forced criticism and self-criticism sessions, sometimes (as in China) involving tens of thousands of people shouting, spitting, and occasionally committing violence against the victim; and being denied information about one's family and other loved ones and knowing that the latter are equally anxious about the prisoner's fate (as in the case of disappeared prisoners).

Psychophysiological Aspects of Torture

Of the methods enumerated, the sustained disruption of sleep patterns—either by complete sleep deprivation or by violently altering the accustomed diurnal cycle—has been singled out as leading not only to dread and disorientation, but eventually to an internalized belief in false confessions. It has been called "probably the most potent of all the debilitating elements of softening up prisoners" (West, 1985, p. 72) and "the ultimate torment" (Ames, 1985, p. 86).

One aspect of physical torture that has received insufficient attention is that of physiological mediators, which in turn may be directly responsible for at least some psychological sequelae. Aside from sleep deprivation, the most obvious example is brain trauma due to being beaten on the head, a very common form of assault against prisoners (Amnesty International, 1984). Some long-term aftereffects of torture, misattributed to noninvasive or psychological techniques, may in fact be caused by nothing more sophisticated or mysterious than such cerebral injuries (cf. Ames, 1985; Fields, 1976, p. 84; Suedfeld, 1980, p. 410).

Similarly, prolonged standing results in reduced blood circulation in the upper body and pooling of blood in the lower extremities. Cardiac output and arterial blood pressure decrease, with an initial overcompensation in heart rate. The eventual redistribution of blood, including reduced blood supply to the brain, leads to vertigo, nausea, alterations in conscious state, and fainting. Being hooded, which may reduce the oxygen supply, also leads to hyperventilation and, in turn, to lightheadedness, giddiness, and feelings of unreality. More subtly, prolonged deprivation of sunlight may affect the secretion of neurotransmitters and increase brain excitability (Ames, 1985).

SUMMARY

It is obvious that although there is a vast variety of specific torture techniques, their goals and common characteristics may be comprehended. The great majority of techniques are simple and brutal, and have been in use throughout history; many others are technologically more sophisticated versions of the same approaches. Still others, which to some observers may appear to be fiendishly original, are traditional or show only slight deviations from tradition in the culture where they are found. Physical pain and its physiological and psychological effects still form the most important category of mistreatment, with more deliberate application of mental and emotional anguish following. It is, therefore, these abuses that psychologists must be prepared to combat and whose aftermath we must learn to treat.

REFERENCES

American Psychological Association. (1985). Bylaws of the American Psychological Association (as amended through August, 1984). *Directory*, (pp. xxi–xxvii). Washington, DC: Author.

Ames, F. (1985). Brain dysfunction in detainees. In A. N. Bell & R. D. A. MacKie (Eds.), *Detention and security legislation in South Africa* (pp. 85–88). Durban, South Africa: University of Natal, Centre for Adult Education.

Amnesty International. (1978). *Political imprisonment in the People's Republic of China.* London: Author.

Amnesty International. (1984). *Torture in the eighties.* London: Author.

Bales, J. (1986, February). U.S. delegation finds intimidation and fear uproot Chilean society. *APA Monitor,* pp. 4–5.

Bendfeldt-Zachrisson, F. (1985). State (political) torture: Some general, psychological, and particular aspects. *International Journal of Health Services, 15,* 339–349.

Biderman, A. D. (1963). *March to calumny: The story of American POWs in the Korean War.* New York: Macmillan.

Crozier, B. (1975). *A theory of conflict.* New York: Scribner's.

Cunningham, C. (1970). Korean War studies in forensic psychology. *Bulletin of the British Psychological Society, 23,* 309–312.

Desbarats, J., & Jackson, K. D. (1985, Fall). Vietnam 1975–1982: The cruel peace. *Washington Quarterly,* pp. 169–182.

Farber, I. E., Harlow, H. F., & West, J. L. (1957). Brainwashing, conditioning, and DDD (debility, dependency and dread). *Sociometry, 20,* 271–285.

Farer, T. J. (1988). Looking at looking at Nicaragua: The problematique of impartiality in human rights inquiries. *Human Rights Quarterly, 10,* 141–156.

Fields, R. M. (1976). *Society under siege: A psychology of Northern Ireland.* Philadelphia, PA: Temple University Press.

Group for the Advancement of Psychiatry. (1956). *Factors used to increase the susceptibility of individuals to forceful indoctrination: Observations and experiments* (Symposium No. 3). New York: Author.

Group for the Advancement of Psychiatry. (1957). *Methods of forceful indoctrination: Observations and interviews* (Symposium No. 4). New York: Author.

Hunter, E. (1951). *Brainwashing in Red China.* New York: Vanguard.

Kinkead, E. (1959). *In every war but one.* New York: Norton.

Klayman, B. M. (1978). The definition of torture in international law. *Temple Law Quarterly, 51,* 449–517.

Koestler, A. (1940). *Darkness at noon.* London: Cape.

Krivitsky, W. G. (1939). *In Stalin's secret service.* New York: Harper.

Lifton, R. J. (1961). *Thought reform and the psychology of totalism.* New York: Norton.

Mayer, W. E. (1956, February 24). Why did many GI captives cave in? *U.S. News and World Report,* 56–62.

Mollica, R. F., Wyshak, G., & Lavelle, J. (1987). The psychosocial impact of war trauma and torture on Southeast Asian refugees. *American Journal of Psychiatry, 144,* 1567–1572.

News Services. (1987, March 4). Eight new ways to torture. *Vancouver Province,* p. 87.

Peking "converts" Vatican's bishop. (1985, July 6). *Vancouver Sun,* p. B-5.

Peters, E. (1985). *Torture.* New York: Basil Blackwell.

Popov, H. (1970). *Tortured for his faith.* Grand Rapids, MI: Zondervan.

Sargant, W. H. (1957). *Battle for the mind.* New York: Doubleday.

Schein, E. H. (1961). *Coercive persuasion.* New York: Norton.

Sprenger, J., & Kramer, H. (1968). *Malleus Maleficarum [The hammer of witchcraft.]* London: Folio. (Original work published 1486).

Stover, E., & Nightingale, E. O. (1985). Introduction. In E. Stover & E. O. Nightingale (Eds.), *The breaking of minds and bodies* (pp. 1–26). New York: Freeman.

Suedfeld, P. (1980). *Restricted environmental stimulation: Research and clinical applications.* New York: Wiley.

United Nations General Assembly. (1984, December 10). *Convention against torture and other cruel, inhuman, or degrading treatment or punishment.* New York: United Nations.

Valladares, A. (1986). *Against all hope.* New York: Knopf.

West, L. J. (1985). Effects of isolation on the evidence of detainees. In A. N. Bell & R. D. A. MacKie (Eds.), *Detention and security legislation in South Africa* (pp. 69–84). Durban, South Africa: University of Natal, Centre for Adult Education.

2

Psychological Consequences of Torture: A Need to Formulate New Strategies for Research

Barbara G. Melamed, Jodi L. Melamed, and Jacqueline C. Bouhoutsos

Torture is defined not only by the acts committed but also by the individual's response to these acts. Thus, the viewpoint taken herein is that the chronic stress associated with torture must be understood as a person–environment interaction. Torture is a crisis that occurs within a system, whether political or personal, and that manifests itself over time. One must consider the situation and individual characteristics that predated its onset, the immediate reaction to change imposed by its occurrence, and its long-term influences. Amnesty International (1984) defined torture partly as "state-induced severe pain or suffering, whether physical or mental, which constitutes an aggravated and deliberate form of cruel, inhuman, or degrading treatment or punishment." Mental suffering, a rather general concept, can be defined in terms of the physiological, behavioral, and subjective experiences that stem from torture episodes.

In this chapter we review the few empirical studies that have attempted to document the psychological effects of political or religious torture on victims and their families. A discussion of psychosomatic illnesses is included, as they often result when there is a prolonged stress experience. In many instances, the victims of torture are not themselves directly involved in the political issues but are symbols of nationality or religion or by association with the groups who come under attack.

In this review we describe the manifestation of torture-related symptoms over time and the similarities and differences with other posttraumatic stress disorder (PTSD) syndromes, such as those exhibited by prisoners of war, hostages taken in terrorist raids, and rape victims. We discuss the methodological weaknesses that limit generalizing from the current data. First, we define the conditions of the

The authors are indebted to Amnesty International for the incentive to understand the phenomenon of torture and for providing the documentation of so many cases. The Rehabilitation Center for Torture Victims, Juliane Maries Vej 34 DK-2100, Copenhagen, Denmark, has provided many resources. Dr. F. Allodi, Director of the Transcultural Psychiatry Division, Toronto Western Hospital, Toronto, Canada M5T 2S8, provided a personal perspective on the assessment and treatment of torture victims. Dr. Peter Suedfeld's persistence, encouragement, and sage editorial advice made this contribution possible.

torture that have been identified as important to the consequences. Then, individual factors that may identify those people who are most vulnerable to the traumatic effects following torture are defined; the individual's response to torture may vary depending upon existing social supports and opportunities to escape the circumstances of torture.

We discuss whether the stress of torture is a unique condition that induces distinctive PTSD or is similar to situations such as hijackings, hostage-taking, combat, thermonuclear leaks, and sexual abuse. These different stressors, which may evoke similar symptoms, vary greatly in terms of the circumstances (e.g., degree of premeditation) of the event and the process by which the accessibility of the victims is achieved. Similarities in the psychological consequences may obscure the clinician's decision on how to treat victims when differences in attitudes, self-perception of threat, or phases accompanying recovery have not been carefully noted. There are often delayed effects. Theoretical conceptions regarding the etiology of the torture syndrome and susceptibility of individuals to torture are very limited.

IDENTIFYING VICTIMS OF TORTURE

Few professionals are trained to recognize the signs and sequelae that characterize victims of torture. Many look only at presenting symptoms, superficially attributable to a variety of causes, and deeper problems may go unnoticed. Consider, for example, the case of a 56-year-old Cuban physician who had left Cuba during the Castro regime. He had some problems adjusting and was referred for treatment of panic disorder. He was divorced and currently having repeated difficulties in a new relationship with a nurse. His predominant complaint was that he would have a panic attack if he drove too far from home or from the hospital where he worked. He also carried a gun under his front seat for protection. He often drove at more than 100 miles per hour in order to return home or to the proximity of the hospital where he was employed. He could not fly on an airplane, and travel was very limited. He was severely depressed and lethargic and was taking an antidepressant. It was not until after he began treatment for the panic disorder that he revealed recurrent nightmares and flashbacks about his experiences in a prison, in which he had both been a torture victim and assisted in the torture of others.

In another case, a young woman from El Salvador asked for assistance. She was feeling that she could not catch her breath. When asked whether she had experienced this before and what other symptoms she had, she described chest pain, anxiety, headaches, sleep disturbance, and loss of feeling for her son and her husband. She also stated that she had gone to the emergency room of a local hospital several nights previously, and an EKG had revealed no heart problems. She also experienced nightmares and flashbacks in which she heard gunfire and voices threatening violence to her husband, her daughter, and herself—events that had actually occurred in El Salvador seven years earlier. She now lived in the United States; had remarried; and had a five-year-old son, a nice home, a job, legal status, and pending citizenship. Externally, all appeared to be going well. The manifest symptomatology indicated a heart problem, and the physician on call had responded to the presenting complaint and dismissed the patient without further exploration of psychiatric problems. It is likely that similar instances occur frequently in emergency rooms and in the offices of most health care providers.

How can we recognize victims of torture? Stress reactions have been found to be the most frequent presenting symptoms of victims. There is an extensive literature available on both the short-term and long-term effects of violent trauma in the cases of Holocaust victims and war veterans. Recent studies have provided us with information about other populations (e.g., Allodi et al., 1985; Padilla & Comas-Diaz, 1986). One major Canadian study showed that although physical symptoms of torture tended to abate with time, psychological difficulties lasted for many years afterward (Allodi et al., 1985).

Such psychological sequelae are designated "delayed or chronic Post-Traumatic Stress Disorders" in the *Diagnostic and Statistical Manual of Mental Disorders*, third edition (DSM-III, American Psychiatric Association, 1980) and by the *Manual of the International Statistical Classification of Diseases, Injuries, and Causes of Death* (ICD-9) of the World Health Organization (1977). The DSM-III specifies that the essential feature of PTSD is the development of "characteristic symptoms following a psychologically traumatic event that is generally outside the range of usual human experience." The manual states further that the most characteristic symptoms of this disorder are the reexperiencing of the traumatic events; numbing of responsiveness to, or reduced involvement with, the external world; and various autonomic, dysphoric, or cognitive symptoms.

Research has revealed that the disorder is more severe and longer lasting when the stressor is of human design. The stressors experienced by Vietnam veterans, Holocaust survivors, and victims of political torture fall within this category. It is not unusual for symptoms to emerge in these victims after many years, and even to occur in the next generation, as has been reported by Holocaust survivors and their families. Researchers report that Australian prisoners of war incarcerated by the Japanese during World War II still suffer guilt, bursts of irrational anger, nightmares, claustrophobia, agoraphobia, compulsive behavior, psychosomatic symptoms such as gastrointestinal upsets and dermatological problems, short-term memory loss, depression, and, in some cases, acute psychiatric disturbances—40 years after the precipitating events (Nelson, 1987). Because of the long time interval before many of these symptoms surface, it is understandable that physicians or psychotherapists may overlook the real etiology and apply treatment measures that deal only with the manifest symptomatology.

In recent years, mental health personnel who have worked with victims of torture have identified a torture syndrome subsumed under PTSD. Symptoms most frequently described include recurrent, painful intrusive recollections of the events while the victim is awake and frequent dreams and nightmares reliving the event while the patient is asleep. Dissociation and disconnection from friends and loved ones for periods of time are also common occurrences. This is frequently called *psychic numbing* or *emotional anesthesia*. There is loss of the ability to feel close; frequently, intimacy and sexuality are not possible. Whereas the most universal symptom described is that of stress, other symptoms of PTSD include anxiety, hyperalertness, lack of concentration, memory disturbances, and other cognitive dysfunctions. Psychosomatic complaints are also frequent.

These symptoms are the same as those that occur following rape and criminal assault, and it is unclear what extra informational value the word *torture* has in terms of identifying a different syndrome. We believe that individuals' susceptibility to torture discriminates the syndrome. In this chapter we argue that there is something unique that occurs in victims of torture, namely, the devaluation of the person's world view and a loss of the ability to maintain an optimistic outlook. Current researchers in psychology (e.g., Kobasa, Maddi, & Kahn, 1982; Kobasa & Puccetti, 1983; Scheier & Carver, 1985) have argued that the failure to maintain optimism puts the individual's immune system at risk for illness. Perhaps a useful addition to our armamentarium of tools to assess consequences of torture would be the inclusion of measures related to the ability to remain optimistic.

FACTORS THAT LEAD TO STRESS IN SURVIVORS

Conditions of Torture

Intensity of Torture

The physical or psychological duration of torture experiences has been postulated to determine the extent of a victim's posttraumatic disturbances. However, physical brutality is not always present in terrorism. In some contexts, the term *terrorism* denotes coercion through domination and fear. Cline and Alexander (1986) defined state-sponsored terrorism as the employment of violence or the threat of it to attain strategic objectives by criminal acts intended to create overwhelming fear in the target population.

Unpredictability

Frequently torture involves removing the victim's sense of control. Comprehension and prediction are both necessary for control and are forms of control in their own right (Seligman, 1975). There is a large body of data that shows that animals and humans prefer predictable to unpredictable aversive events (Badia, Harsh, & Abbott, 1979; Pervin, 1963). In a cognitive theory specific to the victimization experience, Peterson and Seligman (1983) focused on the uncontrollability of the onset and termination of victimization and the effect of this on the development of subsequent cognitive and behavioral deficits. This best explains why some victims become numb and passive. They believe that because the onset is unpredictable and the event unescapable, coping attempts are futile. Low self-esteem and self-blame are associated with this state. If the state becomes chronic, and if the victim believes that the cause of the event is in the nature of humanity, then the symptoms will be more pervasive and exhibited in many situations in which one's self-esteem is questioned.

Lack of Control

In wartime situations, Milgram (1986) argued, the threat of losing one's control of events and control of self is what leads to severe crises. Control over external events may be exercised by the individual acting alone or in concert with significant others to influence outcomes affecting others, one's group, or oneself. Control can also be exercised over internal events. In his attributional analysis of war-related stress, Milgram (1986) argued that control over oneself is essential if one is to persist in solving problems and to function in an appropriate and efficient manner over a long period of time, for example, while in detention as a prisoner of war. Because the enemy intends to destroy us or weaken or destroy our power to control our own destinies, war is rated as a much more powerful stressor than are natural disasters such as earthquakes or floods.

The threat to one's belief system has the adverse effect of demoralizing the individual. Thus, the strength and resilience of one's belief system determines how one withstands threat. Generalizations from the particular to the general are especially powerful. If one generalizes broadly from a particular instance of destruction or powerlessness to a large-scale counterparts of these events, the effect is more devastating than if what is lost is regarded as of limited consequence. According to Milgram (1986), belief systems are highly idiosyncratic. They differ in content, susceptibility to confirmation or disconfirmation, adaptability, and generalizability. Because the type and intensity of the reaction depend on the victim's perception of the trauma, the disturbance is generally presumed to be more severe and to require more skilled and prolonged treatment when the stressor is induced deliberately by other human beings. Suddenness of impact often intensifies the problem because the ego does not have time to prepare for or process such an assault on the psyche (Frederick, 1986).

However, before we put too much confidence in the belief system as a discriminator of the impact of stress, we should look at experimental analogues in situations with both humans and animals where controllability has been systematically altered by operant conditions. Human subjects rate controllable noise as less aversive than uncontrollable noise (Glass & Singer, 1972). In many animals, the certainty of control reduces the autonomic impact of aversive events (Gatchel, McKinney, & Koerbernick, 1977). The behavioral consequences of uncontrollable aversive events on animals, reviewed by Mineka and Kihlstrom (1978), include slowed responding, loss of interest in sex and food, and less aggression. Thus, without any notion of cognitive attribution, it does appear that uncontrollability and unpredictability contribute to the impact of aversive stressors.

Foa, Steketee, and Osolov Rothbaum (1988) reviewed relevant theories and concluded that both the duration and number of uncontrolled traumatic events modified PTSD symptoms in rape victims and combat veterans. In trying to understand why some torture victims may escape the symptoms, it is important to look at the variables of uncontrollability and unpredictability and the importance of the consequences for the victim. Thus, an individual who has had a history of successful control prior to being tortured may have more resistance against the stress-induced symptoms of helplessness. It may also be, however, that individuals who had previously successfully survived an uncontrollable dangerous situation may be inoculated against succumbing to a later version of the experience. This may be one of relatively few hypotheses in this field that can be clearly tested against each other.

Guilt

Guilt may be understood as a direct extension of the three constructs just described. If guilt is defined as a failure to exercise perceived control in a situation to prevent a catastrophe from occurring, then the failure to do something against the perpetrator could lead to a state of guilt. Foa et al. (1988) asserted that the combination of an unpredictable trauma and the perception of unexercised controllability may exacerbate posttraumatic stress reactions. Guilt may also be viewed as an attempt to regain perceived controllability. That is, by feeling guilty over not having exercised sufficient control, the victim can persuade him- or herself that the possibility of control did exist.

Relationships Between Perpetrators and Victims

To understand how the relationship that exists between perpetrators and victims can be a source of stress for survivors, consider the case of survivors of hostage, whose phobias specific to the perpetrator are their most apparent symptom. The hostage may have thoughts, even if unrealistic, that the perpetrator will exact some additional maltreatment on the victim or the victim's family. Frequent psychological symptoms are helplessness and depression, anhedonia, memory deficit, loss of concentration, generalized anxiety, and wavering feelings toward the captors. In this respect, hostage victims suffer from reactions similar to those prisoners of war.

There appears to be a sequence of events that is likely to occur (Frederick, 1986). First, hostages typically talk of attempts to get the captors to recognize them as human beings, rather than as expendable items, by discussing family and other personal topics. Second, victims try to discuss nonthreatening topics such as the weather or sports. Third, they set goals, believing that they will live until some event of personal significance, for example, a son's graduation. Fourth, victims maintain their physical condition by exercising. Fifth, they maintain hope and faith in their family, God, and even their captors.

In extreme cases, identification with the aggressor has been reported. Both in stories of Holocaust survivors and in popularized accounts such as those of Patricia Hearst's capture, the tendency to imitate the perpetrator is evident. In some cases, as the captivity persists over time, the Stockholm Syndrome manifests itself. This phenomenon derives its name from an incident involving some young women who were held hostage in a Stockholm bank. After the incident was terminated, some of the hostages criticized the police and defended the criminals. Such victims frequently perceive their captors as protectors and believe that the perceptions and actions of the police are jeopardizing the victim's life.

Individuals' Susceptibility

Age

Although children and the elderly can be especially vulnerable victims, other age groups are by no means immune to severe long-term effects of trauma. It may be that younger individuals have less experience in dealing with uncontrollable stress and have not acquired coping methods to prolong their resistance. Older people, on the other hand, may actually suffer more punishment and may already have impaired physical health, which may exacerbate their trauma.

Premorbid Psychological Adjustment

Segal and Margalit (1986) studied the level of premorbid risk factors of soldiers with refractory combat stress reactions. They found more pathological interpersonal nuclear family relationships, poor school adjustment, difficulties in intimacy in adolescent and marriage relationships, and more disciplinary problems during military service among soldiers suffering from such reactions. These data were obtained through a retrospective comparison of Israeli soldiers who succumbed and those who did not succumb to combat stress reactions following the conflict in Lebanon. Many of the blind diagnoses made using the DSM-III revealed the presence of a premorbid personality disorder in soldiers who suffered chronic stress reactions. Thus, an individual who is already suffering from neurosis or other borderline personality or affective disorders it likely to suffer more.

Biological Hyperarousability

There are theories that postulate increased vulnerability caused by a hyperactive adrenal system (Kolb, Burris, & Griffiths, 1984). Others, in contrast, postulate that those susceptible to PTSD are parasympathetically dominant (Pena, 1984). In the research of Pena (1983) on Vietnam veterans, self-rated boredom and sensation-seeking scale scores were higher in veterans suffering from PTSD than in age-related controls with insomnia. The veterans with PTSD reported that minor and major central nervous system depressant drugs actually increased their experience of anxiety. Their return to noncombat situations was viewed as a state of inadequate stimulation. The data used to support this theory were primarily the dream activity profiles of the veterans with PTSD.

A more popular theory of physiological susceptibility has to do with central noradrenergic hyperactivity in response to a relative decrease in endogenous opiates (Van der Kolk, Boyd, Krystal, & Greenberg, 1984). This theory is based on the animal analogue of exposure to inescapable and unavoidable shock. Such exposure is postulated to increase norepinephrine turnover, increase plasma catecholamine levels, deplete brain norepinephrine, and increase acetylcholine. This may explain the chronic startle response, an exaggerated neurochemical change in face of new stressors that interfere with response initiation and maintenance (Anisman, 1978). However, the use of beta blockers, including clonodine and propranolol, has not led to long-term relief among human sufferers and, in particular, has not ameliorated the symptoms of guilt and shame.

Family and Environmental Supports

Cohesion and Social Support

Many studies have reported less devastating effects of war-related stress when group cohesiveness had been accomplished during basic training (see Milgram & Hobfoll, 1986). Close personal ties based on mutual trust and friendship serve as a positive stress-resistant factor that reduces the likelihood of succumbing to combat stress situations (Lieberman, 1982); however, the existence of such ties can also increase the degree of victimization experienced when a buddy is maimed or killed or when a soldier becomes an isolated prisoner of war.

Although emotional disturbances occur to some degree in the majority of victims, Frederick (1986) stated that support from significant others and from authorities can aid in ameliorating the distress. When there has been a prior relationship with other victims in a group, sharing and support can be salutary in its effect. In the studies of war hostages in Israel (Ayalon & Soskis, 1986), it was found that helping or taking care of other hostages was a valuable coping response. Successful coping was aided by religious thinking and behavior, or other strategies aimed at maintaining meaning and hope, and by sharing with and caring for other hostages. Eitinger (1980) noted that Norwegian prisoners of war who returned to families that accepted their low level of functioning fared better than did Jewish prisoners who had no families giving similar psychological support.

Emigration

The phenomenon of being forcibly uprooted from one's home and having to resettle somewhere else is thought to contribute to the degree of susceptibility to PTSD. Political persecution and the forced emigration of people from their homeland to a new country constitute a major source of stress for many groups and people (Coelho, Yuan, & Ahmed, 1980). The deleterious effects of having to cut ties with one's familiar surroundings and to establish new ties in unfamiliar and possibly threatening settings are well documented (Tiryakian, 1980).

In a study of the evacuation of Jewish settlers from the Yamit region of the Gaza strip, measures of symptomatology one month after evacuation showed that those settlers who had strong original motivations for settling in Yamit and poor social support systems were more disturbed than were those with weak motivations and strong support systems. Those, however, who were resistors in the sense of having strong ideological and political motivations were insulated from the trauma of evacuation. In assessing the availability of stress-resistance factors in people under crisis, it is important to distinguish between motivation and support systems and between belief systems before and during the crisis in order to evaluate assets and deficits (Toubiana, Milgram, & Falach, 1986).

Period of Separation

In defining the intensity of the trauma, we spoke earlier about the duration of the torture. Along the same lines, we need to look at what else was occurring at the time in the person's existence when separation occurred. For instance, many of the studies to be presented on children of torture victims find a similarity between symptoms of maternal deprivation and the consequences of separation. Thus, the loss of the parents in reality, or because the father has been removed and the mother is only minimally fulfilling the parenting role, would have more devastating effects in children under the age of three than in older children. Cultures or situations such as kibbutz life may provide extended families that would mitigate the foregoing effects.

Societal Reaction

Societal reactions to victims are not a very well-studied phenomenon. With regard to rape victims, we are told that the system reinforces the concept that somehow the victim was to blame: the victim was dressed seductively or gave cues about being available. Blaming the victim would certainly lead to guilt feelings in the victim. Veronen and Kilpatrick (1983) proposed that through attribution and cognitive appraisal, female rape victims blame themselves if they hold the belief that women cannot be raped. Low self-esteem and self-blame are associated with helplessness. Abramson, Seligman, and Teasdale (1978) added the component of internality to their concept of learned helplessness. If a female victim attributes the cause of the event to herself, she will show symptoms that are more pervasive across situations. The response of large (and highly visible) segments of American society to the Vietnam War was hostile and demeaning at worst and ambiguous at best (Milgram, 1986). Thus, deaths and casualties were not represented as acts of heroism.

THE SIMILARITY BETWEEN PTSD
AND THE TORTURE SYNDROME

Many of the psychological problems reported fit in general with the DSM-III's description of PTSD, which is characterized by symptoms that include reexperiencing the traumatic event; a numbing of responsiveness to, or reduced involvement with, the external world; and a variety of autonomic, dysphoric, or cognitive symptoms. There have been several studies of PTSD among Vietnam veterans (Keane, Zimmering, & Caddell, 1985). These studies have documented the similarity of symptoms in victims of torture and those exposed to battle disasters. A number of investigators (Blanchard, Kolb, Gerardi, Ryan, & Pallmeyer, 1986; Blanchard, Kolb, Pallmeyer, & Gerardi, 1982; Dobbs & Wilson, 1960; Malloy, Fairbank, & Keane, 1983) were successful in showing that post-Vietnam combat PTSD patients (like torture victims) showed greater autonomic reactivity in response to standard combat stimuli than did various control groups; however, these studies had design flaws. The subjects varied in age, educational level, and extent of combat experience; some studies used medicated subjects or failed to specify subjects' medication status; and some had or may have had group baseline differences in physiological arousal. In addition, by using standard sets of combat-related stimuli, they may have effectively failed to reproduce what was uniquely stressful about a particular individual's traumatic experiences.

One study that provided an appropriate control group and used a multidimensional assessment battery avoided these problems. It was designed to address the question of who is most vulnerable to the effects of combat stress, manifested in PTSD, among veterans who were exposed to similar combat conditions. Pitman and his colleagues (Pitman, Orr, Forgue, de Jong, & Claiborn, 1987) studied 18 nonmedicated, PTSD-diagnosed veterans and compared their physiological arousal during recollection of traumatic experiences with a control group of Vietnam combat veterans matched in the extent of combat and severity of traumatic experiences who failed to meet the DSM-III criteria for diagnosis as a mental disorder. Thus, Pitman et al.'s research employed the veterans' imagery of their own experiences as the means of eliciting physiological responses. Each veteran also described a traumatic pre-combat experience, a positive experience, and a neutral experience. The Impact of Events Scale (Horowitz, Wilner, & Alvarez, 1979) was used to rate each of the reactions to the scripts.

It was found that skin conductance and frontalis electromyographic responses to scripts of individualized combat-related situations did discriminate between the veterans classified as exhibiting PTSD and those who did not develop this psychiatric condition. However, reactions to the pre-combat traumatic scenes did not differentiate between the two groups. The fact that there was greater autonomic reactivity specific to combat would suggest that this group was more vulnerable to the traumatic revoking of the stress reaction. The PTSD subjects also reported more anger, fear, and sadness in their self-reported emotional responses to traumatic imagery than did control group subjects.

In recent years, psychologists have identified a number of subcategories of

PTSD, including rape trauma syndrome and therapist–patient sex syndrome. Despite their diverse etiologies, these subcategories seem to have very similar symptomatologies (Kilpatrick, Veronen, & Best, 1985). For example, of 11 descriptors of therapist–patient sex syndrome (Pope & Bouhoutsos, 1986), 7 also appear in the literature on the torture syndrome. However, some characteristics have been noted in victims of torture that are not found in other subcategories. For example, these patients manifest symptoms of what has been designated "chronic organic psychosyndrome," an indicator of diffuse brain damage that has affected concentration camp survivors and sailors who had survived battle (Abilgaard et al., 1984; Lunde, 1982; Rassmussen & Marcussen, 1982). The symptomatology is similar to that present in presenile dementia.

Another finding described as specific to torture victims is that both the very young and the elderly appear to suffer more than the middle generation. Allodi and Cowgill (1982) reported that the severity of symptoms is positively correlated with older age in their studies. This may be because mature men were treated more harshly than younger men by the torturers. Older men also had a more difficult time psychologically because most carried the responsibilities for families as well as a concern for their own well-being. Younger people recovered very quickly even if their disturbances were very severe. Foster and Sandler (1985) reported similar findings in their report on Africa.

STUDIES OF VICTIMS OF TORTURE

Victims Who Remained in Their Own Country

It may be anticipated that the degree of disintegration following torture would be lower in individuals who have better social support. Therefore, we compare the psychological sequelae of victims who remained in their own environment, where family or social cohesiveness may buffer them against some of the aversive effects, with the sequelae seen in those who were uprooted subsequent to torture. Two studies, of Greeks (Peterson et al., 1985) and Northern Irelanders (Fields, 1976), represent the only systematic evaluations of individuals who were subjugated to torture and then returned to their own neighborhoods.

The 22 individuals studied in Greece at two points in time, 2 to 8 years after the torture events and again 10 years after the first assessment, provided clear evidence that many symptoms not initially apparent had developed over the years. One must be cautious in interpreting these as direct results of the torture, as there were many lifestyle changes imposed by the remaining physical and psychological trauma. Also, bias may have been introduced: Although the investigations were conducted by the Danish Amnesty International Medical Group, it was Greek clinical psychologists who actually collected the interview and test data. The political views of these researchers may have predisposed them to view the government then in power in Greece unfavorably, perhaps leading to an artifact in the data that they reported. The torture victims who came forward to participate in this study may have been those with a desire to obtain political or other restitution for their suffering.

Within the limits imposed by these possible contaminants, which apply to all studies of this sort, the results revealed that the subjects had sustained organic, locomotor, neurological, and psychological damage. Changes in symptom frequency from the first to the second observation period supported hypotheses regarding the long-term maintenance of symptoms. The finding that 90% of the respondents had psychological symptoms that were unrelated to age, severity of torture, or the lapse of time between torture and the second observation emphasizes the need to define and understand this pervasive syndrome.

Long-lasting psychological effects were also shown in the study of 125 Northern Irish men who had been evaluated by means of a standard battery of psychological tests including the Thematic Apperception Test and the Bender–Gestalt Memory for Designs Test. Results showed that there were psychological effects regardless of exactly when the victims were evaluated, between six weeks and one year after torture. In most of the victims, the symptoms were very similar to those found in the Greek study. These men, aged 16 to 54, suffered recurrent headaches, nightmares, dizziness, disturbed memory, disabling fears and depression, and marked irritability.

Victims Who Emigrated

There exist many more studies of individuals who had been tortured in their home countries and then emigrated than of victims who reestablished their lives in their original community. In these studies (Allodi, 1980; Allodi & Cowgill, 1980) the confound of being in a foreign country is not easy to separate from the psychological sequelae of torture. Because the results are similar to the others even though the groups vary in age, educational level, and time of torture relative to the study, it appears that the syndrome is pervasive. The Latin Americans studied in Denmark, Canada, and the United States have equally high reports of somatic symptoms including sleep disturbances, anxiety, depression, and irritability.

In a large Canadian study of 41 Latin American refugees (Allodi & Cowgill, 1982), all but three of the victims displayed somatic symptoms. Most complained of severe nervousness or insomnia with recurrent nightmares. Many suffered from anxiety, depression, or unspecified, deep-seated fears. Half of the victims mentioned behavioral and personality changes, mainly irritable outbursts, impulsive behavior, or social withdrawal. Four people had attempted suicide. Eighteen of the victims reported changes in mental functioning; of these, 13 reported loss of concentration or attention and blocking of thought processes. Twelve reported difficulty in remembering, and 5 reported episodes of confusion and disorientation. Similar findings have been reported from Denmark, Ireland, Latin America, and Western Europe. A recent study of Chilean émigrés (Padilla & Comas-Diaz, 1986) identified other similar symptoms of helplessness, feelings of disintegration, inability to concentrate, impaired memory, specific or generalized fear, social withdrawal, irritability, loss of appetite, and a variety of additional psychosomatic symptoms.

Records of three groups of torture victims were studied by Somnier and Genefke of the Danish Treatment Center (1986). Group 1 included 200 case reports from Amnesty International medical examinations of torture victims. Descriptions of torture methods were analyzed to obtain information about the procedures used and their impact on victims. Victims were from Latin America, Europe, Africa, and Asia. Group 2 consisted of 24 male torture victims from Latin American countries, treated by the Department of Neurology, Rigshospitalet, Copenhagen. The notes from that treatment group were analyzed. Group 3 comprised the 24 victims from Group 2, plus 4 European and 2 African victims. Twenty-nine of the 30 victims were male. All available victims were selected, and no control group was included. The authors conducted in-depth interviews with many of the victims.

In this research, efforts were made to identify causal relationships between the types of torture used and the sequelae of torture. Two types of torture procedures were differentiated by the authors: weakening and personality destroying. The former taught the victims to be helpless and created feelings of exhaustion. The latter induced guilt, fear, and loss of self-esteem. Specific techniques of torture such as deprivation or reduced environmental stimulation were reported to result in cognitive disturbances, disorientation in time and space, difficulty in concentration, poor memory, and, in some cases, psychotic reactions and hallucinations. Long-term sequelae were described as emotional instability and, ultimately, the "weakening of the identity." There were also feelings of guilt, fear, loss of self-esteem, helplessness, and confusion.

Among victims who had been defined by their captors as mentally ill, admitted to psychiatric institutions, and given various drug treatments against their will, the subsequent symptoms were those just mentioned plus, in some instances, the side effects of the medication. Based on the analyses presented in this study, one cannot conclude that different types of torture lead to distinct symptom patterns.

Research findings from these studies provide important information that can serve as bases for the diagnosis and treatment of victims of torture. Most of the research that has been described here is available through the documentation center in Copenhagen. The Danish Treatment Center is in contact with many countries around the world and collects whatever materials are available regarding research concerning victims of torture. The Center's objective, as stated in its brochures, is to serve as a global resource to interested people, particularly for those who are doing research on the topic of torture. Thus far they have collected and systemized about 2,000 bibliographic materials—journals, newspaper articles, films, and slides—which are catalogued and available from the Center.

The torture study center organized in Toronto by Allodi (1987) provides another resource. There is a specially developed questionnaire (Allodi, 1988) that identifies the types of torture that the client and his or her relatives had experienced. This questionnaire also provides for the collection of information about motivations for emigration and about the social network of the individual. It assesses the current legal status and integration of the immigrant in the new society. Attempts are made to quantify type of torture by whether or not the following elements were present: nonviolent persecution, imprisonment, violent torture, deprivation, sensory manipulation, psychological torture, disappearance, or death. Even though these categories may need refinement, they provide a first step in separating the experiences of torture into categories that may be evaluated to see how they influence the consequences of torture as well as the process of recovery from those consequences.

Child Victims

Another subgroup of victims in the study of torture is children who, although not physically assaulted, were present during the torture of others (usually close relatives, most frequently their parents). Children are often gravely affected by the torture of members of their families. By the usual definition, this cannot be considered to be torture of those children, since there is no deliberate infliction of pain on them by another and this is an integral part of the definition of torture. However, it is important to consider these secondary effects, which in many instances appear to be similar to the symptoms of the victims of torture. Studies of Chilean and Argentine children provide information about these secondary effects (Allodi et al., 1985); three studies are described here.

In one study, 203 children under 12 years of age (65% under 6 years) who had been told that their fathers were in prison were examined and tested. They were administered Goodenough drawing tests and interviewed. Other family members were also interviewed. Not knowing whether the father was dead, the families had undergone a repeated cycle of hope and despair for a number of years. Symptoms reported and observed included withdrawal, depression, intense generalized fear, fear triggered by specific environmental stimuli (such as sirens, uniformed people, or the sound of automobile engines at night), loss of appetite and weight, sleep disturbances, regression in behavior and school performance, dependency and clinging behavior toward mothers.

A second study, by an agency in Santiago, examined nine children of Chilean families that had been subjected to political persecution. Their experiences were similar to those of the group described in the previous paragraph. Most had witnessed the violent arrest and ill-treatment of one or both parents, the destruction of property, threats, and personal violence. One or both parents died or disappeared, and the children had been placed with other relatives or friends. The result was the sudden interruption of psychological development. Fear became the predominant emotion and was involved in all relationships. Profound sentiments of powerlessness, vulnerability, and paralysis pervaded their lives as they witnessed the collapse of parental protection and security. In those instances where the mother remained with the children, she was frequently oppressed by the disappearance of her husband. Grieving for her own loss and coping with her own fear and anxiety seriously detracted from her ability to fill the role of mother, let alone compensate for the loss of the father.

In a third study (Marzolli et al., 1979), similar experiences and symptoms were reported among 29 Argentine families and their 28 children exiled in Mexico. All of the families had been subjected to direct violence (prison and torture); social ostracism and stigma; economic loss (robbery at the time of search or unemployment); or ideological repression (book burning; control of libraries, schools, universities, and media; or the government urging to spy and report on people). The families also had migrated, which is viewed by the authors as a conflict situation, because it entails a loss of affective bonds with family, friends, and community, whereas the demands placed by the new environment interrupt the process of mourning. The method of investigation included interviews, drawing tests, play therapy, intelligence testing, Bender Psychomotor tests, and teachers' ratings.

The most common symptoms reported since the time of the experience were insomnia, eating disorders, behavioral regression or arrested development, aggressiveness, somatic complaints, and overdependence on parents. When the children had been exposed directly to violence, the symptoms were more severe. Older children were more likely to show aggressiveness.

A comparison of these three studies of Chilean and Argentinean children revealed that most of the children under six years of age reacted with similar symptoms: social withdrawal; chronic fear; depressive moods; clinging and overdependent behavior; sleep disorders; somatic complaints; and an arrest of, or regression in, social habits and school performance. Irritability and aggressiveness were observed among the older children and as the younger ones moved on to the later years of childhood.

The author concluded that the symptoms shown by comparable age groups of children were very similar regardless of whether their parents had been torture victims, survivors of Nazi concentration camps (DeGraaf, 1975; Leon, Butcher, Kleinmar, Boldberg, & Almagor, 1981), subjects of political persecution and imprisonment in Northern Ireland during 1969 and the early 1970s, or simply imprisoned for criminal and civil offenses or taken away into exile. Symptoms appear to be primarily related to the loss of the parents or the protective home atmosphere because of the parents' absence, psychological disorganization, or preoccupation. A later Danish study (Aalund et al., 1985) confirmed these results and made some negative predictions. The authors concluded that children suffering serious damage because of the experiences described will probably have lifelong psychological sequelae.

CONSIDERATIONS FOR FUTURE RESEARCH

Future empirical studies should focus on specific gaps in our knowledge. The questions that arise are complicated. These include the following: Who is most susceptible to breakdown in the face of chronic stress? What are the differences due to duration of exposure to the stressor? Does the age of the individual at the time of trauma affect the manifestation of disorders? Are the different forms of torture likely to be related to differences in the symptoms exhibited? Should all victims of acute trauma associated with involuntary detention and physical or psychological abuse be treated to prevent further occurrence of symptoms?

These questions require more rigorous research procedures than most of the literature demonstrates at this time. For example, many researchers recognize the need to obtain information from victims at a standard time. Following this precept in actual studies is something else again. Many factors make it unlikely that one will be able to study people immediately upon their release from detention. The released prisoner may continue to be afraid that informants may report his or her participation in research and that, as a result, the ex-prisoner (or relatives, friends, etc.) will be persecuted. Many victims are moved to new locations, often becoming socially isolated from the support networks of their own cultures and making the effects of torture difficult to disentangle from the problems of alienation and acculturation in a new setting.

In addition, there is little consistency in the use of psychological tools from one investigation to another. Much of the data regarding types of torture used is confounded by memory problems or the simultaneous use of many different means of torture. Compared with speculations and assumptions about cross-generation transmission of trauma, there are too few systematic studies of the effect of torture on families, especially children.

In order to address issues of the specificity of psychological trauma of victims of political torture, we need to develop instruments that will qualitatively and quantitatively allow the multidimensional picture to emerge. Studies in which the sample is recruited on a cross-sectional basis and studied over time can best address the issues of causal relationships and maintenance of trauma. Unfortunately, this ideal is rarely met.

The individuals and families that come forward to be studied may be those that have something to gain, be it monetary reimbursement or psychological therapy. They may represent a biased sample in another way as well, having a higher proportion than the population of torture victims of individuals with serious symptoms and failure to adapt. To minimize another possible source of bias, the design must include control groups, matched for age and other demographic factors, ethnic and cultural origin, and socioeconomic status. The researchers should be blind as to which participants have actually been tortured and which are there as control group subjects.

It is also difficult to determine whether forced migration has severe effects that influence the picture. It would be important therefore that we study parallel immigrant families who leave their country of origin for reasons other than political repression. Perhaps, with the unfortunate increase in innocent victims of hijacking or hostage situations, we can obtain a random selection of individuals to assess the strength of premorbid personality beliefs, family connections, and social support on the coping ability of these groups. There are treatment centers in Canada and the United States that may have access to a population for prospective longitudinal evaluation of adjustment.

The short-term hostage, the rape victim, and the politically tortured as currently all subsumed under the PTSD classification of the DSM-III. This may indicate that there is a common psychological pattern that accompanies feelings of enforced helplessness. However, by developing a systematic battery of psychological tools that would allow us to test finer distinctions, we could make significant advances in differentiating the consequences of these insults to the patient and family and in understanding the adaptation process within unique environments (same country, different country, in family environment, in displacements camps, etc.). This, in turn, would improve our ability to anticipate and plan what preventive actions can be taken to block the development of the post-trauma symptoms or to eliminate them if they do develop. If we want to understand the psychological sequelae of torture, we must learn to view the experience as it occurs: to an individual (but having an impact on others); within a social, political, and personal environment; and with repercussions across a time span of many years.

In terms of research, certain procedures need to be applied.

1. Multivariate analyses are important to clarify the association of factors with outcomes across different stages. Regressiqon approaches, preferably those that control for the time ordering of predictors, seem capable of developing such multivariate predictions.

2. The need for longer term follow-ups is substantiated by the appearance of symptoms over an extended period of time.

3. There is a need for better indicators of preassault psychosocial status of victims.

Large-scale prospective epidemiological studies of groups high in incidence of potential victimization would be useful in looking at the relation between predisposing characteristics and the risk of psychological breakdown. Perhaps the early military records of combat veterans or ex-prisoners of war, especially those who had been given a broad battery of psychological tests for purposes of selection or assignment, could be made available for post hoc analyses of susceptibility to PTSD.

Longitudinal studies comparing a treated group with a nontreated group have not yet been done, because specialized treatment of this population is a fairly recent development. Also, many victims are reluctant to undergo psychological treatment and can be expected to be even more resistant to accepting random selection and assignment to control groups. In addition to patients' concerns, the primary problem for mental health professionals is the ethical issue of placing patients in untreated control groups. All types of research efforts must be looked at with caution. One approach that has been suggested is blind evaluation of the therapy protocols at the start and completion of therapy, and at regular intervals during the course of treatment. The Danish Rehabilitation Center for Torture Victims currently uses this method of evaluation.

REFERENCES

Aalund, O., Cohn, J., Danielson, L., Holzer, K., Koch, Severin, B., & Thogersen, S. (1985). A study of Chilean refugee children in Denmark. *Lancet, 2,* 437–438.

Abilgaard, U., Daugaard, G., Marcussen, H., Jess, P., Petersen, D., & Wallach, M. (1984). Chronic organic psycho-syndrome in Greek torture victims. *Danish Medical Bulletin, 31,* 33–41.

Abramson, L. Y., Seligman, M. E. P., & Teasdale, J. D. (1978). Learned helplessness in humans: Critique and reformulation. *Journal of Abnormal Psychology, 87,* 49–94.

Allodi, F. (1980). The psychiatric effects in children and families of victims of political torture. *Danish Medical Bulletin, 27,* 229–232.

Allodi, F. (1987). *An integrated service approach to the victims of violent oppression.* Paper presented at the meeting of the United Nations Organization, New York, NY.

Allodi, F. (1988). Canadian Center for Investigation and Prevention of Torture. Unpublished questionnaire.

Allodi, F., & Cowgill, G. (1982). Ethical and psychiatric aspects of torture: A Canadian study. *Canadian Journal of Psychiatry, 27,* 88–102.

Allodi, F., Randall, G. T., Lutz, E. L., Quiroga, J., Zunzunegui, M. V., Kolff, C. A., Deutsch, A., & Doan, R. (1985). Physical and psychiatric effects of torture: Two medical studies. In E. Stover & E. O. Nightingale (Eds.), *The breaking of minds and bodies: Torture, psychiatric abuse, and the health professions* (pp. 58–78). New York: Freeman.

American Psychiatric Association. (1980). *Diagnostic and statistical manual of mental disorders* (3rd ed.). Washington, DC: Author.

Amnesty International. (1984).

Anisman, H. (1978). *Psychopharmacology of aversively motivated behavior.* New York: Plenum Press.

Ayalon, O., & Soskis, D. (1986). Survivors of terrorist victimization: A follow-up study. In N. A. Milgram (Ed.), *Stress and coping in time of war: Generalizations from the Israeli experience.* New York: Brunner/Mazel.

Badia, P., Harsh, J., & Abbott, B. (1979). Choosing between predictable and unpredictable shock conditions: Data and theory. *Psychological Bulletin, 86,* 1107–1131.

Blanchard, E. B., Kolb, L. C., Gerardi, R. J., Ryan, P., & Pallmeyer, T. P. (1986). Cardiac response to relevant stimuli as an adjunctive tool for diagnosing posttraumatic stress disorder in Vietnam veterans. *Behavior Therapy, 17,* 592–606.

Blanchard, E. B., Kolb, L. C., Pallmeyer, T. P., & Gerardi, R. J. (1982). A psychophysiological study of posttraumatic stress disorder in Vietnam veterans. *Psychiatric Quarterly, 54,* 220–229.

Cline, P. S., & Alexander, Y. (1986). *Terrorism as a state-sponsored covert warfare.* Fairfax, VA: Hero Books.

Coelho, G. V., Yuan, Y. T., & Ahmed, P. I. (1980). Contemporary uprooting and collaborative coping: Behavioral and societal responses. In G. V. Coelho & P. I. Ahmed (Eds.), *Uprooting and development: Dilemma of coping with modernization.* New York: Plenum Press.

Cohn, J., Holzer, K. I., Koch, L., & Severin, B. (1980). Children and torture: An investigation of Chilean immigrant children in Denmark. *Danish Medical Bulletin, 27,* 238–239.

DeGraaf, T. (1975). Pathological patterns of identification in families of survivors of the Holocaust. *Israel Annals of Psychiatry and Related Disciplines, 13*, 335–363.

Dobbs, D., & Wilson, W. P. (1960). Observations on the persistence of war neurosis. *Diseases of the Nervous System, 21*, 40–46.

Eitinger, L. (1980). The concentration camp syndrome and its late sequelae. In J. E. Dimsdale (Ed.), *Survivors, victims, and perpetrators: Essays on the Nazi Holocaust* (pp. 127–162). Washington, DC: Hemisphere.

Fields, R. M. (1976). Torture and institutional coercion: Northern Ireland: A case study. In (Chair), *Torture and Institutional Coercion.* Symposium conducted at the meeting of the American Sociological Association, New York, NY.

Foa, E. B., Steketee, G., & Osalov Rothbaum, B. (1988). Behavioral/cognitive conceptualizations of posttraumatic stress disorder. *Behavior Therapy.*

Foster, D., & Sandler, D. (1985). *A study of detention and torture in South Africa: Preliminary report.* Cape Town, South Africa: University of Cape Town, Institute of Criminology.

Frederick, C. J. (1986). Psychic trauma in victims of crime and terrorism. In G. R. VandenBos & B. K. Bryant (Eds.), *Cataclysms, crises, and catastrophes: Psychology in action* (pp. 55–108). Washington, DC: American Psychological Association.

Gatchel, R. D., McKinney, M. E., & Koebernick, L. F. (1977). Learned helplessness, depression, and physiological responding. *Psychophysiology, 14*, 25–31.

Glass, D. C., & Singer, J. E. (1972). *Urban stress: Experiments on noise and social stressors.* New York: Academic Press.

Horowitz, M., Wilner, N., & Alvarez, W. (1979). Impact of Event Scale: A measure of subjective stress. *Psychosomatic Medicine, 41*, 209–218.

Keane, T. M., Zimmering, R. T., & Caddell, J. M. (1985). A behavioral formulation of post-traumatic stress disorder in Vietnam veterans. *The Behavior Therapist, 8*, 9–12.

Kilpatrick, D., Veronen, L. J., & Best, C. L. (1985). Factors predicting psychological distress among rape victims. In C. R. Figley (Ed.), *Trauma and its wake.* New York: Brunner/Mazel.

Kobasa, S. C., Maddi, S. R., & Kahn, S. (1982). Hardiness and health: A prospective study. *Journal of Personality and Social Psychology, 42*, 168–177.

Kobasa, S. C., & Puccetti, M. C. (1983). Personality and social resources in stress-resistance. *Journal of Personality and Social Psychology, 45*, 839–850.

Kolb, L. C., Burris, B. C., & Griffiths, S. (1984). Propanolol and Clonidine in treatment of the chronic post-traumatic stress disorders of war. In B. Van Der Kolk (Ed.), *Post-traumatic stress disorder: Psychological and biological sequelae.* Washington, DC: American Psychiatric Press.

Leon, G. R., Butcher, J. N., Kleinmar, M., Boldberg, A., & Almagor, M. (1981). Survivors of the Holocaust and their children: Current status and adjustment. *Journal of Personality and Social Psychology, 41*, 503–516.

Lieberman, M. (1982). The effect of social supports on response to stress. In L. Goldberger & S. Bresnitz (Ed.), *Handbook of stress: Theoretical and clinical aspects.* New York: Free Press.

Lunde, I. (1982, August). Mental sequelae to torture. *Mandeschrift for praktish laegegerning*, 1–14.

Malloy, P. F., Fairbank, J. A., & Keane, T. M. (1983). Validation of multimethod assessment of posttraumatic stress disorders in Vietnam veterans. *Journal of Consulting and Clinical Psychology, 51*, 488–494.

Milgram, N. A. (1986). An attributional analysis of war-related stress: Modes of coping and helping. In N. A. Milgram (Ed.), *Stress and coping in time of war: Generalizations from the Israeli experience.* New York: Brunner/Mazel.

Milgram, N. A., & Hobfoll, S. (1986). Generalization from theory and practice in war-related stress. In N. A. Milgram (Ed.), *Stress and coping in time of war: Generalizations from the Israeli experience.* New York: Brunner/Mazel.

Mineka, S., & Kihlstrom, J. F. (1978). Unpredictable and uncontrollable events: A new perspective on experimental neurosis. *Journal of Abnormal Psychology, 87*, 256–271.

Nelson, M. (1987). The health care needs of refugee victims in New South Wales. In J. Reid & T. Strong (Eds.), *Torture and trauma.* Unpublished report, Department of Health, Western Metropolitan Health Region.

Padilla, A., & Comas-Diaz, L. (1986, November). A state of fear. *Psychology Today*, pp. 60–65.

Pena, A. de la (1984). Post-traumatic stress disorder in the Vietnam veteran: A brain modulated, compensatory information-augmenting response to information underload in the central nervous system. In B. Van Der Kolk (Ed.), *Post-traumatic stress disorder: Psychological and biological sequelae.* Washington, DC: American Psychiatric Press.

Pervin, L. A. (1963). The need to predict and control under conditions of threat. *Journal of Experimental Psychology, 31*, 570–585.

Petersen, H. D., Abilgaard, U., Daugaard, G., Jess, P., Marcussen, H., & Wallach, M. (1985). Psychological and physical long-term effects of torture: A follow-up examination of 22 Greek persons exposed to torture 1967–1974. *Scandinavian Journal of Social Medicine, 13,* 89–93.

Peterson, C., & Seligman, M. E. P. (1983). Learned helplessness and victimization. *Journal of Social Issues, 2,* 103–116.

Pitman, R. K., Orr, S. P. Forgue, D. F., de Jong, J., & Claiborn, J. M. (1987). Psychophysiological assessment of post-traumatic stress disorder imagery in Vietnam veterans. *Archives of General Psychiatry, 44*(11), 970–975.

Pope, K., & Bouhoutsos, J. (1986). *Sexual intimacy between therapists and patients.* New York: Praeger.

Rasmussen, O., & Marcussen, H. (1982, March). The somatic sequelae to torture. *Manedskrift for praktisk laegegerning.*

Scheirer, M., & Carver, C. (1985). Optimism, coping, and health: Assessment and implications of generalized outcome expectancies. *Health Psychology, 4,* 219–248.

Segal, R., & Margalit, C. (1986). Risk factors, premorbid adjustment, and personality characteristics of soldiers with refractory combat stress reactions. In N. A. Milgram (Ed.), *Stress and coping in time of war: Generalizations from the Israeli experience.* New York: Brunner/Mazel.

Seligman, M. E. P. (1975). *Helplessness: On depression, development and death.* San Francisco: Freeman.

Somnier, F., & Genefke, K. (1986). Psychotherapy for victims of torture. *British Journal of Psychiatry, 149,* 323–329.

Tiryakian, E. A. (1980). Sociological dimensions of uprootedness. In G. V. Coelho & P. I. Ahmed (Eds.), *Uprooting and development: Dilemma of coping with modernization.* New York: Plenum Press.

Toubiana, Y., Milgram, N. A., & Falach, H. (1986). The stress and coping of uprooted settlers: The Yamit experience. In N. A. Milgram (Ed.), *Stress and coping time of war: Generalizations from the Israeli experience.* New York: Brunner/Mazel.

Van Der Kolk, B., Boyd, H., Krystal, J., & Greenberg, M. (1984). Posttraumatic stress disorder as a biologically based disorder: Implications of the animal model of inescapable shock. In B. Van Der Kolk (Ed.), *Post-traumatic stress disorder: Psychological and biological sequelae.* Washington, DC: American Psychiatric Press.

Veronen, L. J., & Kilpatrick, D. G. (1983). Stress management for rape victims. In D. Meichenbaum & M. E. Jaremko (Eds.), *Stress reduction and prevention.* New York: Plenum Press.

World Health Organization. (1977). *Manual of the international statistical classification of diseases, injuries, and causes of death* (9th rev., vol.). Geneva, Switzerland: Author.

3

The Effects of Torture and Other Maltreatment: Implications for Psychology

Brian E. Engdahl and Raina E. Eberly

Maltreatment of those held in captivity has continued to occur throughout the ages. The subject of this chapter is its effects, both negative and positive. Maltreatment frequently overwhelms a person's defenses and often produces long-lasting physical and psychological impairments. However, although most captives who are subjected to maltreatment become distressed and preoccupied with their experience, only a minority develop diagnosable mental disorders; positive effects have also been reported. The effects of torture and other maltreatment have been most widely recognized and studied among survivors of World War II German concentration camps. Thus, we review research on those survivors as well as on those held as prisoners of war (POWs) and political prisoners of repressive governments who have been tortured or otherwise severely maltreated.

In this chapter, we outline the psychological issues raised by the long-term consequences of being exposed to maltreatment in captivity. Because these consequences are influenced by the characteristics of the maltreatment itself (e.g., its duration, intensity, and nature) and the characteristics of the individual (e.g., age at exposure, coping mechanisms, and predisposition), these consequences are key areas for psychologists. We outline the status of current knowledge and the methodological dilemmas of research in this area, and we use the Department of Veterans Affairs' (VA) experience in serving a group of survivors of captivity as a backdrop for discussing the directions that research, treatment, and public action should take.

We deeply appreciate the comments of James B. Rounds, Jr., who initially encouraged us to write this chapter; the financial support of the American Contract Bridge League Charity Foundation Corporation; and the comments of Allan Harkness, Matthew McGue, and Peter Suedfeld on earlier drafts of this chapter.

Requests for reprints of this chapter should be sent to Brian E. Engdahl, Psychology Service (116B), VA Medical Center, One Veterans Drive, Minneapolis, MN, 55417.

TORTURE AND MALTREATMENT DEFINED

The maltreatment of captives has been defined by international agreements such as the Geneva Conventions of 1929 and 1949 and United Nations' (1957) standards. The former apply primarily to prisoners of concentration camps or prisoners of war; the latter are most often applied to political prisoners. Maltreatment is most frequently characterized by (a) being subjected to the physical and psychological abuse of torture, (b) prolonged solitary confinement, (c) lack of food (a diet that results in significant weight loss), (d) ill health and lack of adequate medical care, or (e) witnessing the torture or killing of other prisoners. These abuses may occur singly but most often occur in combination. It is not unusual to find individuals who, in captivity, were subjected to torture, lost more than 30% of their body weight, suffered untreated bone fractures or other injuries, and were held in isolation for months at a time.

With the exception of torture, the parameters of maltreatment have not been explicitly defined. Torture is any deliberate infliction of severe physical or mental pain or suffering through cruel, inhuman, or degrading treatment or punishment (United Nations General Assembly, 1984). Torture techniques include not only the use of instruments like whips and clubs, but also the modern technology of electricity; methods of psychological assault (e.g., threats against loved ones and sustained disruption of sleep patterns); and drugs that cause pain, hallucinations, muscle spasms, and paralysis (Amnesty International, 1983).

THEORETICAL CONSIDERATIONS

General Models of Reactions to Torture and Maltreatment

The psychological and physical components of maltreatment are not readily differentiated. Although researchers usually highlight the psychological injuries inflicted during captivity, the physical dimensions of maltreatment also are often noted. Chief among them are direct brain trauma caused by blows to the head and the effects of starvation and untreated physical illness. These may be directly responsible for at least some chronic psychological sequelae. Eitinger (1975) studied a large random sample of Nazi prison and concentration camp survivors living in Norway and Israel, including Jewish and non-Jewish citizens and military personnel. He concluded that the "concentration camp syndrome," which is characterized by anxiety, sleep disturbances, and an array of psychosomatic symptoms, is organic and is caused by trauma and malnutrition. Most camp survivors he studied had one or more major symptoms of the syndrome. Thygesen, Hermann, and Willanger (1970) reached similar conclusions in their work with Danish World War II concentration camp survivors.

Beebe (1975) proposed an explanatory model involving two types of injury: one is somatic and essentially short-term, caused by malnutrition, infection, and physical injury; the other is psychological and is essentially permanent. These lead to a loss of ego strength (decreased feelings of well-being and self-efficacy) and lowered thresholds for both physical and psychological distress. Similarly, Tennant, Goulston, and Dent (1986) attributed their findings of increased psychopathology among Australian former POWs of the Japanese to the prolonged psychological stress and severe physical privation they suffered.

Because the sequelae to such maltreatment resemble posttraumatic stress disorder (PTSD), models of this disorder are relevant. The descriptions of "survivor syndromes" that have evolved from this literature are now represented in the American Psychiatric Association's (1987) *Diagnostic and Statistical Manual of Mental Disorders*, third edition, revised (DSM-III-R) by a separate category of mental disorder, PTSD. The DSM-III-R recognizes that certain stressors such as torture frequently produce PTSD and that its severity and duration may be greater when the stressors are of human design. Among PTSD's frequent features are the victim's continued reexperiencing of the trauma through dreams and intrusive recollections, numbing of emotional responsiveness to the external world, and physiologic reactivity manifested through anxiety, sleep disturbances, hypervigilance, and sensory hypersensitivity. Of all mental disorders, PTSD has been viewed as the most clearly psychologically based. It can be conceptualized readily by learning theory as a psychological disorder in which exposure to a stimulus (catastrophic stress) is followed by a conditioned emotional response and consequent negatively reinforced avoidance behavior (Keane, Fairbank, Caddell, Zimering, & Bender, 1985).

As an alternative to a purely psychological theory of PTSD etiology, Kolb (1987) postulated neuropsychological bases for PTSD, drawing upon the known functional and structural defects in the peripheral nervous (sensory) system caused by high intensity stimulation. He suggested that central cortical changes occur as the consequence of prolonged and excessive sensitizing stimulation. When an individual's capacity to process traumatic, life-threatening stimuli is overwhelmed, the function and perhaps structure of the cortical neuronal barrier is impaired. This leads to both hypersensitivity and impaired habituation learning, and thus impaired discriminative perception and learning, accounting for the range and persistence of symptoms observed in PTSD populations. Those veterans with war-induced PTSD whom he has studied display an ongoing perceptual abnormality whereby they are unable to discriminate nonthreatening sensory inputs from fear-arousing inputs associated with the traumatic events. Their persistent symptoms (e.g., hyperalertness, repetitive fearful nightmares, irritability, and other conditioned emotional responses) may be explained through functional impairments in neuronal and synaptic cortical processing. He theorized that they may suffer from excessive autonomic nervous system arousal of central adrenergic origin.

Kolb integrated divergent experimental and empirical literature and suggested avenues of research that may clarify the mechanisms underlying PTSD and related conditions. He recommended basic animal research on fear-conditioned chronic states and human studies of the psychophysiological, electrophysiological, neuropathological, and neurochemical mechanisms of PTSD. Some of his specific research suggestions include the use of modern imaging technology to study the brain's processing of stress-arousing and neutral stimuli in victim and control groups, and postmortem studies of brain tissue in individuals with PTSD. Watson, Hoffman, and Wilson (1988) also emphasized the biological perspective as being crucial to the understanding of PTSD. Among their recommendations is a call for closer collaboration among researchers in learning theory, neurochemistry, and neurophysiology.

Vulnerability to Captivity Trauma

The assumption that predisposing constitutional or developmental abnormalities are sufficient etiologic factors for the full development of posttraumatic psychopathology among maltreated individuals (a pure diathesis model) has not been supported by the facts. This predisposing defect notion was adopted initially by the German government in providing reparations to victims for injuries sustained in concentration camps (Matussek, 1971/1975). An additional cause for "traumatic neuroses" was thought to be the victim's desire for compensation. Review boards and examining professionals resisted acknowledging survivors' emotional distress as a consequence of imprisonment, attributing it to individual weakness or "compensation neurosis." Pressure from victims and their advocates led to broadened standards for granting such reparations, in which posttraumatic syndromes were recognized as consequences of the imprisonment experience. Similarly, the United States VA now recognizes anxiety, depressive, and PTSD syndromes as being service-related for any former POW.

The diathesis-stress model (Rosenthal, 1970) fits clinical and research observations more closely than the pure diathesis model. Rosenthal was among the first to posit an underlying continuum of vulnerability to stress. According to this model, traumatic captivity exceeds the coping capacities of many individuals, even those who would be stress-resistant under normal circumstances. Many researchers examining the consequences of traumatic captivity advocate a pure stress model, suggesting that maltreatment by itself can precipitate severe mental disorders including depression and chronic anxiety states. Although debate continues (see Breslau & Davis, 1987; Ursano, 1987), this literature indicates that many individuals exposed to significant trauma will develop some chronic psychological symptoms. A smaller but significant proportion will develop persistent diagnosable mental disorders. The role of predisposition remains unclear.

METHODOLOGICAL ISSUES

Sample Composition

Those who survive to give a personal account are clearly a special group. Those studied in most empirical research are unrepresentative of maltreated captives in general in that they are less healthy than the total pool of survivors (being clinical cases or applicants for compensation). Even when selected randomly from nonclinical populations, they are representative only of those who survived until the time of their examination. Thygesen et al. (1970) noted that older prisoners were less likely to survive during their imprisonment in concentration camps and after repatriation, if they survived. Hence differential sampling distorts the picture of cohort effects. Harsher camp conditions led to higher mortality.

Cohen and Cooper (1954) discussed the possible effects of the selective mortality that occurs both during incarceration and during the interval between release and examination among POWs. They speculated that the adverse conditions in Japanese prison camps responsible for the extremely high observed mortality rate could be assumed to have had strong selective effects. Those who survived such conditions presumably were of better than average physical and psychological health prior to captivity and thus theoretically they may produce an overall upward distortion in all population estimates derived from sampling based on them. However, follow-up studies (Beebe, 1975) demonstrated that these subjects bear lasting negative residuals of ill health from the experience, with their morbidity and mortality rates equaling or exceeding that of their non-POW cohorts. Survivor groups could reveal "positive" effects of trauma and positive coping strategies (Antonovsky, 1979), but this possibility has not been systematically examined in research thus far.

Assessment and Diagnosis

Debate surrounds the clinical evaluation of captivity survivors. Standard psychiatric diagnostic interviews such as the Research Diagnostic Criteria (Spitzer, Endicott, & Robins, 1978) typically do not elicit information adequate for a full understanding of the experiences of captivity and its aftereffects. Many survivors undergo psychiatric examinations in which reference to their captivity is minimal or absent, obviously decreasing the quality of assessment and treatment. Mollica, Wyshak, and Lavelle (1987) developed an interview schedule tailored for use with Southeast Asian refugees. The VA's POW History questionnaire (1984) also was developed specifically for use with American POWs. Both are good examples of standardized approaches that directly elicit detailed information about the nature of an individual's captivity experiences and subsequent adjustment, thus improving evaluations and treatment.

Captivity survivors typically display a variety of psychological symptoms upon release from captivity that subside with time. A minority display persistent diagnosable mental disorders, with anxiety symptoms most common. Early evaluation and research on survivors (Eitinger, 1975) loosely described a "concentration camp syndrome" characterized by anxiety, sleep disturbances, and an array of psychosomatic symptoms. The syndrome initially was conceptualized as acute reaction to stress and on that basis was established as "anxiety reaction" in the list of recognized diagnoses in the *Manual of the International Statistical Classification of Diseases, Injuries, and Causes of Death* (ICD-9; World Health Organization, 1977).

The establishment of PTSD in the psychiatric nomenclature, that is, in the DSM-III (American Psychiatric Association, 1980) was initially supported by clinicians who conceived it as a disorder more chronic than ICD-9's "anxiety reaction" and who also were dissatisfied with the absence from DSM-II (American Psychiatric Association, 1968) of a "gross stress reaction" category that originally was present in DSM-I (American Psychiatric Association, 1952). The introduction of PTSD was catalyzed by passage of legislation recognizing the Vietnam veteran (Fuller, 1985). Indeed, shortly after becoming an official diagnosis, PTSD became a compensable disorder as recognized by the VA.

The validity of this diagnostic category has been repeatedly questioned (e.g., Breslau & Davis, 1987). The problem of what constitutes validity of a psychiatric disorder is a difficult one and was laid out clearly by Robins and Guze (1970). They recommended achievement of diagnostic validity through a method consisting of five phases: clinical description, laboratory studies, delimitation from other disorders, follow-up study, and family study. The clinical descriptive work (phase 1) done to date supports the claim of PTSD proponents that it represents a single typical syndrome that repeatedly is found to follow a wide variety of life-threatening trauma. The sufficiency of the etiologic role of trauma in PTSD has generated continuing controversy. In fact, it is curious that in a diagnostic manual that purports to eschew etiologic considerations (on grounds of insufficient knowledge), PTSD is the lone companion of the organic mental disorders in having a purported causal sequence.

Because the DSM-III-R is not intended as a set of unmodifiable rules, PTSD is a provisional or "open construct," as is the case with many other diagnostic categories. The validity of PTSD as a diagnostic category may be judged through its contributions to increased understanding of the effects of the maltreatment of captives and the treatment of adversely affected survivors. The PTSD construct remains open to modification through continued validational research. That such ongoing revision is occurring is suggested by modifications in the diagnostic criteria for PTSD that have appeared in the DSM-III-R, although the evidence that these changes represent refinements rather than tinkering is not apparent.

The laboratory studies (phase 2) are numerous, steadily increasing in number, with findings generally consistent with PTSD's defined clinical picture (see Kolb, 1987, for more detail). In regard to delimitation from other disorders (phase 3), with the introduction of PTSD into the standard nomenclature in 1980 investigators were able to give survivors this diagnosis and did so with frequency, although overlap with other diagnoses is common in many samples. For example, Sierles, Chen, McFarland, and Taylor (1983) found that, among 25 combat veterans with a diagnosis of PTSD, 14 (56%) met the criteria for one additional diagnosis, 5 (20%) for two additional diagnoses, and 2 (8%) for three additional diagnoses. This diagnostic heterogeneity among poorly adjusted survivors of maltreatment in captivity will probably continue to be found, with PTSD the most frequent, but by no means only, diagnosis.

Follow-up study of those with the diagnosis of PTSD (phase 4) is necessarily limited, given its relatively recent introduction. Such studies are underway and are expected to provide additional information on this aspect of validity. Kluznik, Speed, Van Valkenburg, and Magraw (1986) attempted to retrospectively diagnose PTSD in a large sample of American POWs released from captivity more than 40 years prior to their examinations. They concluded that more than half of their sample (67%) fulfilled DSM-III criteria for PTSD within one year of their release, and that more than half of those affected continued to have symptoms more than 40 years later. This consistency, although established retrospectively, lends support to the validity of the PTSD diagnostic category.

No family studies of PTSD (phase 5) have been conducted because of the nature of the disorder being related to the occurrence of a particular stressful event. However, the possibility of family studies exists in circumstances in which several family members experience the same trauma (e.g., natural disasters and Southeast Asian refugees). If an underlying predisposition to develop PTSD or related disorders exists, family or twin studies would be illuminating.

The introduction of PTSD has certainly promoted increased clinical attention and systematic study of survivors of catastrophe. Prior to its introduction, studies examining survivors showed many of them to be suffering a variety of diagnoses, such as anxiety and depressive reactions, adjustment reactions, and delayed bereavement (Beebe, 1975; Thygesen et al., 1970). No epidemiologic data are currently available, and the prevalence of PTSD has been estimated in only preliminary ways with respect to particular stressful events (Merikangas & Weissman, 1986). Research on PTSD is growing rapidly, demonstrating associations among factors related to etiology, treatment, and prognosis (Andreasen, 1985). Contrary to the assertions of its critics, the support for the validity of PTSD as a diagnostic category appears to be steadily growing.

Documentation

Prospective designs are not possible, and in their absence retrospective designs must suffice. The problem of retrospective bias in the recall of traumatic events has been emphasized (Depue & Monroe, 1986) and demonstrated (McFarlane, 1988), which further complicates the study of torture and maltreatment effects to some degree. However, studies in which verification of torture, injuries and weight loss have been available to the investigators (e.g., Speed, Engdahl, Schwartz, & Eberly, 1989) provided findings consistent with those based on only the self-reports of the survivors. This is most easily determined for former POWs who underwent standard military induction medical examinations and for whom records of these examinations remain available to researchers and treatment professionals. Pre-captivity medical records are less likely to be available for survivors of other maltreatment experiences.

STATUS OF CURRENT KNOWLEDGE

Scope of the Problem

The effects of maltreatment in captivity are a significant contemporary social issue. Despite international agreements that forbid it and denials from governments that use it, torture is a regular occurrence in many parts of the world (Amnesty International, 1983). Because torture is almost never officially acknowledged by its perpetrators, and victims are often unwilling or unable to report it, the number of torture victims cannot be estimated accurately.

Solomon (cited in Veterans Administration, 1983) estimated there were 1,000 Canadian former prisoners of the Japanese and 6,000 prisoners of other powers. Stenger (1986) estimated that 76,403 former POWs remained alive in 1987 in the United States. The worldwide number of former POWs is likely to be many times Stenger's figure. Many of them were subjected to intentional harm at the hands of their captors, and still more shared with their captors the damages of armed attack, food and shelter deprivation, and forced relocations.

Civilian prisoners taken during international conflicts include an estimated 75,000 European Jewish Nazi concentration camp survivors (Epstein, 1979) and about one million non-Jews (Ruge, cited in Thygesen et al., 1970). Recent wars and civil upheavals have subjected untold thousands to inhumane imprisonment experiences. For example, Kinzie, Fredrickson, Ben, Fleck, and Karls (1984) described a sample of Cambodian death camp survivors, and Mollica et al. (1987) reported trauma-related symptoms among Southeast Asian refugees, many of whom were imprisoned and tortured.

Studies completed by the United Nations Commission on Human Rights (United Nations, 1984) and by organizations such as the International Commission of Jurists reported a steady escalation of human rights violations, although such increases are difficult to document. Amnesty International (1984) has published dozens of reports on torture in specific countries, including Bolivia, Chile, the People's Republic of China, Colombia, Haiti, Iraq, Northern Ireland, Pakistan, Peru, Spain, the Soviet Union, and Uruguay.

Sources of Our Knowledge

Accounts of Survivors

There exists a body of personal and clinical observations about inhumane incarceration and its effects. The earliest literature was dominated by the writings of psychiatrists and psychologists who themselves were held in Nazi prison camps (Bettelheim, 1943; Frankl, 1959). Authors such as Timerman (1981) provided accounts of maltreatment at the hands of post-World War II governments. Insights developed by clinicians working with survivors of concentration camps (Chodoff, 1980) provided a perspective for examining the experience of survivors.

These accounts document maltreatment, personal methods of coping, and observations of others' coping attempts. They are essentially case studies written from the personal point of view. Such reports are important because they draw attention to a new area, help identify major themes, and arouse the attention of clinicians, researchers, and the public. They are biased, however, in that they were written by those survivors of traumatic captivity who achieved at least some degree of recovery—the "adapted afflicted" (Eitinger, Krell, & Rieck, 1985). These accounts often suggest that individuals emerge from such experiences as better people, having experienced personal growth, with firm identities and life goals. Many reported greater appreciation for freedom, family, and the like. The maladapted afflicted (those who have experienced little recovery) do not write their stories and therefore are not represented in this literature. Their status is, in some ways, better described in the empirical literature.

Empirical Research

Various captivity survivor groups have been examined. Thygesen et al. (1970) intensively studied Danish survivors of the Nazi concentration camps, many of whom were subjected to extended sessions of interrogation and torture, primarily physical torture in the form of blows or kicks to the head. Threats of execution or reprisals against their families were common. Episodes from these sessions often formed part of their recurrent nightmares 20 to 25 years later. They were held 4 months to 4 years under conditions characterized by extreme overcrowding; inadequate shelter and hygiene; and protein- and fat-poor diets of approximately 1,000 calories daily, combined with work that required 3,000–4,000 calories.

Matussek (1971/1975) described the health and psychological adjustment of Jewish survivors of concentration camps who were seeking reparations from the German government. He described a constellation of disorders including a "psychophysical syndrome" (a state of exhaustion with depressive overtones), gynecological and internal disorders, and a "psychic syndrome" (mistrust, isolation, and paranoia) occurring with high frequency among those he studied.

Eaton, Sigal, and Weinfeld (1982) studied the psychiatric status of Holocaust survivors using a community sample drawn at random from all known survivors living in Montreal. A control group was developed that consisted of Jews who were not in Europe during World War II, except those who might have served in the Allied Armed Forces. Survivors were more likely than their controls to exhibit psychiatric impairment even though the study was conducted 33 years later. They noted no differences in physical health status.

In a large national sample of United States former POWs, Beebe (1975) found World War II POWs of the Japanese to be more physically and psychiatrically disabled than their counterparts held by the Germans or the Koreans (during the Korean War). This presumably was due to the harsher treatment suffered at the hands of the Japanese, characterized by a higher incidence and greater severity of beatings, starvation, and untreated disease. Psychiatric disorders were common among all POWs, particularly anxiety reactions and somatization.

In randomly selected Australian World War II POW and non-POW combatant samples, Tennant et al. (1986) found significantly more anxiety and depressive disorders among the POWs. Engdahl (1987) described the physical and psychological status of POWs served by the Minneapolis Veterans Affairs Medical Center (MVAMC). The MVAMC region was thoroughly canvassed, leading to a high participation rate (approximately 70% of all known living POWs), yielding one of the largest POW samples ($N = 455$). In comparison with National Institute on Aging (1986) and National Institute of Mental Health (Robins et al., 1984) statistics drawn from groups comparable in sex, age, and time of survey, no significant differences in prevalence rates for common medical conditions—hypertension, myocardial infarction, diabetes mellitus, or cerebrovascular accident—were found among surviving POWs. Significantly higher prevalences of anxiety disorders, PTSD, and depressive disorders were found, whereas disorders with etiologies less clearly related to traumatic experience—alcohol abuse, schizophrenia, and bipolar disorders—did not occur with increased frequency. Forty-six percent of this group reported at least one positive result of their POW experience, typically an increase in appreciation for freedom, family, or country. This 46% tended to be of higher rank at the time of capture and to describe themselves as being in somewhat better health than those who perceived no positive consequences of their POW experiences.

In a related study (Speed et al., 1989), of 62 MVAMC POWs drawn randomly from the larger group of 455 described by Engdahl (1987), the strongest predictors of persistent PTSD were the experience of torture, beatings, and weight loss. Family history of mental illness, preservice adjustment problems, and severe childhood trauma were not predictive of PTSD development. They identified a subgroup of 7 survivors who did not suffer significant negative aftereffects even though subjected to maltreatment equal to the remainder of the group. Although these 7 men suffered POW experiences that were no less intense than those suffered by the entire group, they were not perturbed by events that their fellow captives found degrading, painful, and frightening.

When asked via questionnaire, 47% of the total sample believed that they had benefited in some way from their POW experience. The perceived benefits were general in nature and included a greater appreciation for freedom, a strong national defense, family, friends, and food. A perception of benefit was more likely among those of higher rank at the time of capture and less likely among those with alcohol problems subsequent to repatriation. A perception of benefit from the POW experience was not related to age at capture; months held captive; being injured as a POW; weight loss while in captivity; subsequent depressive, anxiety, or PTSD diagnoses; self-ratings of health; self-ratings of problems in adjusting to life after the service; number of years employed; or marital status at time of exam. Collectively, the MVAMC work highlights the links between traumatic captivity experience and later adjustment and the continuing needs of some survivors for treatment of these persisting symptoms.

Sledge, Boydstun, and Rabe (1980) described a group of American POWs held by the North Vietnamese who reported psychological benefit from their captivity. They found that "the subjective sense of having benefited from the experience of war imprisonment is positively correlated with the harshness of the experience" (p. 443). Sledge at al.'s POWs were perhaps more stress-resistant as they were highly selected and highly trained Air Force officers. All 221 continued their careers in the supportive environment of active military duty following repatriation.

Reports that focus on torture survivors (as distinct from concentration camp and POW survivors) have appeared only recently. Abildgaard et al. (1984) described a "chronic organic psycho-syndrome" observed in many of the 35 Greek torture victims they examined 6 months or more after their release. Impaired concentration, anxiety, and sleep disturbances were the chief features. Rasmussen and Lunde (1980) summarized the examinations of 135 torture victims, a group that included the 35 Greek nationals just described. Psychiatric symptoms (including impaired memory and concentration and sleep and sexual disturbances) were noted among 75% of the group. Allodi and Cowgill (1982) reported similar findings in their examinations of international victims of torture in their Toronto center. Jensen et al. (1982) reported cerebral atrophy and accompanying neurologic symptoms in 5 young torture victims, which was revealed by detailed x-ray examinations (computerized axial tomography).

THE DEPARTMENT OF VETERANS AFFAIRS' EFFORTS WITH FORMER POWs

Many United States former POWs experienced torture and maltreatment while in captivity. They are a victim population that recently has received increased attention. Follow-up studies, specifically those conducted by the National Academy of Sciences (e.g., Beebe, 1975; Keehn, 1980), previously cast light on the trauma and aftereffects experienced by American POWs of World War II and subsequent conflicts. However, the major impetus for increased research and clinical services targeted at American ex-POWs was provided by enactment of the 1981 Former Prisoners of War Act (Public Law 97-37). It offered complete health examinations and particular benefits to all former POWs, a potential group of 76,400, and established a special category of recognition and responsiveness for them. Using repatriation records, all surviving locatable former POWs were contacted directly to request their participation in thorough, free examinations and follow-up treatment. The use of a standard examination protocol and a standard background history questionnaire yielded uniform data from the more than 23,000 ex-POWs examined to date (Veterans Administration, 1987).

These efforts led to a nationwide increase in clinical services provided to former POWs and their families. A VA survey determined that 5,885 ex-POWs were in active psychological counseling at 146 VA health care facilities, and that approximately 1,240 families of that group of veterans were receiving conjoint counseling. More than 400 VA professional staff were engaged in this program of care. Holmstrom (1987) described a typical multifaceted treatment program developed for this group, the majority of whom were World War II veterans not previously treated for psychiatric problems but who continued to suffer adjustment problems 40 years after the captivity trauma. They would not have sought treatment in the absence of the legislatively mandated exam process. The findings of Engdahl (1987) and Speed et al. (1989) reported previously were made possible through this VA examination procedure.

DIRECTIONS FOR STUDY

More is known about the effects of the maltreatment of captives than is known about effective treatment. Therapists and researchers rely heavily on generalizations drawn from knowledge about victims of related traumatic events (e.g., violent crime and natural disasters) to understand the effects of captivity trauma and to direct the treatment of its victims. In a reciprocal manner, the evolving knowledge of captivity survivors' adjustment processes lends understanding to stress and coping phenomena observed in other traumatized populations. Not surprisingly, people's reactions to starvation, torture, and physical injury are consistent with findings regarding people's responses to other severe trauma. However, many survivors of inhumane imprisonment have undergone trauma that can be distinguished from that of other victims in its severity, duration, and combined threats to physical and psychological integrity. They experienced suffering deliberately inflicted by overwhelmingly strong captors.

Understanding adjustment to maltreatment has implications for teaching people to cope better. However, such research places limits on the commonly held assumption that all individuals can successfully cope with or recover from extreme stresses. Variables that moderate the impact of maltreatment need to be identified, and their roles need to be clarified. A small proportion of people who are exposed to severe trauma appear to benefit from it, and many suffer few negative aftereffects, but it is not clear what factors protect these individuals.

The effect of age on the manifestation of trauma-related disorders is unknown. Speed et al. (1989) found a negative correlation between age at time of capture and symptom severity 40 years after release among former World War II POWs. Kolb (1987) proposed a curvilinear relation between age at the time of trauma and later disorder. He suggested that both younger and older individuals may be more subject to long-term damage than are those of middle age. Younger people have had less experience, and therefore less neuronal activation, whereas older people are already undergoing neuronal inactivation. Middle-aged individuals have numerically larger, more trauma-resistant neuronal networks. Kobasa, Maddi, and Kahn's (1982) concept of hardiness (more mature individuals being more stress-resistant) also is consistent with these observations.

During interviews with more than 2,000 concentration camp survivors, Eitinger (1974) found that one of the most important coping mechanisms was the retention of the ability to make at least a few of one's own decisions. Segal (1986) described similar positive effects among American POWs held by North Vietnam of maintaining some small sense of control. Eitinger concluded that

people who mobilized active coping mechanisms had fewer psychiatric complications than did those who were completely isolated, remained passive, or ascribed survival to mere luck.

Shachak (1986) described "componentiality" as a coping strategy used by
Israeli POWs. Prisoners may cope by reconstructing social reality into highly
differentiated components that suit their own purposes, rather than surrendering
to a view of their plight as a totality, one of hardship and total control by their
captors. They may preserve their sense of self-identity by finding meaning in
their suffering even under the harsh conditions of the concentration camp
(Frankl, 1962).

Antonovsky (1979) formulated the idea of "salutogenesis" in his studies of
successful copers among survivors of extreme trauma. He pointed out that stress
research is dominated by a focus on pathogenesis, the processes by which stressors
lead to undesirable outcomes. Moderating or coping variables are introduced as
buffers, but the outcome variable remains illness. He advocated studies designed
to test hypotheses that explain successful, that is, healthy, outcomes. He reviewed
a wide range of stress studies (Antonovsky & Bernstein, 1986) from his salutogenic point of view and recommended paying increased attention to those who do
well even though they are in the high stressor category. He encouraged openness to
the possibility that stressors may have salutory consequences (the salutogenic orientation). His work on the predictors of health is a contribution to a broad-range
theory of coping. Selye's (1975) position on the positive effects of stress ("eu-
stress"), Kobasa's work on hardiness (Kobasa et al., 1982), and Bandura's self-
efficacy (1977) are other examples of a shift toward interest in coping and positive
outcomes.

IMPLICATIONS FOR TREATMENT

Many individuals who might benefit have not been directly offered the opportunity for treatment. They often are reluctant to seek treatment because of the general stigma attached to receiving mental health services, particularly shame over
their imprisonment (shame associated with being captured in wartime or being
accused of criminal acts as in the case of torture victims themselves accused of
perpetrating torture); being a member of a stigmatized group (e.g., the Korean
POW perceived by many to have succumbed to their captors' brainwashing attempts); or fear of deportation (e.g., refugee illegal immigrants). Although it is
uncertain whether all victims who have been negatively affected should be offered
treatment (some individuals may be unable to benefit from and may even be
harmed by psychological interventions), we must do more than develop programs
and passive remedial or legal structures. Interventions must "beckon victims to
help liberate themselves" (Elias, 1986, p. 221). This is clear from the VA's experience in applying the Former POW Act. Many former POWs and their families now
being served never would have sought psychological treatment in the absence of
the mandated exam process that enticed participation through complete physical
examinations and included referrals for identified treatment needs.

Survivors of traumatic captivity have suffered in obscurity, and only recently
have health care professionals, researchers, and governments focused attention on
their status. Their suffering was not explicitly recognized until the involvement of
activist victim groups (e.g., Vietnam combat veterans) led to the establishment of

the PTSD diagnostic category. Veterans groups provided impetus for the Former POW Act. The formation of the Society for the Study of Traumatic Stress is another example of increasing clinical, research, and political activism on behalf of victims of trauma.

One promising approach to intervention is provided by torture victim treatment centers. Bales (1987) provided an overview of their status. The prototype, the International Rehabilitation and Research Center for Torture in Copenhagen, Denmark, was initiated in 1974 (Somnier & Genefke, 1986). It has been fully operational for 5 years, coordinates the treatment of 200 victims annually, and provides extensive training, education, and research. Similar centers exist in Toronto and Minneapolis (see chapter 11, this volume), and additional centers are in the planning stages.

Those who provide therapy and conduct research with these survivors can become more sensitive to the chronic personal suffering experienced by many of them (Whittaker, 1988). Mollica et al. (1987) highlighted the importance of establishing trust and then conducting a thorough, systematic assessment of the survivors' trauma stories and experiences, as time-consuming and difficult as that may be for both the clinician and the survivor. Considerably more trauma information is thereby elicited—information that is not readily given in standard clinical interviews.

Survivors may have difficulty articulating their symptoms, making the clinician's role even more challenging. Those who have been traumatized both physically and psychologically may manifest their distress primarily through physical symptoms. In other cases, the victim's culture may not provide the vocabulary for describing psychological symptoms and syndromes. Krajick (1986) noted that Southeast Asian languages do not have words for concepts such as stress, anxiety, or mental health. Physical symptoms and sleep disturbances may not be perceived by them as connected to their past traumatic experiences.

Some survivors who have reached a minimal but tolerable level of adjustment tend to deny the long-term effects of trauma on themselves and their family members and therefore are not especially open to psychological intervention. Even if the survivor recognizes the effects of the ordeal, the help offered may be resented because it is perceived as a sign of weakness. As clinicians, we can communicate to both patients and the public that otherwise normal individuals often suffer negative psychological consequences from maltreatment. Those subjected to torture should be informed that confession or breaking down during torture is predictable and not a cause of shame. We may thus alleviate feelings of shame and guilt experienced by victims, many of whom may still believe that personal weakness is to blame for their suffering during and after captivity.

Knowledge that discussion of the traumatic events usually temporarily triggers increased distress, sleep disturbance, and so forth and is an expected part of the healing process is helpful to those in treatment. Support groups for victims (when appropriate) and their families help to increase the sharing of information and emotional support and to reduce the sense that individuals and their families are alone in their suffering.

DIRECTIONS FOR PSYCHOLOGY IN POLICY AND ACTION

The American Psychological Association (APA) recently stated its position on the general problem of human rights (APA Joint Subcommittee, 1984). The APA

Council of Representatives adopted a resolution condemning torture wherever it occurs (Abeles, 1986, p. 661). Rosenzweig (1988) reviewed APA human rights policies and actions and suggested further steps that APA could take to implement its resolution.

APA also has a report on torture (as a special case of human rights violations) and the role of psychology, developed by the Subcommittee on Psychological Concerns Related to Torture. This report forms the core of this volume. Suedfeld's portion of the report (chapter 7, this volume) reveals that charges of psychology's involvement in the assistance of torturers are largely unfounded, and he considers how psychological organizations and individual psychologists can combat the use of torture and help its victims.

At least since World War II, psychologists have been involved in the treatment and scientific study of the effects of the maltreatment of captives. Although a strictly academic approach is insufficient to address the meaning of such suffering inflicted by humanity, maltreatment raises issues relevant to many disciplines, including political science, sociology, law, psychiatry, and psychology. Even though involvement may raise unanswerable moral and philosophical questions, psychology has multiple ways to contribute to understanding the effects, treatment, and reduction of maltreatment. One example of such multidisciplinary involvement is the report of the American Association for the Advancement of Sciences' Committee on Scientific Freedom and Responsibility (Stover & Nightingale, 1985), which focuses on the role of health professionals in the use and prevention of both torture and psychiatric abuse. Another is the Joint Resolution Against Torture of the American Psychological Association and the American Psychiatric Association (see Preface, Table 1, this volume).

The roles for psychologists in this domain parallel those outlined by Siegal (1983). He called our attention to the victims of crime and violence, emphasizing the absence of adequate research in the area and the unique roles that psychology can play in research, treatment, and public education. He urged psychology to take the initiative in entering this neglected psychological arena. In a subsequent APA report (Kahn, 1984), a wide range of policy and practice issues pertaining to victims of crime and violence clearly can be extended to the victims of traumatic captivity.

Information on the maltreatment of captives and its effects may be mustered effectively by psychology to influence national and international policies and thereby protect these human rights. Psychology can reinforce a societal responsibility to victims, ensuring that their emotional upheaval is neither minimized nor forgotten. Psychology must continue research consistent with its reputation for impartiality, present it in a responsible fashion, and highlight its relevance to policy whenever possible. In our roles as scientists, practitioners, and citizens, we can increase our advocacy of and support for policies that seek to prevent oppression.

Historical accounts focus on the number of prisoners who perish at the hands of various cruel captors; far less attention is given to the experience of those who survive. The emerging field of victimology (Elias, 1986) recognizes former prisoners as a subset of a larger population of victims. The maltreatment of captives extracts significant societal costs, having impact not only on its victims but on those around them. Recognition and understanding of these costs will aid efforts to prevent such maltreatment. It is, after all, a preventable cause of human suffering.

REFERENCES

Abeles, N. (1986). Proceedings of the American Psychological Association, Incorporated, for the year 1985: Minutes of the annual meeting of the Council of Representatives. *American Psychologist, 41,* 633–663.

Abildgaard, U., Daugaard, G., Marcussen, H., Jess, P., Petersen, H. D., & Wallach, M. (1984). Chronic organic psycho-syndrome in Greek torture victims. *Danish Medical Bulletin, 31,* 239–242.

Allodi, F., & Cowgill, G. (1982). Ethical and psychiatric aspects of torture: A Canadian study. *Canadian Journal of Psychiatry, 27,* 98–102.

American Psychiatric Association. (1952). *Diagnostic and statistical manual of mental disorders* (1st ed.). Washington, DC: Author.

American Psychiatric Association. (1968). *Diagnostic and statistical manual of mental disorders* (2nd ed.). Washington, DC: Author.

American Psychiatric Association. (1980). *Diagnostic and statistical manual of mental disorders* (3rd ed.). Washington, DC: Author.

American Psychiatric Association. (1987). *Diagnostic and statistical manual of mental disorders* (3rd ed., rev.). Washington, DC: Author.

American Psychological Association, Joint Subcommittee on Human Rights. (1984). Statement by the Joint Subcommittee on Human Rights. *American Psychologist, 38*(6), 676–678.

Amnesty International. (1983). *Amnesty International handbook.* New York: Author.

Amnesty International. (1984). *Torture in the eighties.* New York: Author.

Andreasen, N. C. (1985). Posttraumatic stress disorder. In H. I. Kaplan & B. J. Sadock (Eds.), *Comprehensive textbook of psychiatry* (4th ed., pp. 918–924). Baltimore: Williams & Wilkins.

Antonovsky, A. (1979). *Health, stress, and coping.* San Francisco: Jossey-Bass.

Antonovsky, A., & Bernstein, J. (1986). Pathogenesis and salutogenesis in war and other crises: Who studies the successful coper? In N. A. Milgram (Ed.), *Stress and coping in time of war: Generalizations from the Israeli experience* (pp. 52–65). New York: Brunner/Mazel.

Bales, J. (1987, December). Centers pave long road out of nightmares. *APA Monitor,* pp. 20–21.

Bandura, A. (1977). Self-efficacy: Toward a unifying theory of behavioral change. *Psychological Review, 84,* 191–215.

Beebe, G. W. (1975). Follow-up studies of World War II and Korean War prisoners, II: Morbidity, disability, and maladjustments. *American Journal of Epidemiology, 101,* 400–422.

Bettelheim, B. (1943). Individual and mass behavior in extreme situations. *Journal of Abnormal and Social Psychology, 38,* 417–452.

Breslau, N., & Davis, G. C. (1987). Posttraumatic stress disorder: The stressor criterion. *Journal of Nervous and Mental Disease, 175,* 255–264.

Chodoff, P. (1980). Psychotherapy of the survivor. In J. E. Dimsdale (Ed.), *Survivors, victims, and perpetrators: Essays on the Nazi Holocaust* (pp. 205–216). Washington, DC: Hemisphere.

Cohen, B. M., & Cooper, M. Z. (1954). *A follow-up study of World War II prisoners of war* (Veterans Administration Medical Monograph). Washington, DC: Veterans Administration.

Depue, R., & Monroe, S. (1986). Conceptualization and measurement of human disorder in life stress research: The problem of chronic disturbance. *Psychological Bulletin, 99,* 36–51.

Eaton, W. W., Sigal, J. J., & Weinfeld, M. (1982). Impairment in holocaust survivors after 33 years: Data from an unbiased community sample. *American Journal of Psychiatry, 139,* 773–777.

Eitinger, L. (1974). Coping with aggression. *Mental Health and Society, 1,* 279–301.

Eitinger, L. (1975). Jewish concentration camp survivors in Norway. *Israel Annals of Psychiatry, 13,* 321–334.

Eitinger, L., Krell, R., & Rieck, M. (1985). *The psychological and medical effects of concentration camps and related persecutions on survivors of the Holocaust: A research bibliography.* Vancouver: University of British Columbia Press.

Elias, R. (1986). *The politics of victimization: Victims, victimology, and human rights.* New York: Oxford University Press.

Engdahl, B. E. (1987, August). *Psychological consequences of the WWII prisoner of war experience: Implications for treatment.* Paper presented at the meeting of the American Psychological Association, New York, NY. (ERIC Document Reproduction Service No. CG 020 530)

Epstein, H. (1979). *Children of the Holocaust: Conversations with sons and daughters of survivors.* New York: Putnam.

Frankl, V. E. (1959). *From death camp to existentialism: A psychiatrist's path to a new therapy.* Boston: Beacon Press.

Frankl, V. E. (1962). *Man's search for meaning: An introduction to logotherapy.* Boston: Beacon Press.

Fuller, R. B. (1985). War veterans' post-traumatic stress disorder and the U.S. Congress. In W. E. Kelly (Ed.), *Post-traumatic stress disorder and the war veteran patient* (pp. 3–11). New York: Brunner/Mazel.

Holmstrom, V. L. (1987, August). *Treatment considerations for the WWII prisoner of war.* Paper presented at the meeting of the American Psychological Association, New York, NY.

Jensen, T. S., Genefke, I. K., Hyldebrandt, N., Pedersen, H., Petersen, H. D., & Weile, B. (1982). Cerebral atrophy in young torture victims. *The New England Journal of Medicine, 307,* 1341.

Kahn, A. S. (Ed.). (1984). *Victims of crime and violence: Final report of the APA Task Force on Victims of Crime and Violence.* Washington, DC: American Psychological Association.

Keane, T. M., Fairbank, J. A., Caddell, J. M., Zimering, R. T., & Bender, M. E. (1985). A behavioral approach to assessing and treating post-traumatic stress disorder in Vietnam veterans. In C. R. Figley (Ed.), *Trauma and its wake: The study and treatment of post-traumatic stress disorder* (pp. 257–292). New York: Brunner/Mazel.

Keehn, R. J. (1980). Follow-up studies of World War II and Korean Conflict prisoners. *American Journal of Epidemiology, 111,* 194–211.

Kinzie, J. D., Fredrickson, R. H., Ben, R., Fleck, J., & Karls, W. (1984). Posttraumatic stress disorder among survivors of Cambodian concentration camps. *American Journal of Psychiatry, 141,* 649–650.

Kluznik, J. C., Speed, N., Van Valkenburg, C., & Magraw, R. (1986). Forty-year follow-up of United States prisoners of war. *American Journal of Psychiatry, 143,* 1443–1445.

Kobasa, S. C., Maddi, S. R., & Kahn, S. (1982). Hardiness and health: A prospective study. *Journal of Personality and Social Psychology, 42,* 168–177.

Kolb, L. C. (1987). A neuropsychological hypothesis explaining posttraumatic stress disorders. *American Journal of Psychiatry, 144,* 989–995.

Krajick, K. (1986, November). Healing broken minds. *Psychology Today,* pp. 66–69.

Matussek, P. (1975). *Internment in Nazi concentration camps and its consequences.* New York: Springer-Verlag. (Original work published 1971)

McFarlane, A. (1988). The longitudinal course of posttraumatic morbidity: The range of outcomes and their predictors. *Journal of Nervous and Mental Disease, 176,* 30–39.

Merikangas, K. R., & Weissman, M. M. (1986). Epidemiology of anxiety disorders in adulthood. In Klerman, G. L., Weissman, M. M., Appelbaum, P. S., & Roth, L. H. (Eds.). *Social, epidemiologic, and legal psychiatry* (pp. 169–179). New York: Basic Books.

Mollica, R. F., Wyshak, G., & Lavelle, J. (1987). The psychosocial impact of war trauma and torture on Southeast Asian refugees. *American Journal of Psychiatry, 144,* 1567–1572.

National Institute on Aging. (1986). *Established populations for epidemiological studies of the elderly* (NIH Publication No. 86-2443). Washington, DC: U.S. Government Printing Office.

Rasmussen, O. V., & Lunde, I. (1980). Evaluations of investigations of 200 torture victims. *Danish Medical Bulletin, 27,* 241–243.

Robins, L. N., Helzer, J. E., Weissman, M. M., Orvaschel, H., Gruenberg, E., Burke, J. D., & Reiger, D. A. (1984). Lifetime prevalence of specific psychiatric disorders at three sites. *Archives of General Psychiatry, 41,* 949–958.

Robins, E., & Guze, S. B. (1970). Establishment of diagnostic validity in psychiatric illness: Its application to schizophrenia. *American Journal of Psychiatry, 126,* 983–987.

Rosenthal, D. (1970). *Genetic theory and abnormal behavior.* New York: McGraw-Hill.

Rosenzweig, M. R. (1988). Psychology and United Nations human rights efforts. *American Psychologist, 43,* 79–86.

Segal, J. (1986). *Winning life's toughest battles: Roots of human resilience.* New York: McGraw-Hill.

Selye, H. (1975). Confusion and controversy in the stress field. *Journal of Human Stress, 1,* 37–44.

Shachak, O. (1986). Componentiality as a survival strategy in a total institution: Case study of a POW in solitary confinement in a Syrian prison. In N. A. Milgram (Ed.), *Stress and coping in time of war: Generalizations from the Israeli experience* (pp. 216–229). New York: Brunner/Mazel.

Siegal, M. (1983). Crime and violence in America: The victims. *American Psychologist, 38,* 1267–1273.

Sierles, F. S., Chen, J. J., McFarland, R. E., & Taylor, M. A. (1983). Posttraumatic stress disorder and concurrent psychiatric illness: A preliminary report. *American Journal of Psychiatry, 140,* 1177–1179.

Sledge, W., Boydstun, J., & Rabe, M. (1980). Self-concept changes related to war captivity. *Archives of General Psychiatry, 37,* 430–443.

Somnier, F. E., & Genefke, I. K. (1986). Psychotherapy for victims of torture. *British Journal of Psychiatry, 149,* 323–329.

Speed, N., Engdahl, B. E., Schwartz, J., & Eberly, R. E. (1989). Posttraumatic stress disorder as a consequence of the prisoner of war experience. *Journal of Nervous and Mental Disease.*

Spitzer, R., Endicott, J., & Robins, E. (1978). Research diagnostic criteria: Rationale and reliability. *Archives of General Psychiatry, 35,* 773–782.

Stenger, C. A. (1986). *American prisoners of war in WWI, WWII, Korea, and Viet Nam.* Washington, DC: Veterans Administration Central Office, Advisory Committee on Former POWs, Department of Medicine and Surgery.

Stover, E., & Nightingale, E. O. (Eds.). (1985). *The breaking of minds and bodies.* New York: Freeman.

Tennant, C., Goulston, K., & Dent, O. (1986). Clinical psychiatric illness in prisoners of war of the Japanese: Forty years after release. *Psychological Medicine, 16,* 833–839.

Thygesen, P., Hermann, K., & Willanger, R. (1970). Concentration camp survivors in Denmark: Persecution, disease, disability, compensation. *Danish Medical Bulletin, 17,* 65–108.

Timerman, J. (1981). *Prisoner without a name, cell without a number.* New York: Knopf.

United Nations. (1957). *Standard minimum rules for the treatment of prisoners.* New York: Author.

United Nations. (1984). *Report of the Commission on Human Rights.* New York: Author.

United Nations General Assembly. (1984). *Convention against torture and other cruel, inhuman or degrading treatment or punishment.* New York: United Nations.

Ursano, R. J. (1987). Commentary: Posttraumatic stress disorder: The stressor criterion. *Journal of Nervous and Mental Disease, 175,* 273–275.

Veterans Administration. (1983, June). *POW: Study of former prisoners of war.* Washington, DC: Veterans Administration, Office of Planning and Program Evaluation.

Veterans Administration. (1984). *Former POW medical history* (VA form 10-0048). Washington, DC: U.S. Government Printing Office.

Veterans Administration. (1987, May). Services provided to former POWs. *The VA Today,* p. 6.

Watson, I., Hoffman, L., & Wilson, G. (1988). The neuropsychiatry of post-traumatic stress disorder. *British Journal of Psychiatry, 152,* 164–173.

Whittaker, S. R. (1988). Counseling torture victims. *The Counseling Psychologist, 16,* 272–278.

World Health Organization. (1977). *Manual of the international statistical classification of diseases, injuries, and causes of death* (9th rev., vol. 1). Geneva, Switzerland: Author.

4

The Psychology and Culture of Torture and Torturers

Ervin Staub

What psychological processes and motivations allow or lead to torture? How are the inhibitions lost that human beings usually develop about inflicting pain and suffering, and about killing other human beings, which in the modern use of torture is frequently the ultimate fate of those who are tortured? What social and cultural characteristics of groups, what personal characteristics of individuals, give rise to torture or make it possible? It is not enough to consider torturers and torture in a narrow sense, as if they were independent as individuals and as phenomena from the nature of a society and from what is happening in the society at a particular time. Understanding the psychological processes of torture and of both direct perpetrators and decision makers in a broad sense, including their origins in culture and society, is important for future efforts to diminish torture in the world. The motivations for and psychological possibility of torture in either decision makers or direct perpetrators do not suddenly appear. Normally, they evolve. What are these motivations, what are their origins, and how do they evolve?

We must differentiate between torture in earlier times and in the current era, starting with its wide-ranging use in the Soviet Union (which followed the use of torture in tsarist Russia in the late 19th and early 20th century) and in Nazi Germany. Although the psychological principles that I describe apply to torture in general, they apply more directly to the current era, which is the focus of this chapter. In the Western world in three earlier time periods, in ancient Greece, in the Roman Empire, and then in the Middle Ages from about the 12th to about the 18th centuries, torture was part of the judicial process, used to collect evidence and to extract confession (Peters, 1985). In China as well, torture was a long-standing aspect of the judicial system, used to extract confession, which was required before anyone could be convicted of a crime. In the modern era torture has been separate from the judicial process, at times contrary to existing laws, at other times in the domain of the law that dealt with political crime. The focus of this chapter is on the systematic use of torture, primarily for political reasons.

Frequently torture is one aspect of the destructiveness of a murderous system that commits other atrocities as well. The policy of torture and killing, including mass killing, often go together. This was true in Nazi Germany, a country that established the widespread use of sophisticated techniques of torture against political opponents (Colligan, 1976; Reitlinger, 1953) and later brutalized and killed Germans who were regarded as genetically inferior—Jews, gypsies, and others. It was true in the Soviet Union, where millions of people were deliberately starved to death on the way to enforced collectivization, and millions more were killed in repeated purges (Beck & Godin, 1951). It was true in Cambodia at the time of the "autogenocide" between 1975 and 1979 (Staub, 1989b). It was also true in Argentina, where many thousands of people were kidnapped and savagely tortured. Some were later released, but most of them were subsequently murdered (Argentine National Commission on the Disappeared, 1986; Staub, 1989b).

Although the same systems often both torture and kill (and they may do so indiscriminately or first torture and then kill people), at times they differentiate among types of victims. For example, in Cambodia, the population, especially the "new people," former city dwellers who were forced to move into the country and to work on the fields, were brutally treated. Many were killed: people who worked for the previous government, educated people, or those who deviated from the strict rules of life laid down by the communists. However, the people who were tortured before they were killed were communists, members of the Khmer Rouge who were the victims of infighting or somehow became suspect (Etcheson, 1984; Staub, 1989b). This suggests that in addition to shared psychological sources of torture and killing, there are differences. One of them is a practical one: Some people are in a position, or perpetrators believe they are in a position, to provide valuable information. In addition, intense negative feelings, hatred, and the desire for revenge may at times motivate perpetrators to torture their victims before killing them.

Inflicting physical pain is the most usual form of torture, with the accompanying threat to life and loss of control by victims over their bodies and lives. There are also other forms. In the Soviet Union political dissidents have been placed in mental hospitals, many subjected to painful or disorienting treatments to cure their "mental illness" (Block & Reddaway, 1977, 1984; chapter 11, this volume). Although torture seems substantially more frequent in repressive societies, its use is widespread and can also be found in democratic systems (Peters, 1985; Suedfeld, 1989). In November 1984, Amnesty International announced that half the member nations of the United Nations practice torture.

To generate a conception of the psychology of torture and torturers, one must draw on varied sources. A substantial amount of psychological research has bearing on it. Analyses of societies during periods of great destructiveness is another source (see Argentine National Commission on the Disappeared, 1986; Staub, 1989b). The study of former torturers, interviews with them, and the assessment of their personalities is a further source. However, this type of information has potential biases. Perpetrators are usually studied after the world has condemned their actions, and frequently after they were jailed or in other ways punished. Consequently, the information they give is likely to be distorted by rationalizations and justifications. Frequently, they stress their obedience to either legitimate or coercive authority (Dicks, 1972). Although obedience and coercion to obtain it are important, this may lead to overestimation of their role in torture.

There are many reasons or motivations for torture, some seemingly more rational or in the service of practical self-interest, others more psychological.

Among the former, eliciting information about opponents, bringing about admission of guilt, the desire to intimidate political opponents, or eliciting confession for "show trials" that serve to intimidate opponents or to justify repression, all can serve political control. Among the more psychological motivations are revenge for real or imagined harm or the desire to establish one's superiority and elevate the self.

There are certain basic psychological processes and motivations that seem common both to torture, regardless of the exact reason for it, and to extreme violence of other kinds, as is indicated both by research findings and by the study of societies, of groups of perpetrators, and of individual perpetrators at times of extreme destructiveness (Staub, 1989b). Therefore, what follows is a discussion of extreme harm doing by groups and their members (dominant subgroups of society or the state) with a focus on torture and torturers. Another reason for such a more inclusive approach is the recent, tragic development of the use of death squads, kidnapping and disappearances, and outright murder in dealing with political opponents, practices that in part seem to have replaced torture as a political tool. The killing of children has also become a political tool ("Children," 1988), its apparent purpose to terrorize communities and stop them from political action.

There are a number of basic questions that I examine in this chapter. First, what are the psychological processes and motivations that underlie and make possible torture and other extreme harm doing? Second, do perpetrators have special personal characteristics, and what are they? What leads to their self-selection or to their selection by those in authority for the role of perpetrators? Third, what training prepares potential perpetrators for torture and killing? Fourth, what is the nature of their psychological evolution in the course of their training and their early "steps along a continuum of destruction" (Staub, 1989a, 1989b)?

The perpetration of torture or harm doing can be analyzed on three levels. At one level is the psychology of individual perpetrators. At the second level, perpetrators and decision makers may be studied as a group. Such analyses may focus on the processes within subgroups of a society (such as the military in Argentina and Greece, or the Nazis and the SS in Germany) or within the movement that they are part of. Such subgroups at times set the policy of torture, at times execute the policy, and at times do both. The third level of analysis is the exploration of the characteristics of culture and historical processes within a society that give rise to psychological processes and motivations that are likely to lead to extreme harm doing. At times torture is part of a general societal process which may lead to torture as well as mass killing or genocide; at other times it is more delimited and as a result claims fewer and a more restricted group of victims. In special instances torture and other violence may be widespread without a general societal process leading to it, as in the case of a colonial power acting outside its own borders.

To explore the psychology of torture and torturers, including the processes that occur on the level of society, I draw on a conception of extreme human destructiveness and its application to the in-depth analysis of group violence in four instances—the genocide of the Armenians in Turkey, the Holocaust in Nazi Germany, the autogenocide in Cambodia, and the disappearances in Argentina—that I presented elsewhere (Staub, 1989b). I also refer to basic research and to a few existing studies of perpetrators. I use a variety of examples but do not discuss the specifics of torture in all nations and time periods. Although the principles that I discuss are broadly generalizable to instances of systematic torture of members of political, racial, or religious groups, the limits of generalizability will have to be established in further research.

UNDERLYING PSYCHOLOGICAL PROCESSES AND MOTIVATIONS IN EXTREME HARM DOING

The Role of Differentiation, Devaluation, and Moral Exclusion

It is a very basic human tendency to differentiate people into members of in-groups and outgroups, into "us" and "them." There may be genetic building blocks at the root of this tendency, such as the simultaneous appearance in infants of attachment to caretakers and fear of strangers[1] (Ainsworth, 1979; Shaffer, 1979). Humans tend to fear and dislike the unfamiliar, the strange, and especially what is greatly discrepant from their own experience (Hornstein, 1976). In the course of their socialization, children's dispositions for us—them differentiation is enlarged: They are taught to like some people and to dislike and mistrust others.

Most cultures come to develop strong stereotypes, exaggerated beliefs about the characteristics of a group (Allport, 1954), or images, frequently devaluative, of some groups of people, that are maintained and expressed in literature, arts, and the media. Children acquire these stereotypes and devaluative images (Piaget & Weil, 1951). Children, as well as adults, also experience intense satisfactions associated with their identification, and their experience of unity, with varied ingroups, for example, with their baseball team, their school, their town, or their nation. This is often in the context of some form of conflict (minimally, competition) with an outgroup.

Thus the tendency for ingroup–outgroup differentiation becomes strengthened. It is not surprising, therefore, that people come to easily make or accept divisions into ingroups and outgroups, even if the basis for the division is trivial, such as being told that some people prefer the same modern painter they do, whereas others prefer a different modern painter, or that some people group dots on a page as they do, and others group them differently. Such differentiations, once made, lead to devaluation of members of the outgroup relative to the ingroup and to discrimination against outgroup members in dividing rewards (Brewer, 1978; Tajfel, 1982; Tajfel, Flamant, Billig, & Bundy, 1971). Discrimination occurs even when participants are told that they have been randomly assigned to one group or another and will never meet members of either group (Brewer, 1978).

Devaluation makes it easier to harm people, given that a motivation or reason exists for doing so. Intense devaluation may by itself generate the desire to harm. In one experiment, participants gave more intense shocks to people about whom they overheard devaluative comments and less intense shocks to people about whom they overheard positive comments, in comparison to a control group (Bandura et al., 1975). Devaluation can include at least two somewhat separate

---

[1]With regard to attachment, except under the most extreme conditions such as lack of caretaking by a constant caretaker, the infant develops a close affectional tie to the caretaker. This indicates a strong genetic predisposition for attachment. However, the quality of caretaking and the infant–caretaker relationship affects the quality of attachment; this and the variety and nature of the infant's experience with other people affects the degree of stranger anxiety. Thus, even in case of a strong genetic predisposition, there is malleability.

components: one is a dislike, or a negative view of the capacities, intentions, and moral character of a group, and the second one is a view of the other as an enemy that seeks to harm or destroy one's group, oneself included, or endangers it by its very nature. At times the second component can enlarge into an "ideology of antagonism," a system of beliefs that identifies the other as the enemy and requires self-defense and superiority in power for the sake of security (Staub, 1989b).

Whereas defining people as "them" and devaluing them motivates or allows harming them, defining or perceiving them as "us," as similar to or like oneself, generates caring for them and empathy with them. People so seen are more likely to be helped and less likely to be harmed (Hornstein, 1976; Krebs, 1975). Christian militia that, upon entering Palestinian camps, would kill inhabitants repeatedly spared Palestinians who were Christian (Kuper, 1981). Sometimes opponents in war are humanized, with a change in feelings and behavior toward them. In *Homage to Catalonia,* George Orwell described a profound change in his feelings when he saw an enemy soldier in the Spanish Civil War pull down his pants and relieve himself.

A great deal of research shows that a positive evaluation of human beings is a source of positive actions toward them. People who have a *prosocial value orientation,* which consists of a positive evaluation of human nature and human beings, a concern about others' welfare, and a feeling of personal responsibility for others' welfare, tend to help other people more, whether they have physical problems (Erkut, Jaquette, & Staub, 1981; Staub, 1974) or are in psychological distress (Feinberg, 1978; Grodman, 1979; see Staub, 1978). Temporary positive and negative evaluations of human beings that result from specific experiences also affect one's willingness to help others (Hornstein, 1976).

Similarly, individuals may devalue others because of their own negative orientation to other human beings (part of an *antisocial value orientation,* see Staub, 1989b). They may have acquired devaluative stereotypes in their group toward human beings in general or toward specific groups. Or they may do so as a result of specific experiences, or a combination of these factors. A sharp differentiation between one's own group and another group and intense devaluation of the latter not only limits caring and empathy for members of the other group but also excludes them from the *range of applicability* of moral values (Staub, 1980). People do not apply moral values such as justice or responsibility for the welfare of other humans equally to all people. Some people are excluded from the universe of moral concerns, and moral values become inapplicable to them.

The role of ingroup–outgroup differentiation, devaluation, and moral exclusion in torture is also suggested by the categories of people whose torture was prescribed or allowed in earlier eras, when torture was part of the judicial process. Almost invariably these categories included groups excluded from societal processes, such as slaves, and the lower strata of society, such as the poor. The upper strata were not to be tortured. As it is often the case with destructive practices (see the sections on experiential learning and on steps along the continuum of destruction in this chapter), they became more inclusive over time, with a wider range of victims.

In the current era, the use of torture by colonial powers in their colonies was widespread. It is reasonable to assume that in most instances the colonized people were regarded as "them" rather than "us" and were devalued. In addition, the judicial processes and other institutions that protect human rights were usually less carefully established in colonies (Peters, 1985). Additional elements also entered, such as a history of torture in some colonized societies, which may have made the colonial governments believe that the population would tolerate and respond to torture.

A sharp differentiation between the ingroup and an outgroup and profound devaluation of this outgroup preceded all four genocides that I examined (Staub, 1989b). This combination was also evident in other cases of group violence, for example, against American Indians, or more recently against Indians in Paraguay. Differentiation usually precedes torture, as it did in Argentina, Cambodia, and Nazi Germany (Staub, 1989b), and in Greece (Gibson & Haritos-Fatouros, 1986; Haritos-Fatouros, 1988), and could probably be documented in most other instances.

Devaluation can vary in nature and intensity. In Argentina, the greater the devaluation of victims the more ferociously they were tortured. Communists were regarded as the most direct enemy, while Jews were the subject of intense anti-Semitism. Both were especially cruelly tortured. Amnesty International (1980) quotes one torturer explaining the special cruelty toward Jews: "In here, some people are mercenaries and others aren't, but we are all fascists." According to the Argentine National Commission on the Disappeared,

> All kinds of torture were applied to Jews, especially one which was extremely sadistic and cruel: the "rectoscope," which consisted of inserting a tube into the victim's anus or into a woman's vagina, then letting a rat into the tube. The rodent would try to get out by gnawing at the victims's internal organs. (1986, p. 72)

One focus of the training of would-be perpetrators is the devaluation of the victim group. This seems to have been true in all known instances and even characterizes the training of soldiers when the enemy or potential enemy is known (Dyer, 1985).

The Experiential Learning of Devaluation and Harm Doing

Perpetrators select themselves or are selected; they often receive multifaceted training that prepares them for their roles; and they further evolve in the course of their activities as they exercise power over and inflict harm, physical suffering, and death on other people. People learn by doing, by participating in varied activities. In a number of experiments with children, my associates and I found that guiding children to engage in activities that benefit others increased their later helpfulness. Children who repeatedly made toys for poor, hospitalized children or taught things to younger children were more likely to extend effort or sacrifice material rewards in order to help needy others (Staub, 1975, 1979, 1986). A variety of research findings with adults also indicate that prior helping acts or, as research on the "foot-in-the-door" hypothesis shows, even prior agreement to help, increase later helping (DeJong, 1979; Freedman & Fraser, 1966). Helping acts can lead to a positive evaluation of the beneficiaries and to an increased concern about their well-being. It can also lead to a changed self-concept in the helpers, a view of themselves as able and willing to help others (see Eisenberg & Cialdini, 1984; Grusec, Kuczynski, Rushton, & Simutis, 1978; Staub, 1979).

People also learn violence by participation and evolve an increasing capacity to harm others. Apart from evidence provided by the gradual expansion of violence in the history of torture (Peters, 1985) and in that of genocides and mass killings (Staub, 1989b), a number of experiments show this. When "teachers" administer electric shocks to "learners" and they themselves select shock levels, over trials the level of shock they administer progressively increases (e.g., Buss, 1966; Goldstein, Davis, & Herman, 1975). Some of these and other experiments show that having harmed people, harm-doers derogate, diminish, and devalue their victims (e.g., Berkowitz, 1962; Goldstein et al., 1975; Staub, 1978; Sykes & Matza, 1957).

A study by Zimbardo and his associates (1974), in which students who were assigned the role of prison guards came to mistreat other students who were assigned the role of inmates, although in some ways flawed, does provide a case study demonstration of both the influence that roles can exert and of learning by doing. The guards, in fulfilling their assigned roles, used extreme prison procedures that dehumanized the inmates. The prisoners were "stripped naked, skin searched, and deloused"; had to memorize and follow rules restricting freedom of speech and movement; and had to ask permission for the simplest activities such as writing letters or going to the toilet. Practices by torturers that diminish and dehumanize victims in much more extreme ways than this are common. It is probably impossible to act in this way toward other human beings without a progressive devaluation of them, without a spread of disregard for their welfare and their humanity. This results in their further mistreatment, which in turn leads to further psychological changes in the perpetrators.

In the prison simulation, some of the guards became extremely punitive, whereas others passively accepted their actions. They made prisoners gather at any time of day or night for the count, the duration of which they increased from the original ten minutes to several hours, spontaneously recreating practices used both in Russian labor camps and German concentration camps. They reacted to a "rebellion" by stripping prisoners naked, by placing the leaders in solitary confinement, and by harassing and intimidating prisoners.

One aspect of the role of guard, especially when the victims are placed outside the rule of law, as torture victims usually are, is tremendous power. Without clearly drawn limits and accountability, power can lead to a feeling of limitless right to determine the fate of victims and to unbridled excess. Less systematic use of torture, especially against the lower strata of society, often occurs when enforcement agents such as the police are not carefully supervised and made accountable (Peters, 1985). Such torture is made easier and more likely by existing devaluation of lower social groups. The limitations in the rights and power of such groups reduces the accountability of the police and other authorities.

Just-world Thinking

A substantial amount of research shows that when people witness the suffering of others, for example, observe other people receive electric shocks, they tend to devalue the victims (Lerner, 1980; Lerner & Simmons, 1966). This is especially so when the suffering (e.g., the shocks) is likely to continue and when the witnesses themselves are unable, or because of the circumstances are unlikely, to do anything about it. Wanting to believe both in a just world and that they themselves will not become victims of random circumstance, people tend to view those who suffer as being responsible for and deserving their fate because of their character or prior conduct.

Although bystanders—people who are witness to but are not the cause of others' suffering—tend to devalue the sufferer, not all of them do so. In research studies, some blame the experimenter (Lerner & Simmons, 1966). Individuals differ in their tendency to see the world as just, and those with a stronger belief in a just world are more likely to devalue people who are poor, underprivileged (Rubin & Peplau, 1975), and presumably victims of violence as well.

Research findings mentioned earlier and life events (Staub, 1989b) indicate that perpetrators also devalue victims, even though (or especially because) they themselves cause their suffering. Usually victims are devalued before they are harmed. Such devaluation is likely to be insufficient, however, to justify intense violence like torture. Further devaluation of the victims is one way for the perpetrators to justify their actions. In addition, victims of torture are usually helpless and unable to resist; they are made bloody, dirty, undignified. They can easily be seen as less than human, especially because that can protect the torturer from feeling sympathy and guilt.

The case of Jacobo Timerman offers an example of bystanders' use of just-world thinking. The former editor of an Argentine newspaper, Timerman published a highly influential book describing his abduction and torture, one of the first in-depth stories of the disappearances in Argentina (Timerman, 1981). However, a number of responses to the book implied that he somehow brought his troubles on himself and that he invited and perhaps deserved his torture (Peters, 1985). These reactions, while blaming the victim, also denied the widespread use of abduction, torture, and disappearance.

Ideology and Higher Ideals

Often a group's devaluation of another group evolves over a long period of time and becomes a firmly established part of group culture that is also expressed in discrimination and societal institutions that serve discrimination. At times the devaluation is part of an ideology that either evolves within the group or comes to be accepted by the group in a relatively short time period. Especially when life is difficult and a society or a subgroup faces persistent problems, a group may adopt an ideology that provides a vision of a better future, that creates hope. Frequently, such ideologies invoke or genuinely aim to fulfill what are believed to be higher ideals and offer those who work for them a sense of significance. Unfortunately, such better world ideologies identify enemies, people who by their actions or by their very existence are seen to hinder the ideology's fulfillment. As individuals give themselves over to a group or movement guided by the ideology, and as the fulfillment of the ideology becomes their overriding goal, constraints about methods are lost; torture, murder, and mass killing become possible.

There are components of many ideologies in which the potential for destruction is inherent. The Nazi ideology had a number of such components. One of them, the racial theory, ultimately led to the attempt to kill whole groups of people, as well as many Germans who were identified as genetically inferior, in order to purify the German race and even humanity in general. An especially destructive variant of Communist ideology led to autogenocide in Cambodia: Its aim was the creation of the ideal society based on agriculture and on complete equality. An anti-Communist ideology, a world view that depicts Communism as evil and a profound threat to society, has been one important source of violence in South and Central American countries, in Indonesia, and elsewhere. In the Argentine military, especially in the officer corps that decided on a policy of torture and mass killing and together with members of some paramilitary groups provided most of the perpetrators, there was deep-seated anti-Communism which regarded all those who were concerned with social change as Communists or left leaning (Argentine National Commission on the Disappeared, 1986; Potash, 1970; Staub, 1989b).

Fascist Italy in the 1920s, the newly created Soviet Union in 1917, and Nazi Germany, all highly ideological revolutionary states, all held the view that the state, or the people, or the revolution embodied a superior morality. In the face of this superior morality, lesser moral concerns had no claim. The ideologies of these states substituted the rights of the state, people, or revolution, for the rights of the individual (Peters, 1985). The first head of the Soviet Secret Police proclaimed: "We stand for organized terror. . . . terror being absolutely indispensable in current revolutionary conditions. Our task is to fight against the enemies of the Soviet Government and the new order of life" (Leggett, 1981, cited in Peters, 1985). The use of torture was intense between 1917 and 1922 and again after 1936, with Stalin explicitly supporting and justifying its use. The superior purposes of the revolutionary state justified torture and made torture and other violence in fighting its enemies not only acceptable, but valued.

Perpetrators both select themselves for their role and are selected by those in authority. An important basis of selection is ideology. In interviews after World War II, former SS members described their reasons for joining the SS as follows: ideological attraction to national socialism; liking for military and paramilitary activities that they could not satisfy by joining the army, because the size of the German Army was greatly restricted by the Versailles peace treaty; and tangible benefits associated with a career in the SS (Steiner, 1980). In Greece, the perpetrators of torture were selected from army conscripts who were known to come from strongly anti-Communist families, and who also showed strong obedience to authority (Gibson & Haritos-Fatourous, 1986; Haritos-Fatouros, 1979). Ideologically reliable Nazi doctors were selected to participate in the euthanasia killings and then in the killings in the death camps of Nazi Germany (Lifton, 1986).

All members of a political–ideological movement usually receive ideological education or indoctrination. This was part of the training of perpetrators, whether they were SS members (Kren & Rappoport, 1980), Greek military police, or the Khmer Rouge in Cambodia. (In Cambodia the mistreatment of people was great and killing widespread. The increasing cycle of violence and civil war that preceded this prepared soldiers in the Khmer Rouge to be its perpetrators— Staub, 1989b.)

The Defense of the Physical or Psychological Self

A substantial body of laboratory research shows that threat to or attack on either the physical or psychological self result in anger, hostility, and aggression. When people receive electric shocks from others or are threatened with aggression, when they are insulted or in other ways diminished, they respond with anger, hostility, and aggression (Averill, 1982; Baron, 1977). Attack on either one's body or one's self-concept, values, and ways of life generates the motivation to defend the self. One way to defend the psychological self or to deal with a diminished self is to elevate oneself over others. Threat to one's societal or group self-concept brings forth similar reactions. To varying but usually substantial degrees people define themselves by their group memberships—as Germans or Americans, as members of civil organizations, of church groups, of the SS, or the Ku Klux Klan. A threat to the group can be as profound in its meaning or effects as a threat to the self. Moreover, a threat to individual self-concept can be dealt with by elevating one's societal or group self-concept or by joining and giving oneself over to a new group.

As a specific example, consider the case of the Argentine military (Staub, 1989b). Between 1976 and 1979 the military kidnapped and intensely tortured a large number of people; at least 9,000 of these people (but possibly three to four times as many) never reappeared and are believed to be dead (Argentine National Commission on the Disappeared, 1986). The societal conditions that preceded the military takeover in 1976 and the policy of disappearances strongly threatened the self-concept of the military. Part of the Argentine culture following World War II, but especially part of the culture of the military, was a view of Argentina as a country of great potential: as having a population different, more European, and better than those of other South American countries; having great natural resources and being potentially very wealthy; and as having great potential power, even world power. Moreover, over time the military came to regard itself as a protector of the nation not only from external but also from internal enemies, as responsible for the well-being, internal stability, and even values and ways of life of the nation. This evolved as a result of the increasing practice since 1930 of military takeovers whenever the military deemed this necessary for the national well-being, and the increasing influence of the military in political life even when a civilian government ruled.

The military's beliefs about Argentina and its members' views of themselves were greatly threatened by the deteriorating economic conditions over several decades, by political chaos, and by the threat to the stability and internal order presented by more than 600 kidnappings and murders by terrorist guerillas. However, most of those kidnapped, tortured, and murdered by the military had nothing to do with the terrorists. Their crime was showing concern for the poor or an interest in social change. This tremendous overgeneralization in the definition of the enemy was seemingly due to a combination of elements: a strong anti-Communist ideology and the ideologically based national security doctrine, which saw the nation as being profoundly threatened by internal enemies who were the agents of, and supported by, external forces; the threat to the existence of the military; and the threat to the self-concept of its members, including their view of themselves as defenders of the nation and its Christian ideals. As a consequence, people advocating *any* social change, and even those suspected of subversive *thought,* came to be regarded as enemies to be destroyed.

The Need for Control and Personal Power

When people face persistent problems in their lives that they cannot effectively deal with, when they lose control over their lives and the circumstances surrounding them, their need for control can become intense. A number of writers such as

Rank (1941/1958) and Becker (1975), have proposed that the incapacity of human beings to accept death and their resulting feeling of vulnerability results in their seeking power over life by destroying others. This gives them a feeling of invulnerability. I believe that it is a feeling of helplessness and lack of control over their lives, which comes from their inability to defend themselves from threat and attack or to fulfill their important goals, that makes people seek a feeling of invulnerability through power over others' well-being, bodies and lives.

Obedience to Authority

Milgram's (1965, 1974) research, in which large percentages of participants proceeded to administer increasing and seemingly extremely painful and life-threatening electric shocks to another person under the guidance and insistence of an experimenter, called attention to the role of obedience to authority in human violence and destruction. Fromm (1965) suggested that the need or desire for guidance by authority, arising in part from varying degrees of difficulty people have in using their freedom and standing on their own, can lead groups of people to give themselves over to leaders.

Although obedience to authority plays an important role in the execution of a policy of torture and murder, two important qualifications are necessary. First, the characteristics of individuals affect the degree of their obedience. For example, scores on the F scale, a measure of the authoritarian personality, were associated with more obedience in the Milgram paradigm (Elms & Milgram, 1966). In contrast, an advanced level of moral reasoning was associated with less obedience (Kohlberg & Candee, 1984). Second, societies vary in the extent to which they encourage obedience to authority and thus in the extent to which people in that society tend toward obedience or develop authoritarian personalities. Moreover, certain subgroups in most societies, such as the military, embody a strong authority orientation.

Perpetrator groups are often selected and shaped with a focus on authority and obedience. However, when difficult conditions of life in a society and certain characteristics of culture join, psychological processes and motivations arise in members of the group that lead them to join leaders, or even to select leaders, with destructive ideologies and practices. Thus, rather than reluctantly obeying their leaders, there is shared motivation and a *joining* with those in authority. A number of studies indicate that perpetrators frequently are characterized by a strong tendency toward obedience, a valuing of obedience, or even an authoritarian personality. The latter refers to a personality constellation characterized by a preference for hierarchical systems, with a willingness and even desire to obey higher authority and an enjoyment of power over those lower in the hierarchy. The authoritarian personality is characterized in part by a lack of awareness or acceptance of certain feelings, desires, or impulses in the self, such as hostility or sexual desire, and the projection of these unacceptable feelings onto other people (Adorno, Frenkel-Brunswik, Levinson, & Sanford, 1950; Cherry & Byrne, 1977).

Many Greek torturers were selected because of their extreme obedience even to senseless orders in their first few days as conscripts in the military police (Gibson & Haritos-Fatouros, 1986; Haritos-Fatouros, 1988). A study by Dicks (1972) of a group of former SS men who served in concentration camps and similar units showed that these men were raised by highly authoritarian, punitive fathers. Not surprisingly, they devalued their victims and saw them as deserving their punishment. Nonetheless, they also saw performing their tasks as merely following orders. They claimed to have had doubts about what they had to do. As I suggested earlier, given the perpetrators' need to justify themselves, some of these claims must be regarded with caution.

This study does not tell us how different these SS men were from other Germans, especially because authoritarian upbringing (Miller, 1983) and strong respect for authority (Craig, 1982; Staub, 1989b) were prevalent in Germany. The tendency for obedience, which appears to contribute to predisposition for group violence, was a shared characteristic of Germans. In addition, however, Steiner (1980) found that former members of the SS scored higher on a measure of authoritarianism than did former members of the regular German army. This may partly reflect selection factors, but it may also reflect the training of SS men and their experience in the SS.

People may have joined or been selected for the role of perpetrators because of their already exiting authoritarian tendency. However, perpetrators also receive training in obedience and in following extreme orders. This was the case with the SS as well as the Greek torturers. In both cases, rituals of group identification served not only to strengthen in-group bonds but also to enhance respect for and obedience to leaders. In the SS this was also served by the ideology of the Fuhrerprinzip (leader principle), the absolute authority of Hitler, and by the special loyalty oath to him. As part of their training, the Greek torturers were themselves physically abused, perhaps both as further training in submission and to make violence a normal standard of conduct.

A focus of basic military training as well, for example, training in the U.S. Marine Corps, is an unquestioning obedience to superiors (Dyer, 1985). Although all U.S. soldiers, including marines, are instructed to disobey inappropriate orders, this receives little emphasis, and there is no training to help soldiers judge when an order is illegal and immoral (Gibson, chapter 5, this volume; Padgett, 1986). The focus is on obedience, loyalty, commitment to the group, and creating a willingness to strike at and kill the enemy.

At times self-selection occurs, by people with certain personal characteristics, for *roles* that lend themselves to an evolution that ends in torture and killing. For example, the early SS members joined Hitler in the 1920s to be his bodyguards. They protected him at political meetings against attack and attacked members of other groups. Devotion to Hitler at a time when he had no power and as yet little influence, and an inclination for physical violence, must have characterized these early volunteers. Following either self-selection or selection by authorities, the personality of perpetrators would evolve further as a result of their experience in hierarchical-authoritarian systems and their special training, and as they progress along a continuum of destruction.

The perpetrators' respect for and submission of self to authority was utilized and their task made easier by their leaders assuming responsibility. For example, in a famous speech by Himmler, SS troups were told that the leaders, Hitler and Himmler, assumed responsibility for what the SS were doing (Dawidowicz, 1975). Himmler described the killings by the SS as heroic devotion to a difficult task for the sake of a higher good. In Argentina, superior officers signed release forms that authorized kidnapping, thus assuming responsibility and releasing the kidnappers from responsibility (Amnesty International, 1980). Admiral Massera, the chief of the Argentine navy, personally participated in the first kidnappings, both demonstrating his commitment and implicitly assuming responsibility (Argentine National Commission on the Disappeared, 1986).

Political Control and the Defense of Self-Interest and Power

The use of torture is frequently regarded as a means of political control. A particular group wants to maintain (or at times to gain) power and uses torture to deal with its actual or potential enemies to gain information that helps in controlling the enemy, to intimidate the enemy, and so on. Some people may find torturing others easy; some may enjoy it. But for most people, torturing other people because it serves their interests or the interests of their group is impossible without psychological preparation before and evolution in the course of it. For example, it would be extremely difficult to torture someone whom one identifies with and highly values. Psychological self-defense of a probably essential kind requires the torturer to separate the self from victims, to devalue victims, and regard them as deserving their fate.

In addition, conflicts of interest between classes, power groups, and even nations usually involve more than real conflict—that is, the division of power or material resources and wealth. They usually involve values, world views, ideologies, and self-concepts. Decision makers who set a policy of torture and killing, and followers as well, often see themselves as patriots or as defenders of essential ideals and values. In Argentina, large-scale terrorism by the Montonero guerillas and other leftist groups arose partly from real conflict of interest—from the motivation to right social injustice, to reduce the power of the elite and the military, and presumably to gain power. Members of the military and the elite, and even trade union leaders, were killed. The military acted to defend the lives of its members as well as its power and privilege and to avoid social disorganization.

Its longstanding power and privilege also made the existing social order, including their own power and privilege, right in the eyes of the military. Their self-concept as defenders of the nation and the social order and their beliefs and values were greatly threatened. The military felt that the essence of the nation was threatened by Communist and antireligious elements. As was noted earlier, varied elements combined to lead to a tremendous overgeneralization in the definition of the enemy: Even people suspected of thoughts that the military considered leftist or subversive were singled out (Argentine National Commission on the Disappeared, 1986; Staub, 1989b). The tortures and death squad murders in many other South American and Central American countries, prevalent in the 1970s and still continuing, had similar bases (Caviedes, 1984).

Secondary Motives

A number of motives are secondary, that is, they are not the source of the policy of torture or killing—although they may be a primary motive for certain individual perpetrators. Material rewards are often provided by the system or can be acquired by looting the victims' possessions. Prestige and status are often conferred on direct perpetrators: The SS in Germany had special, elite status, whereas the Greek perpetrators were indoctrinated into seeing themselves as an elite and were given special privileges. The enjoyment of others' suffering, of power and control over other people, and sexual opportunities with victims (e.g., rape) may attract some people to the perpetrator role.

Cultural and Societal Processes

A number of motivations that lead to torture or killing arise from a pattern of characteristics of a culture and of social organization, especially when they are combined with difficult conditions of life that the society faces (see Staub, 1989b). Such conditions include persistent economic problems; political violence among subgroups of society or political parties, war, or widespread criminal violence; great cultural change, because of technological or other developments; and chaos and disorganization in society that follow such events. Destructive, violent reactions become probable given a certain pattern of cultural–societal characteristics, described as follows.

1. A history of *devaluation of a subgroup* of society and discrimination against this subgroup that preselects the group as a victim of scapegoating or ideological persecution.

2. *Strong respect for authority,* which makes it unlikely that people question the definition of reality provided by those in authority or that they resist authorities who lead them to torture and killing. A strong respect for and reliance on authority also makes it difficult for people to stand on their own when as a collectivity they face difficulties (Fromm, 1965; Miller, 1983).

3. A *monolithic culture or social organization,* with certain dominant values and goals and limitations in the freedom to express conflicting values and goals. Together with strong respect for authority, this makes a uniformity of views within society more likely and counterreactions by members to early actions against victim groups less likely.

4. *Cultural self-concepts* such as a belief in cultural superiority (which at times, as in the case of Germany, was accompanied by a belief in the nation's right to dominate others, a form of entitlement), especially when this is belied by life conditions. Another is a shaky cultural self-concept that requires constant defense. Frequently, these self-concepts coexist: a veneer of superiority masks underlying self-doubt. Self-doubt may be due to a superior self-concept that has never been fulfilled by reality as in Argentina or Germany,[2] or to past glory or greatness that is long gone but remains part of the national memory and national self-concept, as in Turkey or Cambodia (Staub, 1989b). This is a complex characteristic but possible to assess by a careful examination of the products of a culture.

5. An *ideology* that designates as enemy is another important characteristic,

---

[2]In Germany, some of the self-doubt and insecurity may have been the result of devastation in wars, such as the Thirty Year War (Craig, 1982). A longstanding belief in German superiority may have been to some degree fulfilled and strengthened with victory in the Franco-Prussian War, unification in 1871, and Germany's role as a military power and cultural leader. The defeat in World War I and the tremendous life problems that followed would have represented, therefore, a great loss, a great blow to the national self-image.

at times existing in the culture for a long time, but frequently speedily evolving in response to life problems.

Given these predisposing characteristics, the members of a society are likely respond to difficult life conditions with a variety of intense needs, including the need (a) to protect their physical self, their body, and their material well-being; (b) to protect their psychological self, self-concept, values, and ways of life; (c) to protect their societal self-concept and their image of their group, which represents an important component of their individual self-concept; (d) to regain a comprehension of reality that provides them with a coherent view of the world; and (e) for human connections that were disrupted by the feelings of threat and by competition for scarce resources.

Because constructive problem solving to resolve persistent life problems of a society is difficult, given the cultural characteristics that I have described, other avenues become more likely. One of them is the protection of the psychological self, the creation of an in-group, and the creation of a (usually false) sense of control by scapegoating some group that is made responsible for life problems. Another avenue is to create ideologies or join groups or movements guided by ideologies. Usually such ideologies promise a better life and thereby provide hope. Their blueprint for a new social organization and new mode of existence provides a new understanding of the world, a renewed comprehension of reality. Joining a group also makes it possible to gain a new group identity while relinquishing a burdensome self that is frustrated and diminished by life problems. Usually the ideology identifies an enemy that interferes with the fulfillment of the ideology and the creation of a better world and leads the group to turn against this "enemy."

Such ideologies could, but usually do not, present realistic solutions to life problems. Communism could promote equality, justice, and the fulfillment of human needs, but as it has been practiced, it has reduced freedom and choice and led to persecution and murder. Anti-communism could defend a valued system, but it tends to be unrealistic in resisting, at times with great violence, social change in general. Even when the enemy that the ideology identifies is real, there is overgeneralization in the identification of the enemy group. In addition, the attempt to fulfill ideologies often leads to fanaticism and violence. The ideology becomes an overriding shared goal, a group goal around which other group goals and personal goals can be organized. Its ideals become abstract and removed from the welfare of real people. This makes it possible to torture and kill for the sake of the "higher ideals" it embodies.

When many people who share certain characteristics, and a whole society or important subgroups are affected by difficult life conditions, they will share a *cultural tilt*: Similar motivations will arise in them, with similar inclination for certain avenues to satisfy these motivations. Some will join leaders who offer extreme ideologies and extreme solutions to life problems, whereas bystanders tend to passively accept or even support the perpetrators. An important characteristic of the decision makers is their creativity and leadership in synthesizing or extending an ideology that fits the culture. The needs they satisfy, the avenues they choose for their satisfaction, and the values they stress express and in some ways carry on the culture.

THE EVOLUTION OF TORTURERS: STEPS
ALONG A CONTINUUM OF DESTRUCTION

Whether they initially have strong or weak inclinations, all perpetrators evolve as they increasingly harm other people. So do bystanders who accept the torture or killing of others without opposing it. Whole societies evolve (see Staub, 1989b). Their motivations and the conduct that is possible for them change. Individual decision makers and direct perpetrators progress from lesser harm-doing to the motivation and willingness to do greater harm. At times, when the group that comes to perpetrate torture or killing on a broad scale comes to power, society as a whole has already progressed far along a continuum of destruction, as in Turkey, where the Armenians had been the objects of discrimination, persistent violence, and even mass killing. In other instances, such as in Nazi Germany and the Soviet Union, by the time they gained power the perpetrators had evolved an ideology that advocated and justified violence. Their psychological preparation—the us—them differentiation and the devaluation of others—may be well advanced. This makes their progress along a continuum of destruction faster.

As a group engages in lesser harm doing—for example, in Nazi Germany, boycotting Jewish stores, breaking personal relations with Jews, or engaging in torture that is limited in scale or level of destructiveness—psychological changes result. As I noted earlier, people learn by participation; they change as a result of their own actions (Eisenberg & Cialdini, 1974; Grusec et al., 1978; Staub, 1975, 1979, 1986). Just-world thinking and further devaluation, and exclusion from the range of applicability of moral values makes it possible to harm victims more and to feel less responsibility for their suffering. The self-perception of the perpetrators is likely to change; they come to see themselves as willing and able to torture and kill, usually for a higher purpose. Frequently perpetrators develop an intense, fanatic commitment to some higher good and supposed higher morality, in the name of which they commit atrocities. Although understanding what conditions and personal characteristics make people more likely to join radical movements and adopt ideologies is important, once people develop a fanatic commitment it is their commitment rather than their personality that becomes a primary determinant of their conduct.

Such an evolution sometimes takes place in a whole system, as when a society participates in mistreating a group of people. At other times a progression is intentionally created by leaders to shape perpetrators, as in the training of torturers in Greece. After they were selected and subjected to violence themselves, they were

> . . . *first brought into contact with prisoners by carrying food to them and "occasionally" were ordered to "give the prisoner some blows." The next step was to place them as guards in the detention rooms where they watched others torturing prisoners; they would occasionally take part in some group-floggings. Later they were asked to take part in the "standing-ordeal" during which they had to beat the prisoner (on the legs mainly) every time he moved. (Haritos-Fatouros, 1988, p. 117)*

Finally they became the torturers (Gibson & Haritos-Fatouros, 1986; Haritos-Fatouros, 1988; Peters, 1985).

Mistreatment of a victim group, or a cycle of violence between opposing groups, results in changes that make increasingly greater levels of violence possible. Almost universally, with progression along the behavioral and psychological continuum of destruction, both the range of victims and the intensity of violence against them expand. For example, in earlier eras when torture was part of the judicial process, over time it came to be used for a wider range of reasons and against a wider range of victims: first against low-status defendants, later against people of higher status, and then even to gain information from witnesses (Peters, 1985). In Argentina, the many different kinds of victims, including adolescents, teenage girls, nuns, and pregnant women, made it impossible to differentiate between more or less worthy human beings. Over time it became possible to casually torture kidnapped people, to torture as a private whim, and to kill as a private whim (Staub, 1989b).

When torture is practiced, over time a variety of personal motives can enter. A former torturer, an officer of the Uruguayan Army who at some point refused to participate further, observed that torture can first serve the purpose of gaining information, but then comes to be practiced for its own sake, "as part of a routine and also as an act of vengeance against the detainee" (Stover & Nightingale, 1985, p. 7). Another torturer described "personal success" in fulfilling the task, that is, in gaining information, as a motivator of extra effort in continuing with torture, to the point of the torturer's exhaustion. Letting someone else take over might

> let the bird go to the next chap after he [the victim] is softened up nicely, when of course the other chap would get the honor and glory of it. It is a question of personal success. You see, you're competing with the others. (Fanon, 1968, pp. 268–269)

As perpetrators evolve, the feeling of responsibility for the welfare of other humans that people normally possess diminishes or is lost in relation to the victims. Most people acquire such feelings of responsibility. This can lead them to help others in need (Latane & Darley, 1970; Staub, 1978) or inhibit them from harming others. Lifton (1986) offered the concept of "doubling," the notion that perpetrators develop a second, separate self, as an explanation of the great discrepancy in who they appear to be and how they act in relation to victims and the rest of the world. In my view, instead, people develop a more differentiated self and a more differentiated orientation to different groups of people. Through devaluation and other processes, some groups are excluded from the moral universe. It then becomes possible to harm and even to kill their members in the service of the needs and motives discussed previously.

Nonetheless, some direct perpetrators suffer aftereffects (Amnesty International, 1975) that can be similar to posttraumatic stress disorder. One torturer heard screams at night that prevented him from sleeping. One day, walking around the hospital grounds while waiting for his doctor's appointment, he had an anxiety attack upon seeing a former victim who was under treatment in the hospital. Another torturer had the impulse to beat and fantasies of torturing people who crossed him or interfered with him to the slightest degree. He beat his children and went to see a doctor after he tied up and beat his wife, stating that "before, he wasn't like that" (Fanon, 1968, p. 268).

It would be useful to ascertain the frequency of such aftereffects and to explore whether initial differences in personality, incomplete training of torturers, or very large steps along the continuum of destruction make them probable. One torturer, quoted earlier, believed that his problems stemmed from his inability to stop and rest, from continuing with the work of torture too long, driven by the desire for personal success. Knowledge of the factors that contribute to distress reactions in torturers might offer avenues for discouraging people from participating in torture.

THE PERPETRATION OF TORTURE AS A GROUP PROCESS

Systematic torture is performed by groups of perpetrators who are frequently part of an ideological movement or system. The group often fulfills important personal needs that arise from difficult life conditions and shared goals that are embodied in the ideology. In becoming a member of the group, through rituals, sacrifices demanded by the group, and shared experience, the members' individual goals will often be subordinated to, supplanted by, or integrated with group goals. Members come to identify themselves with the group. Their individual self-concept, the "I," will be embedded in and defined by their group concept, the "We," to a substantial degree. With the boundaries of the self weakened, there will be emotional contagion, or "empathic joining" (Staub, 1987a), the spread of feelings in the group and thus shared reactions to events. The members' perception of reality will be shaped by their shared belief system and by the support they receive from each other in interpreting reality. The power of the group to define the "correct" or morally acceptable reality becomes great and deviation from the group unlikely (Staub, 1989b; Toch, 1965).

Leaders can lead only when their purposes, mode of thinking, and ideology are accepted by their followers (see Staub, 1989b, on "leadership" and "followership"). When that is so, they can exert great influence. They can influence group practice, both directly and indirectly. In Vietnam, by instituting the practice of the body count, of search and destroy missions (Egendorf, 1986), and by silence in the face of atrocities about which at least rumors must have existed,[3] army leaders made brutality and the killing of civilians more acceptable.

Brutality by perpetrators is often fostered to keep victims demoralized, to limit their resistance, and to diminish them and thereby make it easier for perpetrators to harm them and kill them (Hilberg, 1961; Sereny, 1974; Staub, 1989a). Although individual sadism may be discouraged, the possibilities for it clearly exist, and it is likely to be accepted within broad limits. Rape may be discouraged, either because it is too evidently self-serving, or because ideology makes sexual contact with inferiors a breach of racial purity (as in Nazi Germany). However, frequently rape goes unpunished (Argentine National Commission on the Disappeared, 1986). Looting is often part of the official policy, but attempts

---

[3]The courage that is required to limit violence is frequently not physical courage, the willingness to put one's life on the line, but the courage to oppose one's group and to endanger one's status in the group or one's career. Many army leaders in Vietnam reported after the war that they disagreed with and disliked the policy of the use of body count (the count of the number killed) as an index of success and the practice of search and destroy operations. In a 1974 survey "almost 70 percent of the army generals who led the war in Vietnam believed that body counts, kill ratios . . . were inflated and invalid" (Egendorf, 1986, p. 102). They seem to have kept quiet, according to researchers, because their careers were at stake. However, the psychological difficulty of standing apart and opposing one's group, its policy and practices, probably also entered.

may be made to define its acceptable limits, in part to apportion what goes to the group and what goes to its individual members (Hilberg, 1980).

Zimbardo (1969) suggested that in groups individuals lose their personal identity and experience deindividuation, with a lessening of the power of social prohibitions. Some practices of torturers serve both to deindividuate them and, by hiding their identity, to diminish their concern about blame and retribution. For example, torturers wore masks in Algeria (Peters, 1985), and they blindfolded prisoners in Argentina (Argentine National Commission on the Disappeared, 1986). The use of jargon or euphemisms in talking about torture is common. This both creates a shared group culture and lessens the torturer's confrontation with the meaning of his or her actions. In Brazil, suspending victims from a bar was called the "parrot perch," the electric chair the "dragon chair." In Greece and other places, torturers referred to each other as "doctor" (Lippman, 1982).

Another process that is affected by group membership is *moral equilibration*. I had proposed (Staub, 1987b; 1989b) that people frequently try to resolve conflict between a personal goal or motive and a moral value by replacing the moral value with one that allows the expression of the goal or motive in behavior. For example, perpetrators of torture may replace the value of respect for individual welfare with the value of loyalty and obedience, or with the value placed on group welfare, or with the value of maintaining a revolution. Such a conflict resolution process may take place without conscious deliberation, in a relatively automatic fashion. The elevation by the group as a whole of these "replacement" values should make moral equilibration easier.

THE EVOLUTION OF BYSTANDERS

Bystanders also progress along a continuum. They are usually exposed to at least some degree of propaganda and indoctrination. They also engage in just-world thinking and devalue victims. Just like perpetrators, bystanders learn from experience and change as a result of their own actions and inaction. They are likely to progressively accept the perpetrators' conduct if they remain passive in the face of witnessing or knowing about torture or other harm inflicted on victims.

Although fear of a repressive and violent system may inhibit opposition by bystanders to torture and murder, the shared culture and life conditions, the shared cultural tilt with perpetrators', and the bystanders' own evolution are also important. In Germany there was strong reaction against the euthanasia killing of Germans once it became known (Dawidowicz, 1975; Lifton, 1986), but there was little reaction to the mistreatment of Jews. This may have been partly because of differences in attitudes toward (e.g., in the evaluation of) the two groups and partly because of the more gradual, step-by-step mistreatment of Jews. In Turkey, Argentina, and many other countries, bystanders on the whole remained passive.

Some bystanders evolve into perpetrators. This often begins with their involvement with the system, which represents a starting point for change. For example, although most German psychoanalysts left after the Nazis came to power in Germany, some remained in Berlin. Obviously, there had to be self-selection, not only by religion, but also by attitudes and beliefs. Perhaps with that as a starting point, there was an evolution in the thinking and actions of these analysts. In the end, some of them helped select victims for the euthanasia killings of the Nazis (Friedrich, 1989; Staub, 1989a).

Involvement with the system and the resulting psychological evolution may explain why some doctors and other professionals cooperate with torture. Some have an ideological affinity as a starting point. Others are called upon to participate in their capacity as doctors. Although their participation may be seemingly humane, it usually serves the perpetrators not the victims—by helping to revive or keep alive victims for more torture or selecting methods of torture to minimize visible signs. As they participate in these ways, rather than protest and resist, doctors must employ psychological processes—such as justification of the torture, moral equilibration, and just-world thinking—to make their participation bearable to themselves. Almost certainly, psychological changes result that make greater involvement in the torture process possible.

Even though Argentinian perpetrators abducted and killed some priests and nuns, they claimed the support of Christian values and ideals as part of their motivation. This may explain why some priests were present at the interrogation of victims and even participated in them. Some were even present during tortures, supporting the perpetrators (Argentine National Commission on the Disappeared, 1986). In Germany, a history of service for, and subordination to, the state contributed to an inclination by doctors to serve the state in euthanasia killings and genocide (Lifton, 1986). The evolution of strong professional group ethics may over time lessen the influence of forces, external or psychological, that lead doctors to serve torturers (see Stover & Nightingale, 1985).

Sometimes new laws and procedures are created soon after a radical, ideological system gains power. Psychological changes are likely to follow as these are put into practice. At other times, as a whole society moves along the continuum of destruction, societal norms, values, and institutions change. The whole society undergoes a resocialization of beliefs, values, and standards of conduct. Once new institutions emerge, such as those in Nazi Germany and Russia that dealt with political opposition or the Department of Technical Investigation in Guatemala, a civilian group that killed and abducted on orders from the intelligence division of the Guatemalan army (Nairn & Simon, 1986), these represent new realities that maintain torture or killing.

External groups, including other nations, can also be seen as bystanders who evolve over time. Their views of national self-interest, the usual view that nations are not moral agents that have moral obligations, and unwillingness to interfere with other nations' supposedly internal affairs often lead nations to remain passive when another nation mistreats its own citizens. Nations as a whole are also affected by just-world thinking, tending to assume that victims somehow deserve or brought on themselves their fate. Furthermore, nations are affected by the propaganda of the perpetrators, who aim to further this belief. These interpretations are supported when relevant data and analyses are available, as in the case of the Holocaust and the reactions of the rest of the world to it (Wyman, 1984). For example, there was an increase in anti-Semitism in the United States and elsewhere during the 1930s (Wyman, 1968).

Because bystanders can have substantial influence, probably more so if they react early in the perpetrators' progress along the continuum of destruction, understanding why bystanders allow persistent harm doing is highly important (Staub, 1985, 1989a, 1989b).

It is worth noting that frequently torture and other mistreatment begins with certain ideas and ways of thinking. This is obvious with regard to destructive ideologies. However, sometimes seemingly innocent ideas evolve into a source of maltreating or destroying people. In Soviet psychiatry, the evolution of certain theories of schizophrenia probably both contributed to, and was used to justify, the incarceration of political dissidents in mental hospitals (Block & Reddaway, 1977; Suedfeld, in press). In Germany, the evolution in medical thinking of killing as a form of healing, the view that killing certain individuals affirmed life and strengthened the community, contributed to the involvement of German doctors in the euthanasia program and possibly to the very existence and extent of the euthanasia program (Lifton, 1986). This, in turn, represented a step in the progression toward genocide. The freedom of expression of ideas is essential to counteract early steps along a continuum of destruction. This freedom also places responsibility on bystanders to combat ideas and world views that dehumanize and carry a destructive potential.

THE ROLE OF PERSONALITY

I stressed the role of personal characteristics both in self-selection by perpetrators, and in their selection by authorities. This seems to contrast with the widely held assumption by social psychologists that the situation—for example, the pressure of authority or being placed in certain roles (e.g., Zimbardo, Haney, Banks, & Jaffe, 1974) is the more important influence in leading people to harm others (see Gibson, 1987; chapter 5, this volume). However, the contrast is not as great as it seems. First, this chapter stresses that perpetrators and bystanders, given their shared culture and shared life conditions, share a psychological situation. Second, in this analysis I considered ideological inclination to be a personal characteristic. Third, in contrast to research situations, in which people are unexpectedly asked to shock others, perpetrators usually select if not their roles as perpetrators, then roles such as SS member or a career officer in the military, which evolve into perpetrator roles. The Greek torturers, who were exceptions to this, were selected from among conscripts on the basis of certain characteristics. Finally, even in some of the research studies, selection factors probably operated. For example, people with certain characteristics are more likely to volunteer for a study on prison life (Staub, 1989b).

I described characteristics of perpetrators that lead to their self-selection or selection by those in authority: a positive orientation to authority, an enjoyment of military activities, and a belief in ideology. Others were implied by a description of psychological processes, motivations, and cultural-societal characteristics that lead to harm-doing, such as a negative evaluation of human beings, strong in-group–out-group differentiations, the devaluation of specific groups, and certain self-concepts that easily give rise to the need to defend or elevate the self. Usually a pattern of characteristics, not a single characteristic, represents a predisposition.

A predisposition to be a torturer need not be evident in other contexts. A person coming from a family that strongly opposes communism and respects and obeys authority may be someone "about whom everyone said was a 'diamond'" as the father of Alexander Lavranos, one of the defendants at the Greek torture trials in 1975, described him (Peters, 1985, p. 179). Nonetheless, inherent in the very characteristics that make a person such a "diamond" may be an enhanced potential to become a torturer. Obviously, different ideological orientations can predispose people, if they fit the ideology of a destructive group or system.

Other considerations about personality are speculative. Frequently, the direct perpetrators are a subgroup of participants in a mass movement. The participants in mass movements, such as the French Revolution or the Nazi movement, are frequently quite heterogeneous, belying early notions that members of certain classes or subgroups would primarily participate, those whose interests the movement especially serves (Platt, 1980). Because of this heterogeneity, it may be more useful to consider personality, rather than class or other group membership, and how people with different characteristics are affected by life problems. People with weaker identities, with stronger needs for comprehension of reality and for control, or who require a reliable social structure in order to feel safe may be most affected. They may be most in search for solutions, most in need of a new comprehension of reality and a new identity, the most willing to join movements and give themselves over to ideologies.

The role of personality as a predisposing factor may also be present when already existing groups become the torturers. In Argentina, for example, many of the torturers were career soldiers. People who choose a military career must have some liking for hierarchical, authoritarian institutions and a willingness to fight. Their training further promotes these dispositions. The early members of the SS did not yet have to torture and kill enemies of the state, but as bodyguards of Hitler who volunteered to fight for him they were willing to engage in and possibly enjoyed violence.

People who gain enjoyment from others' suffering are likely to be attracted to the role of perpetrator, but we have little evidence about the presence or frequency of such characteristics. Although some torturers apparently relish the role, their satisfaction may arise from their elevation over other people, their power over their lives, or other factors. Moreover, the prescribed role of a torturer, that on the one hand demands task orientation and on the other hand furthers a seeming abandon—which partly serves to intimidate the victims (Argentine National Commission on the Disappeared, 1986; Peters, 1985; Staub, 1989b)—makes it difficult to infer personality as a predisposing factor from the torturers' conduct as reported by victims.

Some personality disposition is likely to be present in most people who select themselves, who are selected, and who proceed through all the requirements of training and group bonding. Even if they somehow get involved, people with strong disinclination can usually get out of such roles; they are eliminated because of their inclinations, inadequacies, or incompetence, which they may purposely create. Even at a late stage, with some cost to themselves, people can usually opt out of such roles, claiming constitutional weakness or the like (Lifton, 1986). However, once in the role, there can be immense pressures operating on them to fulfill their functions: rewards for doing so, their bonding with the group, and the possibility of not only the loss of privilege but also of severe punishment for resistance and opposition.

Can Anyone Become a Torturer?

The conception that I have presented suggests that torturers tend to have some of a variety of predisposing personal characteristics. It also suggests that with steps along the continuum of destruction the psychological processes and motivations that facilitate torture evolve, even in torturers who initially possessed them only to a minimal degree. People who have strong separate identities and strong universal moral values would probably not become torturers, regardless of the pressures on them. Although a majority of people can probably be led to torture others, they require different degrees of pressure—the threat of force, motivation arising from culture and life conditions, or the promise of rewards. When a whole society moves along the continuum of destruction, as individuals are resocialized, the mistreatment and destruction of others become easier and more possible for many people.

"Justified" Torture

Peters (1985), among others, described views and arguments that torture is justified in certain instances. Circumstances or military necessity can justify it, as General Massu claimed in his defense of the use of torture in Algeria by the French (cited in Peters, 1985). The information gained by torture can protect innocent lives. Those who present such views claim that torturers can be responsible agents of the state or that they can be objective and dispassionate (see Levin, chapter 6, this volume).

My analysis (as well as the few statements by torturers themselves referred to earlier) suggests that the existence of such "ideal" torturers is highly unlikely (if we can regard disinterested, uninvolved torturers as ideal), because of the personal changes that inevitably occur in the course of torturing people. At times torture may save lives, for example, when members of terrorist groups are captured who have important information about other terrorists or about impending terrorist acts. As was noted earlier, however, the range of victims, the motivations, and the intensity of torture, tend to expand. The psychological requirements for and changes resulting from torture make it unlikely that is practice remains circumscribed.

The psychological changes that lead to greater destructiveness are not limited to the direct perpetrators. They also characterize the decision makers. Thus, people in authority, even if they initially set narrow limits, may progressively expand the circle of victims and raise the level of violence. In Germany, over time the racial ideology led to plans for killing jailed criminals who were ugly (Hilberg, 1980). Although exceptions may exist, and theoretically it is possible to define narrow limits, and the pressure to use torture to save innocent lives may at times be intense, instances of torture are likely to become steps along a continuum of increasing violence.

Another aspect of justified torture is that it rarely fulfills its intended purpose: At least over the long run, it rarely, if ever, increases the security of the state or of its people. As Barber (1985) noted, "cruelty arouses revulsion . . . and adds support to the resistance" (p. 17). Most killing and genocide do not contribute to the strength or success of the state either; on the contrary, they tend to weaken it and contribute to its downfall (Staub, 1989b).

CREATING A WORLD WITHOUT TORTURE

It is beyond the scope of this chapter to explore two important issues. Briefly, the first one is the psychology of those who resist being placed in the role of torturers, oppose torture and the torturers, or attempt to help the victims. The literature on rescuers, people who helped victims of the Nazis (London, 1970; Oliner & Oliner, 1988; Tec, 1986; Staub, 1989b) together with the voluminous literature on helping behavior, can be one guide to the exploration of this issue. The second issue is the elimination of torture, the creation of a world without torture. These concluding paragraphs offer some suggestions.

The potential influence of active bystanders, even individuals, groups, institutions, or nations, is enormous. In several Latin American countries the frequency of torture declined following an international campaign (Stover & Nightingale, 1985). A persistent policy by nations that demands respect for human rights is of great importance. Unfortunately, countries frequently support other countries that engage in torture. They provide training, equipment, and experts (Lippman, 1982) and thereby also express acceptance and approval. Policies that are contrary to this are likely to have significant effects. One goal must be to influence nations so that they will make decisions about aid, commerce, and other relations partly on the basis of other nations' respect for human (and civil) rights. For such a policy to work, contact with offending nations must be maintained, with the possibility of reestablishing positive relations. The support of such a policy among many nations is likely to have substantial effects, not only because of material consequences or loss of credibility, but also because it forcefully brings the values of respect for human life and welfare to the attention of the perpetrators, values that lost influence on their conduct, at least toward the victim group.

Actions by institutions, such as churches or corporations that do business in a country that tortures or kills its citizens, are also important. Unfortunately, such institutions rarely speak out. One case study of the difficulty in moving institutions to act, specifically the International Medical Association to condemn the Soviet practice of putting dissidents into mental hospitals, was described by Bloch and Reddaway (1984). A central aim of citizen groups, such as Amnesty International and others, ought to be to influence governments and institutions so that they set policy on the basis of, and speak out in defense of, human rights. The evolution of strong international norms prohibiting torture, with sanctions against deviators by the community of nations, is required to diminish torture in the world.

We must also have long-term goals and work to develop the values of caring and connection among individuals and between groups and an international system based on them. To create such basic change requires, on the individual level, certain socialization practices in the home and in the school. It also requires providing opportunities for and guiding both children and adults to engage in actions that benefit others. On the group level, it also requires cross-cutting relations among subgroups of societies and members of nations, whereby members of different groups work and play together (Deutsch, 1973). Groups need to create joint projects and develop shared goals, superordinate to conflicting interests and goals (Sherif, 1958; Sherif, Harvey, White, Hood, & Sherif, 1961; Worchel, 1979). With steps along the continuum of benevolence, the values of caring, nonaggression, and mutual help can evolve—a system of relating among groups and their members that make torture and other atrocities unlikely. Although this is a slow, long-term process, it is an essential one to reduce the many forms of group violence (Staub, 1988; 1989b).

The analysis in this chapter points to many influences contributing to torture and mass killing: the characteristics of culture and the organization of society and its institution; the conditions of life in a society and emerging life problems; the characteristics of individuals, both those who become perpetrators and the bystanders; and the behavior of both internal bystanders and external ones, other nations or groups of people in other nations. Changes in any of these categories can diminish the likelihood of groups turning against other groups.

REFERENCES

Adorno, T. W., Frenkel-Brunswik, E., Levinson, D. J., & Sanford, E. N. (1950). *The authoritarian personality.* New York: Norton.

Ainsworth, M. D. S. (1979). Infant–mother attachment. *American Psychologist, 34,* 932–937.

Allport, G. (1954). *The nature of prejudice.* Reading, MA: Addison-Wesley.

Amnesty International. (1975). *Report on torture.* New York: Farrar, Straus & Giroux.

Amnesty International. (1980). *Testimony on secret detention camps in Argentina.* London: Author.

Argentine National Commission on the Disappeared. (1986). *Nunca Mas.* New York: Farrar, Straus & Giroux.

Averill, J. R. (1982). *Anger and aggression: An essay on emotion.* New York: Springer-Verlag.

Bandura, A. (1973). *Aggression: A social learning analysis.* New York: Holt.

Bandura, A., Underwood, B. & Fromson, M. E. (1975). Disinhibition of aggression through diffusion of responsibility and dehumanization of victims. *Journal of Research in Personality, 9,* 253–269.

Barber, J. D. (1985, November). Rationalizing torture: The dance of the intellectual apologists. *The Washington Monthly,* 12–17.

Baron, R. A. (1977). *Human aggression.* New York: Plenum Press.

Beck, F., & Godin, W. (1951). *Russian purge and the extraction of confession.* New York: Viking Press.

Becker, E. (1975). *Escape from evil.* New York: The Free Press.

Berkowitz, L. (1962). *Aggression: A social psychological analysis.* New York: McGraw-Hill.

Bloch, S., & Reddaway, P. (1977). *Psychiatric terror: How Soviet psychiatry is used to suppress dissent.* New York: Basic Books.

Bloch, S., & Reddaway, P. (1984). *Soviet psychiatric abuse: The shadow over world psychiatry.* London: Victor Gollancz.

Brewer, M. B. (1978). Ingroup bias in the minimal intergroup situation: A cognitive–motivational analysis. *Psychological Bulletin, 86,* 307–324.

Buss, A. H. (1966). The effect of harm on subsequent aggression. *Journal of Experimental Research in Personality, 1,* 249–255.

Caviedes, C. (1984). *The Southern cone: Realities of the authoritarian state in South America.* Totowa, NJ: Rowman & Allenheld.

Cherry, F., & Byrne, D. (1977). Authoritarianism. In T. Blass (Ed.), *Personality variables in social behavior.* Hillsdale, NJ: Erlbaum.

Children around the world killed and tortured, rights groups says. (1988, January 6). *New York Times,* p. A-6.

Colligan, J. (1976). New science of torture. *Science Digest, 44.*

Craig, G. A. (1982). *The Germans.* New York: The New American Library.

Dawidowicz, L. S. (1975). *The war against the Jews: 1933–1945.* New York: Holt, Rinehart & Winston.

DeJong, W. (1979). An examination of self-perception mediation of the foot-in-the-door effect. *Journal of Personality and Social Psychology, 34,* 578–582.

Deutsch, M. (1973). *The resolution of conflict: Constructive and destructive processes.* New Haven, CT: Yale University Press.

Dicks, H. V. (1972). *Licensed mass murder: A socio-psychological study of some SS killers.* New York: Basic Books.

Dyer, G. (1985). *War.* New York: Crown.

Egendorf, A. (1986). *Healing from the war: Trauma and transformation after Vietnam.* Boston: Shambhala.

Eisenberg, N., & Cialdini, R. B. (1984). The role of consistency pressures in behavior: A developmental perspective. *Academic Psychology Bulletin, 6,* 115–126.

Elms, A. C., & Milgram, S. (1966). Personality characteristics associated with obedience and defiance toward authoritative command. *Journal of Experimental Research in Personality, 2,* 282–289.

Erkut, S., Jaquette, D., & Staub, E. (1981). Moral judgment–situation interaction as a basis for predicting social behavior. *Journal of Personality, 49,* 1–44.

Etcheson, C. (1984). *The rise and demise of democratic Kampuchea.* Boulder, CO: Westview Press.

Fanon, F. (1968). *The wretched of the earth.* New York: Grove Press. (Original work published 1961)

Feinberg, J. K. (1978). *Anatomy of a helping situation: Some personality and situational determinants of helping in a conflict situation involving another's psychological distress.* Unpublished doctoral dissertation, University of Massachusetts, Amherst.

Freedman, J. L., & Fraser, S. C. (1966). Compliance without pressure: The foot-in-the-door technique. *Journal of Personality and Social Psychology, 4,* 195–202.

Freidrich, V. (1989). From psychoanalysis to the "Great Treatment." Psychoanalysts under National Socialism. *Political Psychology, 10,* 3–26.

Fromm, E. (1965). *Escape from freedom.* New York: Avon Books.

Gibson, J. T. (1987, August). *The psychology of torture and other atrocious acts: Etiology, dynamics, prevention.* Paper presented at a preconvention workshop at the meeting of the American Psychological Association, New York, NY.

Gibson, J. T., & Haritos-Fatouros, M. (1986). The education of a torturer. *Psychology Today, 20,* 50–58.

Goldstein, J. H., Davis, R. W., & Herman, D. (1975). Escalation of aggression: Experimental studies. *Journal of Personality and Social Psychology, 31,* 162–170.

Grodman, S. M. (1979). *The role of personality and situational variables in responding to and helping an individual in psychological distress.* Unpublished doctoral dissertation, University of Massachusetts, Amherst.

Grusec, J. E., Kuczynski, L., Rushton, J. P., & Simutis, Z. M. (1978). Modeling, direct instruction, and attributions: Effects on altruism. *Developmental Psychology, 14,* 51–57.

Haritos-Fatouros, M. (1988). The official torturer: A learning model for obedience to the authority of violence. *Journal of Applied Social Psychology, 18,* 1107–1120.

Hilberg, R. (1961). *The destruction of the European Jews.* New York: Harper & Row.

Hilberg, R. (1980). The nature of the process. In J. Dimsdale (Ed.), *Survivors, victims, and perpetrators: Essays on the Nazi Holocaust* (pp. 5–54). Washington, DC: Hemisphere.

Hornstein, H. A. (1976). *Cruelty and kindness: A new look at aggression and altruism.* Englewood Cliffs, NJ: Prentice-Hall.

Kohlberg, L., & Candee, L. (1984). The relationship of moral judgment to moral action. In W. M. Kurtines & J. L. Gewirtz (Eds.), *Morality, moral behavior, and moral development* (pp. 52–73). New York: Wiley-Interscience.

Krebs, D. L. (1975). Empathy and altruism. *Journal of Personality and Social Psychology, 32,* 1134–1146.

Kren, G. M., & Rappoport, L. (1980). *The Holocaust and the crisis of human behavior.* New York: Holmes & Meier.

Kuper, L. (1981). *Genocide: Its political use in the twentieth century.* New Haven, CT: Yale University Press.

Latane, B., & Darley, L. (1970). *The unresponsive bystander; Why doesn't he help.* New York: Appleton-Crofts.

Lerner, M. (1980). *The belief in a just world: A fundamental delusion.* New York: Plenum Press.

Lerner, J. J., & Simmons, C. H. (1966). Observer's reaction to the "innocent victim": Compassion or rejection? *Journal of Personality and Social Psychology, 4,* 203–210.

Lifton, R. J. (1986). *The Nazi doctors: Medical killing and the psychology of genocide.* New York: Basic Books.

Lippman, M. (1982, June 25). *Torture and the torturer: An overview of the findings.* Paper presented at the meeting of the International Society for Political Psychology, Washington, DC.

London, P. (1970). The rescuers: Motivational hypotheses about Christians who saved Jews from the Nazis. In J. Macaulay & L. Berkowitz (Eds.), *Altruism and helping behavior.* New York: Academic Press.

Milgram, S. (1965). Some conditions of obedience and disobedience to authority. *Human Relations, 18,* 57–76.

Milgram, S. (1974). *Obedience to authority: An experimental view.* New York: Harper & Row.

Miller, A. (1983). *For your own good: Hidden cruelty in child-rearing and the roots of violence.* New York: Farrar, Straus, and Giroux.

Nairn, A., & Simon, J. M. (1986, June). Bureaucracy of death. *The New Republic,* pp. 13–18.

Oliner, S. & Oliner, P. (1988). *The altruistic personality. Rescuers of Jews in Nazi Europe.* New York: The Free Press.

Padgett, V. (1986). *Predicting violence in totalitarian organizations: An application of eleven powerful principles of obedience to authority.* Unpublished manuscript, Marshall University, Huntington, WV.

Peters, E. (1985). *Torture.* New York: Basil Blackwell.

Piaget, J., & Weil, A. (1951). The development in children of the idea of the homeland and of relations with other countries. *International Social Science Bulletin, 3,* 570.

Platt, G. M. (1980). Thoughts on a theory of collective action: Language, affect and ideology in revolution. In M. Albin, R. J. Devlin, & G. Heeger (Eds.), *New directions in psychohistory: The Adelphi papers in honor of Erik H. Erikson.* Lexington, MA: Lexington Books.

Potash, R. A. (1970). Argentina. In L. N. McAlister (Ed.), *The military in Latin American sociopolitical evolution.* Washington, DC: Center for Research in Social Systems.

Rank, O. (1958). *Beyond psychology.* New York: Dover Books. (Original work published 1941)

Reitlinger, G. (1953). *The final solution.* London: Sphere Books.

Rubin, Z., & Peplau, L. A. (1975). Who believes in a just world? *Journal of Social Issues, 31,* 65–89.

Sereny, G. (1974). *Into the darkness: From mercy killing to mass murder.* New York: McGraw-Hill.

Shaffer, D. R. (1979). *Social and personality development.* Monterey, CA: Brooks-Cole.

Sherif, M. (1958). Superordinate goals in the reduction of intergroup conflict. *American Journal of Sociology, 63,* 349–358.

Sherif, M., Harvey, D. J., White, B. J., Hood, W. K., & Sherif, C. W. (1961). *Intergroup conflict and cooperation: The Robber's Cave experiment.* Norman: University of Oklahoma Book Exchange.

Staub, E. (1974). Helping a distressed person: Social, personality and stimulus determinants. In L. Berkowitz (Ed.), *Advances in experimental social psychology* (vol. 7). New York: Academic Press.

Staub, E. (1975). To rear a prosocial child: Reasoning, learning by doing, and learning by teaching others. In D. DePalma & J. Folley (Eds.), *Moral development: Current theory and research.* Hillsdale, NJ: Erlbaum.

Staub, E. (1978). *Positive social behavior and morality: 1. Social and personal influences.* New York: Academic Press.

Staub, E. (1979). *Positive social behavior and morality: 2. Socialization and development.* New York: Academic Press.

Staub, E. (1980). Social and prosocial behavior: Personal and situational influences and their interactions. In E. Staub (Ed.), *Personality: Basic aspects and current research.* Englewood Cliffs, NJ: Prentice-Hall.

Staub, E. (1985). The psychology of perpetrators and bystanders. *Political Psychology, 6,* 61–86.

Staub, E. (1986). A conception of the determinants and development of altruism and aggression: Motives, the self, the environment. In C. Zahn-Waxler (Ed.), *Altruism and aggression: Social and biological origins.* New York: Cambridge University Press.

Staub, E. (1987a). Commentary. In N. Eisenberg & J. Strayer (Eds.), *Empathy and its development.* New York: Cambridge University Press.

Staub, E. (1987b, August). *Moral exclusion and the evolution of extreme destructiveness.* In S. V. Opotow (Chair), *The moral community: Implications for the psychology of justice.* Symposium conducted at the meeting of the American Psychological Association, New York, NY.

Staub, E. (1988). The evolution of caring and nonaggressive persons and societies. In R. Wagner, J. DeRivera, & M. Watkins (Eds.), *Positive approaches to peace. Journal of Social Issues, 44,* 81–100.

Staub, E. (1989a). Steps along the continuum of destruction: The evolution of bystanders, German psychoanalysts and lessons for today. *Political Psychology, 10,* 39–53.

Staub, E. (1989b). *The roots of evil: The origins of genocide and other group violence.* New York: Cambridge University Press.

Steiner, J. M. (1980). The SS yesterday and today: A sociopsychological view. In J. Dimsdale (Ed.), *Survivors, victims and perpetrators: Essays on the Nazi Holocaust* (pp. 405–456). Washington, DC: Hemisphere.

Stover, E., & Nightingale, E. O. (Eds.). (1985). *The breaking of minds and bodies: Torture, psychiatric abuse and the health professions.* New York: Freeman.

Sykes, G. M., & Matza, D. (1957). Techniques of neutralization: A theory of delinquency. *American Sociological Review, 75,* 664–670.

Tajfel, H. (1982). Social psychology of intergroup relations. *Annual Review of Psychology, 33,* 1–39.

Tajfel, H., Flamant, C., Billig, M. Y., & Bundy, R. P. (1971). Societal categorization and intergroup behavior. *European Journal of Social Psychology, 1,* 149–177.

Tec, N. (1986). *When light pierced the darkness: Christian rescue of Jews in Nazi-occupied Poland.* New York: Oxford University Press.

Timerman, J. (1981). *Prisoner without a name, cell without a number.* New York: Knopf.

Toch, H. (1965). *The social psychology of social movements.* New York: Bobbs-Merrill.

Worchel, S. (1979). Cooperation and the reduction of intergroup conflict: Some determining factors. In W. G. Austin & S. Worchel (Eds.), *The social psychology of intergroup relations.* Monterey, CA: Brooks-Cole.

Wyman, D. W. (1968). *Paper walls: America and the refugee crisis, 1938–1941.* Amherst: University of Massachusetts Press.

Wyman, D. S. (1984). *The abandonment of the Jews: America and the Holocaust, 1941–1945.* New York: Pantheon Books.

Zimbardo, P. G. (1969). The human choice: Individuation, reason, and order versus deindividuation, impulse and chaos. In *Nebraska symposium on motivation.* Lincoln: University of Nebraska Press.

Zimbardo, P. G., Haney, C., Banks, W. C., & Jaffe, D. (1974). The psychology of imprisonment: Privation, power and pathology. In Z. Rubin (Ed.), *Doing unto others.* Englewood Cliffs, NJ: Prentice-Hall.

5

Factors Contributing to the Creation of a Torturer

Janice T. Gibson

Torture, as described by the United Nations General Assembly (1984), is an act by which the perpetrator intentionally inflicts severe physical or mental pain. The perpetrator's purposes vary and include obtaining information or confessions, punishing, intimidating, and coercing. Although torture is condemned publicly by governments and religions, it has, nevertheless, been conducted throughout history, and its practice has recently been reported by Amnesty International in at least 90 countries, often at the instigation or with the consent of people acting in official capacities (Power, 1981). Torture that is initiated or condoned by officials is the subject of this chapter.

In recent years, torture has been practiced by regimes reflecting an enormously broad spectrum of ideologies and religions and governing an equally broad spectrum of cultures. The following excerpts illustrate.

Greece: "When a new political prisoner came, the usual order was that five or six men should go into his cell and give him a good beating . . . with their clubs and with their fists."—ex-military policeman and torturer Michaelis Petrou (Preisler, 1982)

Brazil: "She was submitted to electric shocks on various parts of the body, including her arms, legs and vagina."—ex-prisoner Elsa Lianza (Dassin, 1986)

Argentina: "The doctor . . . removes my blindfold. . . . He tells me he's proud of the way I withstood it all. Some people die on their torturers."—ex-political prisoner Jacobo Timerman (1981, p. 54)

Russia: "The prison doctor was the interrogator's and executioner's right hand man. The beaten prisoners would come to on the floor only to hear the doctor's voice: 'You can continue, the pulse is normal.'"—ex-political prisoner Aleksandr Solzhenitsyn (1973, p. 208)

Vietnam: "You tied them to a tree and got the dog handler to let the dog jump and bite at them. Or . . . you wired the field telephone to ears, nose, genitals. . . .

I've seen it done to women."—American military veteran Michael McCusker, describing methods of interrogation that he observed in the field in Vietnam (Vietnam Veterans Against the War, 1972, p. 32)

An act of torture requires two people: a victim and a torturer. Bales (1987) reported recently that far less is known about the impact of acts of torture on victims than about the acts themselves. Even less is known about the individual soldiers, police, physicians, and others who commit the atrocious acts. The few psychological studies of individual torturers that exist have usually been conducted long after the fact, and they have examined people who have already been convicted and punished for committing acts for governments or institutions that no longer held power or even existed. A prime example is studies of Nazi war criminals.

PERSONALITY AND THE TORTURER

A number of researchers have attempted to determine the type of person who became a torturer in Nazi Germany by isolating personal factors that might differentiate individuals who had committed atrocities from individuals in the same situations who had not. Kelley (1946) interviewed and took Rorschach records of war criminals during their trials in Nuremberg after the war. Arendt (1964) analyzed the testimony of Adolph Eichmann during his war crimes trial in 1961. Harrower (1976) sent the Rorschach records of 8 top Nazi war criminals taken earlier in Nuremberg, together with 8 Rorschach records of ordinary Americans, to 15 Rorschach experts who were not given the identities of any of the individuals whose responses were described. Lifton (1982, 1986) studied physicians who played major roles in the Nazi atrocities through "medicalized" killing, mass murder, and torturing.

It might be comforting to assume that torturers are, in fact, peculiar monsters who can be explained away as the sort of freaks of nature who commit mass murders in periods of insanity. However, the conclusions of the researchers mentioned previously show clearly that this is not the case: They hold that, although it is true that, in some situations, deranged and sadistic individuals have committed acts of torture for pleasure, in most cases in which torture is committed at the instigation of government officials, the torturers can best be described as normal individuals. A deranged person who receives gratification primarily from feelings of power or from personally inflicting pain on others is usually too unreliable to be counted on by authorities to follow orders.

Kelley (1946), in fact, was unable to find anything unique or insane in the personalities of the Nuremberg war criminals. He reported that their personalities could be duplicated in any country in the world. Arendt noted that the troops of the Einsatzgruppen used on the Eastern front in World War II for the purpose of killing Jews had been drafted from the armed SS, a military unit with "hardly more crimes in its record than any ordinary unit of the German army" (1964, p. 105). Arendt concluded that they were not insane sadists, but, on the contrary, had been carefully selected by a process designed to weed out those who derived pleasure from what they did. Harrower (1976) discovered that the Rorschach experts, when they did not know the identity of their subjects, rated Nazi war criminals equally in all categories with ordinary Americans. Finally, Lifton (1982, 1986) concluded that the Nazi physicians he interviewed, who had played active roles in mass murder and torturing in the Nazi concentration camps, were also, in fact, ordinary.

The author of a study of individual perpetrators of torture in more recent times reached a conclusion similar to that of researchers who had studied Nazis. Haritos-Fatouros (1983), in an investigation of Greek military police convicted of committing atrocities during the 1967–1973 reign of the military junta, found nothing unusual in their family or school backgrounds. She also found nothing unusual in their personal characteristics that could differentiate them in any way from the rest of the Greek male population of their age at the time.

Controlled simulation studies also provide evidence consistent with the ordinariness of individuals who commit atrocious acts. In the well-known study by Haney, Banks, and Zimbardo (1973), students in an American university were selected for normal personality characteristics, physical and mental health, and family background, and then were subjected to daily simulations of prison experience. Half of the subjects were assigned randomly the role of guard, the other half the role of prisoner. Mock guards were given uniforms and nightsticks and told to act as guards. Prisoners were treated as dangerous criminals: Local police rounded them up, fingerprinted and booked them, and brought them to a simulated cellblock. Guards made them remove their clothing, deloused them, gave them prisoner uniforms, and put them in cells. After only six eight-hour simulations, the behavior of the two groups showed striking changes: Prisoners became passive, dependent, and helpless. Guards, who could not be differentiated in any way from prisoners by the researchers before the study began, became aggressive and abusive within the prison, insulting and bullying the prisoners. Later, many were surprised and dismayed at the extent of their abusive behavior, reporting it to be "degrading" and "sick."

The conclusion of these studies is that individual personality characteristics and background information about individuals, by themselves, cannot distinguish individuals who will commit torture or other cruel acts from those who will not. According to Arendt, for example, Adolph Eichmann was not emotionally disturbed; rather, he was far more interested in "getting ahead" in his bureaucratic job than he was in facing the reality of the situation around him and the immorality, and consequences, of his acts. Lifton (1982, 1986) argued that the Nazi physicians he studied, like physicians who cooperated in torture in other countries, were, in fact, ordinary people who committed atrocious acts. No researchers, however, explained what made the people they studied who cooperated in committing torture so different in their behavior from the very few individuals of the same culture and regime—individuals who not only maintained the ability to distinguish right from wrong, but were also capable of acting on that distinction.

SITUATIONAL FACTORS AND THE TORTURER

The Role of Obedience to Authority

Although many researchers have been frustrated in their attempts to differentiate individual torturers from ordinary people in terms of identifiable personal factors, others have been successful in identifying situational factors that can explain how ordinary individuals become torturers. Torturers have sometimes described themselves, and have sometimes been described by those studying them, as obedient followers of orders:

"I was simply doing my job. . . . I respected the Resistance. . . . War is war."—Klaus Barbie, accused of torturing Jews and French Resistance members before deporting them to Nazi death camps, at his 1987 trial in Lyons, France

"The authorities constantly enjoined on us the need to [commit torture to] obtain confessions. . . . [It] was . . . a means to an end."—Uruguyan ex-military officer and torturer Julio Cesar Cooper (Stover & Nightingale, 1985, p. 7)

Both of these statements, made by ex-torturers, were taken after-the-fact and presented to persons who, the ex-torturers knew, condemned their atrocious acts. For this reason, it is unclear just how much of the arguments presented were due to attempts to justify individual actions or to rationalize behavior. As unsatisfying to their victims and to society as it may be, however, researchers who study the testimony of ex-torturers often conclude that those who torment others and later experience no guilt actually view their own actions, at least in part, as following orders.

He (Adolph Eichmann) left no doubt (during his testimony at his Jerusalem trial) that he would have killed his own father if he had received an order to that effect. . . . He remembered perfectly well that he would have had a bad conscience only if he had not done what he had been ordered to. (Arendt, 1964, pp. 22, 25)

Laboratory research demonstrates that obedience to authority can, in fact, play a major role in the decision to commit acts of torture. Milgram (1963, 1965) showed, for example, that ordinary people not disposed to cruelty will administer pain if instructed to do so by someone who professes to be in charge. In Milgram's laboratory, ostensibly scientific, white-coated authority figures directed ordinary adult Americans to impose a series of electric shocks on other people. The subjects were told that they were using the shocks to teach and that the purpose of the study was to measure the effects of punishment on learning. In fact, no real shock was administered, although the subjects did not know this. Sixty-five percent of those directed to go ahead obediently used what they thought was dangerously high shock. The closer they were physically to their victims, the less likely they were to administer what they thought were high levels. However, 30% continued to administer the shock even when they were in physical contact with their victims; 2.5% administered what they thought to be high shock even when the same authority figure told them that they could choose their own level of shock intensity. Milgram reported that subjects responded similarly, regardless of their age, political party, religion, or sex.

Nazi torturers and ordinary Americans are not alone in their obedience to authority; they are typical. Mantell (1971), Kilham and Mann (1974), Shanab and Yahya (1977), and others, replicating Milgram's work in a variety of countries and cultures and with different age groups, found that subjects continued to administer what they believed was powerful shock even under conditions in which they had nothing to fear if they disobeyed and nothing to gain if they obeyed. In the Haney et al. study (1973) cited previously, the subjects chosen for the guard role behaved abusively, seemingly without any authority figure who ordered them to do so. In this study, however, the mock guards were directed to behave as guards. They knew from television and movies what they were supposed to do, including punishing prisoners.

Factors That Influence Obedience

Milgram proposed a theoretical model with the following three groups of situational factors to explain the mechanisms that control the decision to obey authority figures.

1. Antecedent conditions: Those aspects of family or school history that form a predisposition for obedience or disobedience. Milgram (1974, p. 136) argued that antecedent conditions predispose most people to be obedient to authority. As children, they first learn obedience at home from parental regulations that inculcate a sense of respect for adult authority. The belief that deference is the only appropriate and comfortable response to authority is reinforced in school.

2. Binding factors: Conditions that make people comfortable in situations in which they are learning and then maintaining new obedient behaviors. An example of a factor that might have increased binding in Milgram's experiments, as well as in the Haney et al. study, was the obligation subjects felt that they incurred when they accepted money (even though, in each case, it was a small amount) and agreed to participate in the study.

3. Strain: Uncomfortable feelings that result when obedience produces adverse consequences. According to Milgram, the often extreme anxiety that was manifested by subjects when they did decide to obey authority was evidence of strain. If high enough, he thought, strain would produce disobedience.

Predispositions for obedience, binding factors, and strain were present in all of the cases of torturers described earlier. Levi pointed out, for example, that, in addition to "terrifying miseducation" provided by schools throughout Hitlerian Germany to predispose students to obedience to the wishes of Hitler,

> drill . . . was turned against the German people themselves. Newspapers of the period. . . . describe exhausting marches imposed on adolescent boys and girls within a framework of up to 50 kilometers a day, with knapsacks on their backs and no pity for stragglers. (1988, p. 118)

Arendt (1964, p. 137) noted that children and adults in Nazi Germany were taught systematically at home and in the workplace as well as at school to go a step farther than obedience by acting as if they were, in fact, the legislators of the laws they obeyed. Haritos-Fatouros's study of Greek torturers showed that, earlier in their lives, these men had all been obedient sons and well-behaved students. There are many binding factors among most modern torturers. Saluting, taking oaths, and many other initiation rites and military ceremonials (including ranks and promotions) psychologically bound the Nazi recruits and the Greek recruits to their peers as well as to the officers in charge, just as they bind military recruits to peers and officers in other societies today.

Finally, the perpetrators of torture or killing often demonstrated symptoms of severe strain on the job, particularly when they had to commit their acts in close contact with their victims. Arendt (1964, p. 105) reported that the Nazi Einsatz-gruppen troops who were required to shoot their prisoners at close range regularly became physically ill during missions. Lifton (1986, pp. 193–197) described Nazi physicians who personally had to select people for the gas chambers at Auschwitz as suffering considerably and using alcohol to help deal with their stress.

According to Milgram's model, when the factors that bind people to authority figures are greater than the strain caused by obeying, people remain obedient. When the strain is greater, they disobey. This hypothesis seems to explain short-term obedience to authority under laboratory conditions, and it also seems to describe some of the variables operating in long-term institutional torturing and killing. It fails, however, to explain why the strain that should have been associated with the atrocities committed by some normal individuals for long periods of time did not stop the perpetrators.

The Role of Moral Disengagement

Some of the most interesting explanations of torture deal with mechanisms through which individuals reduce the strain of obedience. Bandura (1987) argued that, in addition to displacing responsibility to authority figures, torturers reduce the strain associated with their acts by disengaging themselves morally from what they do. Bandura outlined the following specific mechanisms:

1. Disengagement of internal controls, including moral restructuring and psychological justification of whatever atrocious acts are being committed.
2. Euphemistic labeling, a linguistic device that further disengages the individual morally and reduces strain by creating the appearance that the abhorrent act is the work of nameless forces, rather than of specific people.
3. Dehumanizing the victims and blaming them for what happens to them. According to laboratory studies, subjects who are made responsible for punishing others tend to devalue their victims and view them as deserving of the punishment they receive (Lerner & Mathews, 1967). Studies have also shown that devaluing potential victims by making them appear less than human makes it easier to apply torture (Bandura, Underwood, & Fromson, 1975).

Psychological descriptions of torturers that we have today demonstrate that they made use of the three mechanisms described by Bandura. The Nazi physicians in Lifton's study (1986, p. 175), for example, restructured morality to the point that they actually discussed ways to carry out their tasks (planning of mass murder) "humanely." These same physicians used a psychological process similar to what Lifton (p. 419) referred to as "doubling," in which they "split into separate selves" in order to cope with their own contributions to mass murder, while at the same time continuing their personal and family lives away from the concentration camp. Euphemistic labeling was used extensively: Torturing became "hard inter-rogation"; mass murder became "the final solution."

Staub (chapter 4, this volume) has argued that devaluation of potential victims always occurs before a society begins to purge a group. In Nazi Germany as in other countries, victims were dehumanized to make them easier to hurt: Jews, Gypsies, and others were described as "vermin" by their torturers. Today, in fascist regimes in which torture is practiced, victims become "bloody Communists"; in Communist regimes, they become "reactionaries" or similarly evil subgroups.

The Role of Specialized Military Training

According to Amnesty International (Power, 1981), torture as a systematic activity is conducted with the approval of many governments. Amnesty International believes that torture is made possible, in part, by specialized military training designed to create torturers. Gibson and Haritos-Fatouros (1986) accepted as valid both Milgram's factors and Bandura's mechanisms in a model that describes the steps used to create official military torturers. The model incorporates the following elements.

1. Screening new candidates (or potential recruits) is performed to find normal (ordinary) people with the physical, emotional, and intellectual attributes necessary for the task.

2. During training, the following two techniques are used to increase binding among these prospects. (a) Initiation rites that isolate trainees from their families, friends, and, in general, all important previous relationships. The trainees meet new colleagues and a whole new social order with different rules and values. (According to Bandura, 1987, initiation rites assist in moral restructuring of the task.) (b) Elitist attitudes and in-group language that highlight differences between the prospects and the rest of society. (Bandura pointed out that euphemistic labeling also creates the appearance that atrocious acts are not being described.)

3. Also during training, the following techniques are used to reduce the strain arising from obedience: blaming the victims and dehumanizing them, so that it is less disturbing for torturers to hurt them; harassing recruits, because constant physical and psychological intimidation of prospective torturers prevents them from using logical thinking based on their life-long moral experience and promotes the instinctive responses needed for acts of inhuman cruelty; rewarding obedience and punishing noncooperation; social modeling of violence through observation of other group members committing violent acts and then receiving rewards; and systematic desensitization to repugnant acts by gradual exposure to them, so that they come to appear routine and normal, reducing conflicts with previous moral standards.

Haritos-Fatouros (1988) developed a model for obedience to an authority of violence using information taken from interviews of former Greek military policemen who had been involuntarily drafted, first into the ordinary military of the 1967–1974 period and then into specialized units in which they were trained for service as torturers. She found that their training included all of the steps listed. Screening to find suitable prospects was based, first, on tests of physical strength and stamina and, second, on recruits' reported political beliefs. (Only those with negative attitudes toward Communists—their future potential victims—were selected.) Later screening was based on measures of trustworthiness, willingness to report on others, and willingness to follow orders blindly.

Initiation rites included brutal cursing, punching, kicking, and flogging of recruits as well as swearing an allegiance to a totem-like symbol of authority used by the junta. Initiation took place in isolated sites in which moral displacement could occur without interference. Recruits were helped to develop elitist attitudes by being informed in varieties of ways that theirs was the most elite corps of the regime. They developed the habit of using in-group language by being encouraged to use nicknames for themselves and, later, for their victims and for each of the different methods of torture. For example, "tea party" meant the beating of a prisoner by a group of military policemen using their fists. "Tea party with toast" meant a more severe group beating in which the police used clubs. Recruits came, eventually, to speak of all people not in their group as belonging to the "outside world."

Basic training included daily lectures on "national ethical education" with indoctrination against communism and the enemies of the state. Recruits were taught that Communists were the cause of the nation's problems, and that prisoners were "worms" that had to be "crushed." Recruits were harassed in a variety of ways, including being beaten and being restricted from drinking water and from urinatng or moving their bowels. Some interviewees reported partial or complete retention of urine, sometimes for up to 4 days, and retention of feces for up to 15 days at the beginning of training.

Rewards for obedience included loosened military rules following completion of training, leaves of absence after success in forcing confessions from their prisoners, bonuses such as free rides on busses or meals in tavernas, and promises of job placement when military service was over. Punishment for noncooperation included intimidation and threats, both to servicemen and their families: "An officer used to tell us that if a warden helps a prisoner, he will take the prisoner's place and the whole platoon will flog him" (Haritos-Fatouros, 1988, p. 1117).

Social modeling of violence first took place in basic training where trainers flogged and psychologically degraded the trainees. Even after graduation from basic training, older servicemen continued to harass more junior men. When trainees were promoted to interrogation units, they were first assigned the task of guard in detention rooms, where they watched other servicemen torture. Servicemen were desensitized to the acts of torture by enduring it themselves, and later by watching the torturing of victims. Servicemen were initially brought into contact with political prisoners when they carried food to the cells. Eventually, they were required to give the prisoners "some blows," and then to participate with other servicemen in group beatings of prisoners. Finally, they were required to carry out individual tortures such as the "standing-ordeal" (a prisoner is required to remain standing while the torturer beats him whenever he moves). When they were ready, they were assigned full responsibility as torturers.

These same steps can be shown in other situations of officially condoned military torture and atrocities. Troops selected to torture and kill civilians in Nazi Germany were screened carefully in advance of training for political beliefs or backgrounds that would make it easier for them to commit the acts for which they were to be trained. In Nazi Germany, feelings of elitism among torturers were deliberately enhanced through elaborate initiation ceremonies that bound recruits on entrance into their special corps. Blaming the victim was a major part of all rituals, and initial Nazi military training (like military training the world over) included harassment.

There were also rewards and punishments. If any aspect of Eichmann's testimony is to be believed, the most potent reward for obedience, for many individual torturers, may have been simply "getting ahead." All societies practicing torture punish those who do not cooperate, some more severely than others. Punishment meted out to disobedient Greek military was sometimes as harsh as that meted out to prisoners. Fear of reprisal has been given as a reason for cooperating by military all over the world. It has also been used as a reason for cooperating by civilians, as for example, some of the Russian psychiatrists who treated political prisoners in mental institutions with pain-inducing drugs. Unlike the punishments used by other repressive regimes, however, punishment for disobedience among troops in Nazi Germany was not always as harsh as that meted out to "enemies": Arendt (1964) reported (p. 91) that it was a relatively easy matter for members of extermination squads to quit their jobs without serious penalty. In Nazi Germany, social modeling and gradual desensitization to violent acts also played major roles.

Recent Examples of Military Training

In recent years, reports from a number of countries have described formalized training of military interrogators that includes techniques of torture in order to obtain information from prisoners. Although less is known of the details about most of these training programs than about the training of interrogator–torturers in Greece, it appears that the formal lessons are designed not only to make the act of torture efficient by utilizing new scientific information about the body and its nervous sytem, but also to reduce the strain of committing torture by providing prospective torturers with social modeling and systematic desensitization to acts of violence. Dassin (1986, p. 13), for example, described formal classes for police and military torturers in Brazil between 1964 and 1985. They included slides as well as practical demonstrations in which prisoners were used as guinea pigs and tortured in front of large audiences. Stover and Nightingale (1985, p. 11) described similar Argentinean military training programs for torturers and executioners. Known as "task forces," the Argentinean torturers worked together in hundreds of secret detention centers from 1976 to 1983.

The training of soldier interrogator–torturers has been reported in democratic as well as in totalitarian regimes, although not in the former as official policy. American veterans have reported the teaching of techniques of torture to military interrogators in the field in Vietnam as well as to trainee-interrogators on bases in the United States (Lane, 1970, pp. 85, 144–146; Vietnam Veterans Against the War, 1972, p. 119). However, the methods were not officially condoned.

The Training of Regular Armies

The Brazilian and Argentine military interrogator–torturers just described, like most military interrogator–torturers in other countries, began their training as recruits in regular armies. As Dyer (1985) demonstrated, the training of regular armies throughout the world is designed to create soldiers obedient to all orders, even when those orders require them to commit acts that they were taught throughout their lives were repugnant. In order to accomplish this goal, military training makes use of many of the steps outlined in the model presented by Gibson and Haritos-Fatouros and designed to increase binding and reduce strain. In unpublished tape-recorded interviews with ex-servicemen of regular U.S. Army, Marine, and Green Beret units in 1985, for example, Gibson and Haritos-Fatouros found that these veterans described all the steps of the model as part-and-parcel of regular American military training.

The fact that armies train soldiers to commit brutal acts when ordered and provide mechanisms to increase binding and help soldiers reduce the strain of obedience has led some governments to use their trained military as recruits for the training of torturers. The same fact that explains why trained soldiers, when ordered, are able obediently to torture or kill, also explains why those who have witnessed a great deal of violence during war can generalize their training for battle and act in brutal ways in other situations without having been ordered to do so.

SUGGESTIONS FOR FUTURE RESEARCH ON TORTURERS

The models outlined in this chapter suggest that three factors need to be investigated in order to understand the creation of a torturer: personal factors, situational factors, and military training. Studies of the personal characteristics of individual torturers and nontorturers have not been able to isolate any factor that, by itself, can discriminate between those who commit atrocities (either in wartime or in stressful domestic security situations) and those who do not. Factors considered in the studies cited in this chapter have included personality differences, as measured by Rorschach records, as well as family and school backgrounds. Milgram declared that, although he had not been able to isolate specific factors, he was confident of a personality basis to obedience and disobedience. Staub (chapter 4, this volume) has proposed that a complex set of personality characteristics, which includes the individual's stage of moral reasoning, is necessary to describe the obedient torturer. Gibson (1987) noted, in addition, that other characteristics that are known to be related to obedience and that should be examined further are locus of control and level of self-esteem.

The models also suggest situational factors that need to be investigated. Milgram suggested that antecedent conditions exist in both the early family life and the school life of most individuals that predispose them to be obedient to authority. Two of the many aspects of family life and school life that should be examined in this regard are the treaching of obedience as opposed to prosocial values and of moral education once social values are being learned.

Another factor that should be examined is the relation between moral development and ability to commit torture. Kohlberg (1971) contended that young people who are taught moral reasoning tend to be able to solve moral dilemmas at higher levels than are those whose educations include no such study. Others, such as Papalia and Bielby (1974), have argued that informal experiences in interacting with peers, both inside and outside the family, play more critical roles in moral development. Either way, a clear understanding of how a torturer is created requires knowledge of the relation between moral development and ability to commit torture. It also requires understanding of the lessons taught through a lifetime of interactions with others that are governed by the social milieu as well as through schooling. It should be easier to become an obedient torturer in a society like Nazi Germany that not only taught citizens to be obedient but provided opportunities for them to disengage themselves from internal controls than in a society that stresses moral education and teaches moral responsibility.

Other questions raised by these models and noted by Gibson (1987) deal with the role that certain types of military training can play in the creation of a torturer. Another issue is how governments might restructure military training so as to reduce the possibilities that soldiers will either obey immoral orders or will generalize behaviors learned for war to new situations without orders. Padgett (1986) noted that, although military authorities agree that it is appropriate for soldiers to disobey immoral orders, they do not usually provide soldiers with training about how to discriminate between moral and immoral orders. Soldiers are not normally trained to discriminate between situations in which brutal responses are appropriate and situations in which they are not. It might be worth exploring ways to do that.

REFERENCES

Arendt, H. (1964). *Eichmann in Jerusalem: A report on the banality of evil.* New York: Viking Press.

Bales, J. (1987, December). Torture methods ancient; Studies on victims few. *APA Monitor,* pp. 20–21.

Bandura, A. (1987, spring). *Mechanisms of moral disengagement.* Paper presented at the meeting of the Woodrow Wilson International Center, Washington, DC.

Bandura, A., Underwood, W., & Fromson, M. (1975). Disinhibition of aggression through diffusion of responsibility and dehumanization of victims. *Journal of Research in Personality, 9*(4), 253–269.

Dassin, J. (Ed.). (1986). *Torture in Brazil.* New York: Random House.

Dyer, G. (1985). *War.* New York: Crown.

Gibson, J. (1987, August). *The psychology of torture and other atrocious acts: Etiology, dynamics, prevention.* Paper presented at a preconvention workshop at the meeting of the American Psychological Association, New York, NY.

Gibson, J., & Haritos-Fatouros, M. (1986, November). The education of a torturer. *Psychology Today,* pp. 50–58.

Haney, C., Banks, C., & Zimbardo, P. (1973). Interpersonal dynamics in a simulated prison. *International Journal of Criminology and Penology, 1,* 69–97.

Haritos-Fatouros, M. (1983). *Antecedent conditions leading to the behavior of a torturer: Fallacy or reality.* Unpublished manuscript, University of Thessaloniki, Greece.

Haritos-Fatouros, M. (1988). The official torturer: A learning model for obedience to an authority of violence. *Journal of Applied Social Psychology, 18*(13), 1107–1120.

Harrower, M. (1976). Rorschach records of the Nazi war criminals: An experimental study after 30 years. *Journal of Personality Assessment, 40*(4), 341–351.

Kelley, D. (1946). *Preliminary studies of the Rorschach records of Nazi war criminals.* Paper presented at the meeting of the Rorschach Institute, New York City.

Kilham, W., & Mann, L. (1974). Level of instructive obedience as a function of transmitter and executant roles in the Milgram paradigm. *Journal of Personality and Social Psychology, 29,* 696–702.

Kohlberg, L. (1971). Stages of moral development as a basis for moral education. In C. Beck, B. Crittendon, & E. Sullivan (Eds.), *Moral education,* (pp. 23–92). Toronto, Canada: University of Toronto Press.

Lane, M. (1970). *Conversations with Americans.* New York: Simon & Schuster.

Lerner, M., & Mathews, G. (1967). Reactions to suffering of others under conditions of direct responsibility. *Journal of Personality and Social Psychology, 5*(3), 319–325.

Levi, P. (1988). *The drowned and the saved* (R. Rosenthal, Trans.). New York: Simon & Schuster. (Original work published in 1986)

Lifton, R. (1982). Medicalized killing in Auschwitz. *Psychiatry, 45,* 283–297.

Lifton, R. (1986). *The Nazi doctors.* New York: Basic Books.

Mantell, D. (1971). The potential for violence in Germany. *Journal of Social Issues, 27*(4), 101–112.

Milgram, S. (1963). Behavioral study of obedience. *Journal of Abnormal Social Psychology, 67*(4), 277–285.

Milgram, S. (1965). Some conditions of obedience and disobedience to authority. *Human Relations, 18*(1), 55–57.

Milgram, S. (1974). *Obedience to authority.* New York: Harper & Row.

Padgett, V. (1986). *Predicting violence in totalitarian organizations: An application of eleven powerful principles of obedience to authority.* Unpublished manuscript, Marshall University, Huntington, WV.

Papalia, D., & Bielby, D. (1974). Cognitive functioning in middle- and old-age adults: A review of research based on Piaget's theory. *Human Development, 17,* 424–443.

Power, J. (1981). *Amnesty International: The human rights story.* New York: McGraw-Hill.

Preisler, E. (1982). *Your neighbor's son* [Film]. (Available from TV Studios, Vesterbrogade 37, D K 1620, Copenhagen, Denmark)

Shanab, M., & Yahya, K. (1977). A behavioral study of obedience in children. *Journal of Personality and Social Psychology, 35*(7), 530–536.

Solzhenitsyn, A. (1973). *The Gulag archipelago.* New York: Harper & Row.

Staub, E. (1990). The psychology and culture of torture and torturers. In P. Suedfeld (Ed.), *Psychology and Torture* (pp. 49–76). Washington, DC: Hemisphere.

Stover, E., & Nightingale, E. O. (Eds.) (1985). *The breaking of minds and bodies.* New York: Freeman.

Timerman, J. (1981). *Prisoner without a name, cell without a number.* New York: Knopf.

United Nations General Assembly. (1984, December 10). *Convention against torture and other cruel, inhuman or degrading treatment or punishment.* New York: United Nations Publications.

Vietnam Veterans Against the War. (1972). *The winter soldier investigation: An inquiry into American war crimes.* Boston: Beacon Press.

6

Torture and Other Extreme Measures Taken for the General Good: Further Reflections on a Philosophical Problem

Michael Levin

THE CASE FOR JUSTIFYING TORTURE WITHIN LIMITED CONTEXTS

A few years ago I defended torture as a permissible tool of interrogation in certain emergencies, such as that created by a terrorist refusing to disclose where an atomic bomb is planted (Levin, 1982). I subsequently extended this defense to the torture of the terrorist's innocent wife and children should timely disclosure require such measures (Levin, cited in Spieler, 1982). This argument stirred some discussion, not all of it focused on the underlying philosophical issues. Some critics noted the relatively greater efficacy of certain psychoactive drugs for prompting disclosure—a point I readily concede, but also one likely to raise much the same ethical issue raised by torture itself. Many who deny the state's right to inflict pain to get information will also deny the state's right to administer truth drugs forcibly. The larger question of individual rights versus the general good remains.

Other difficulties involved the uncertainty that may be felt by the authorities that their prisoner is really the bomb-planter, or that he knows where the bomb is. In my original article I relied on terrorists' penchant for self-advertising and advocated torture only of those who publicly announce their intention to harm innocents. This standard, though strict, would still sanction torture of those many evil-doers who brandish weapons before television cameras in efforts to manipulate mass emotions. Unfortunately, standards however strict still admit borderline cases. What of them? I am not competent to draw up model legal guidelines for torture or any other method of interrogation, but I see no difference in principle here from other cases: Be sure the likelihood of benefit to society in general outweighs the likely harm to innocents. Although it can be damaging to reputation and psyche, detaining a suspect overnight on a false charge is permissible so long as there is "probable cause."

It was not always realized that I defended torture as a form of interrogation, not punishment. It is far from clear why torture *cannot* be used to punish, especially if a major goal of punishment is deterrence and if fear of torture deters. I have encountered the question, "Would you sanction the torture of known-to-be-innocent nonterrorists or their families to deter future terrorism?" Obviously not, for the same reason that no punishment of the innocent of any sort can ever serve deterrence. Punishment as a deterrent is a tax imposed on forbidden behavior to decrease its occurrence. Punishing those who have not emitted the behavior is as pointless as taxing gingerale to reduce the consumption of beer. My artificially narrow focus on interrogation does, however, force the critic to address a difficult question ad hominem: What would *you* do were you in a position to discover the bomb's location by torturing the terrorist?

Among the many evasions of this question there are a few honest answers, the most interesting of which runs thus: Torturing the terrorist is justified and necessary, but torture as a general practice must never be institutionalized. Regulating torture legitimizes it and other forms of brutality. Like all rules, those permitting torture would be subject to abuse by mischievous officials. Anyway, what sort of person would be attracted to a job the duties of which entailed torture (cf. chapters 4 and 5, this volume)?

Although I remain personally uncertain as to the feasibility of torture regulations, the foregoing position against them should be given its full weight. In particular, it is, despite appearances, quite consistent to hold that torture is sometimes right but always to be forbidden. This holding would seem to put society in the absurd position of threatening to punish right action. Indeed, police officials, who are surely obliged to obey the law and are also, we are assuming, obliged to torture the terrorist, would have incompatible obligations.

In fact, however, these puzzles do no more than illustrate the moral dilemma treated by Melville in *Billy Budd* and Anouilh in his *Antigone*. Following a rule that is good on the whole may sometimes yield an unacceptable result in a particular case; should such conflict be resolved in favor of the rule, or of justice in the particular case? According to Melville, as I read him, Captain Vere is right to see Billy hanged despite Claggart's provocations, because naval discipline must be maintained in wartime. Anouilh's Creon makes a good case for punishing Antigone lest society disintegrate for lack of strict laws.

The two sides of conflicts of this sort are known to philosophers as *act-utilitarianism* and *rule-utilitarianism*. Act-utilitarians hold the moral agent obligated to do, in the particular case at hand, what will lead to the best consequences overall. Rule-utilitarians hold moral agents to be obligated to follow those rules that will in the long run lead to the best consequences if always followed, even in exceptional cases in which deviation from those rules would lead to better results. Captain Vere is a rule-utilitarian; in choosing to break the fugitive slave laws to help his friend Jim, Huckleberry Finn is an act-utilitarian.

The conflict between act- and rule-utilitarianism could be avoided if legitimate exceptions could be built into otherwise good rules. That such incorporation is often not possible appears to be an intrinsic feature of the human condition. Legitimate exceptions to good rules may be unforeseeable, too difficult to define, or themselves liable to abuse. What degree of provocation extenuates the killing of a superior officer? Oddly enough, we may know that there are exceptions to some good rule, but we may never be justified in taking an apparent exception to be genuine. It may always be more reasonable to construe the appearance of exceptionalness as deceptive, and therefore always to follow a rule we know to be occasionally unjust, than to believe that a real exception has been found. This near-inconsistency[1] in our moral beliefs is created by a number of familiar factors that distort moral judgment, chiefly emotion and partiality toward one's own interests. Thus, I may sometimes be entitled to more than strict equity permits; but any time I am tempted to think that such a case has arisen, I need only reflect on my self-serving bias to realize that this temptation is more likely caused by the bias than by the facts of the case at hand. So I am justified in believing that there are cases in which equity shortchanges me *and* that I should nonetheless follow strict equity in every case.

It can thus be argued that legitimate exceptions to good rules are "blind spots," in Sorenson's phrase (1988). They are there, but we cannot recognize one when one is before us. And perhaps the most sophisticated objection to institutionalizing torture is not the possible bad consequences of doing so, but the impossibility of knowing when torture is justified. Torture is so brutal and prone to misapplication that, although it may sometimes be justified, we are never entitled to think that any such case has arisen. Justified cases of torture are blind spots, the argument concludes.

I think this argument as stated is far too strong, because I believe that we know torture is justified in the original bomber-terrorist case I outlined. I chose it for its very obviousness. It remains possible, however, that permissible cases of torture cannot be described systematically and therefore cannot be written into law. Perhaps this question can be settled only experimentally: draft torture regulations and see what happens. (But perhaps the experiment itself is too dangerous to try?)

There are affinities between the problems that beset utilitarianism and slippery-slope arguments. This is only natural, since many objections to torture are slippery-slope arguments. Once you get started torturing, where do you stop? The utilitarian arguments that justify torture also justify patent wrongs if pushed to their logical extreme, do they not? Moreover, just as arguments for rule-utilitarianism come in two forms—the practical and the knowledge-based—so do slippery slopes. More precisely, although all slippery slopes have the same structure—an attractive peak, a horrific abyss, and a long series of tiny steps between—the slippery stuff underfoot may be of two sorts.

On one hand, it may be contended as a matter of psychological fact that anyone who accepts the peak position will accept the nearby lower positions, then the positions just below those, and so on, until he ends up in the abyss. A familiar example of this "psychological" slippery slope runs that anyone who accepts abortion will soon embrace euthanasia, then infanticide, and sooner or later will endorse death camps for genetic undesirables. An equally familiar example from the other side of the ideological spectrum runs that anyone who seriously acknowl-

---

[1]A collection of beliefs containing the generalization "something is an *F*" but containing no specific instance of *F* is said to be omega-inconsistent. It may well be, then, that our moral beliefs are (or ought to be) omega-inconsistent. Omega-inconsistency does not imply inconsistency. For instance, the set of sentences "2000 comes after 1999; 2001 comes after 1999; and some year comes before 1999" is omega-inconsistent but obviously consistent (indeed, all the sentences are true). Omega-inconsistent beliefs may be not only consistent but reasonable. Most people believe, of a lottery with 10,000 tickets, that ticket #1 will not be chosen, that ticket #2 will not be chosen . . . and that ticket #10,000 will not be chosen—*and* that one of these 10,000 tickets will be chosen. So a utilitarian can rationally adopt strict rules that he believes, omega-inconsistently, will not maximize utility.

edges innate biological sex differences will soon acknowledge innate biological racial differences—and sooner or later will endorse death camps for genetic undesirables. So many slopes bottomed out in the Third Reich that Max Hocutt and George Graham called this style of reasoning "argumentum ad Naziam" (Hocutt, 1986).

Yet however persuasive they may prove in debate, psychological slippery slope arguments establish nothing. They not only trade on dubious empirical psychology—friends of abortion and critics of feminism do not characteristically admire Treblinka—they also fail even to address the positions they purport to refute. For even if acceptance of premise *P* always leads to acceptance of dreadful conclusion *Q*, it follows at most that *accepting P* is dreadful, not that *P* itself is erroneous. It all depends on why acceptance of *P* leads to acceptance of *Q*. Such psychological inevitability as there is in the slide impugns *P* itself only if no rational line bifurcates the troublesome intermediate steps—only if the way down is clear because there is no logical barrier to stop it. A logical slippery slope argument against a position like the acceptability of torture is the claim that no principled demarcation exists between the position in question and a suitably chosen abyss. Logical slippery slopes are the only ones worth worrying about.

So the serious critic of my view on torture forgoes speculation about where such a position is likely to lead people. Instead, he mounts a challenge: Your argument (the critic says) appears to rest on a broadly utilitarian outlook favoring the well-being of the many over the rights of the possibly innocent few. Show why this broad utilitarianism does not sanction other forms of expedience that are objectionable from the perspective of common sense. Why, for instance, are you not committed to telling a father to rescue ten infants he does not know instead of his own son, if he must choose between the two courses of action in a burning building?

PHILOSOPHICAL ARGUMENTS FOR MAKING EXCEPTIONS

What I just called "a broad utilitarian outlook" has lately been dubbed "end-state maximization" (Nozick, 1975). I will adapt Nozick's trenchant terminology and call a moral theory "maximizing" if it advocates the maximization of some specified value as the fundamental obligation of moral agents. Commands to increase happiness, the satisfaction of preferences, liberty, knowledge, love, or obedience to God are all maximizing. The classical utilitarianism of Mill and Bentham is the command to maximize pleasure. Note that the theory that human morality is maximizing is *not* a theory about any particular value, but about the form or structure of morality. (I will examine a competing theory about the structure of morality shortly.)

Because I find the idea of maximizing pleasure incoherent and that of maximizing satisfaction implausible,[2] I would, if forced to pick a maximizing theory, select the maximization of negative liberty, or noncoercion. I would ask that the total amount of uninterfered-with action be maximized or, equivalently, that the total

---

[2]My views on pleasure-maximizing, and its more contemporary counterpart preference-maximizing, are based on the contention that *pleasure* does not name a psychological state and hence cannot be the goal of any action. For a complete treatment of this argument, see Levin (1985).

amount of interference and aggression in the world be minimized.[3] It is aggression-minimizing that justifies torture: the aggression the terrorist is preparing to unleash outweighs the aggression involved in torturing the terrorist or his family.

Although they agree in form, liberty-maximizing and happiness-maximizing could hardly differ more in content. For instance, if state seizure and redistribution of property acquired in market transactions increased overall happiness, happiness-maximizing would sanction such seizure, whereas liberty-maximizing would forbid it. Such seizure aggresses against nonaggressors (those who acquired property through voluntary transactions) without in turn preventing further aggression, thereby increasing the net amount of aggression and thus violating the principle of aggression-minimization.

A happiness-maximizing defense of torture (a defense not mine) concentrates exclusively on the happiness it stands to produce; a liberty-maximizing defense (which is mine) concentrates exclusively on the aggression it stands to prevent. This difference between utilitarianisms works all in favor of my version, since the standard slippery-slope objections to utilitarianism are largely directly against its happiness-maximizing version. Happiness-maximizing does decree, implausibly, that a father should rescue ten strangers rather than his own child from a fire, but aggression-minimizing carries no such implication. So long as he aggresses against no one, the father can rescue whom he pleases. Similarly, the happiness-maximizer is bound to find some value in child-molesting, whereas the aggression-minimizer does not.

The chief threat to liberty-maximizing comes not from less plausible maximizing principles, but from a competing conception of the nature of morality itself that has traditionally gone under the name "Kantian rigorism" (e.g., Kant, 1797/1964). Fully recognizing the failure of this characterization to do justice to the subtlety of Kant's thought, I will nonetheless call a moral theory Kantian if its basic imperative categorically forbids the violation of certain rules of personal behavior, or categorically commands obedience to such rules. Thus, for instance, although honesty-maximizing tells the moral agent to do what he can to increase honesty, the Kantian version of honesty tells each moral agent to be honest, period.

The difference is that honesty-maximizing allows (indeed, favors) lying in cases in which lying can be expected to decrease lying elsewhere on the whole, whereas Kantian honesty forbids lying even in such cases. Similarly, Kantian nonaggression forbids aggressing even when a little aggression stands to decrease aggression overall. It thus forbids torture of the terrorist's family in the case I originally outlined. Depending on how Kantian nonaggression is elaborated to handle preemptive strikes, the behavior of proxies, and other tricky matters, it might well forbid torture of the terrorist. Certainly the thrust of Kantian morality is all against torture, as is the turn of mind of those who find themselves attracted to Kantian

---

[3]The distinction between "negative" liberty, or freedom from interference, and "positive" liberty, or freedom to have what one wants, was given its classic statement in Berlin (1969), although one or the other concept or their interplay permeates the ethico-political thought of Aristotle, Hobbes, Locke, Hume, Kant, Hegel, Marx, Hayek, Rawls, Nozick, and most other figures in the Western tradition. Notable exceptions are Plato, whose ideal society rests primarily on order, and Spinoza, for whom freedom is acceptance of God's nature. For a systematic defense of "negative" liberty, see Levin (1984).

morality; see for instance Thomas Nagel's remarks on torture (Perry & Bratman, 1986, p. 612).

These two opposing conceptions of morality—the maximization of some value or range of values versus categorical obedience to personally directed rules—both rest on truisms in perfect balance. If it is wrong to aggress against the innocent, declares the Kantian, it is wrong to aggress against the innocent to prevent further aggression. If aggression is bad, declares the minimizer, the less of it the better. Not only is the winner of this debate unclear, so are the criteria by which a winner might be chosen. At such an impasse, consistency with our actual, nonphilosophical moral convictions becomes the touchstone for moral philosophy. Of two competing moral theories, the one that agrees with reflective common sense in the greater number of cases, or better "explains" moral intuition, is superior. (Philosophers have followed social scientists and statisticians in extending the word *explanation*, which usually implies the presence of a causal mechanism, to successful curve-fitting. A moral theory can of course also explain particular moral convictions in the usual causal sense if people consciously or unconsciously derive the conviction from the theory.)

The theory that best describes how people actually think about morality is best overall. It is violation of this canon that leads philosophers to reject Kant's own extreme absolutism, which, contrary to common sense, condemns lying to a would-be murderer to protect the innocent victim. I appealed to this same canon in citing the burning building case as an objection to happiness-maximizing. The question before us now is whether libertarianism conceived as a maximizing rule or as a Kantian rule better captures how we actually think about the duty not to aggress.

One is likely to respond to this way of putting the problem by agreeing that common sense is Kantian, while denying the decisiveness of common sense as a test of ethical theories. We do not test scientific theories by their conformity to common sense, so why should we test ethical theories this way? To infer what people should approve from what they do approve appears to be a clumsy blunder, a collision with the barrier separating *ought* from *is*. That the majority favor a course of action can hardly be supposed by itself to render that course of action right. Such an inference requires some further normative premise, the discovery of which is precisely the job of moral philosophy.

Although this reaction is natural, it gets things completely wrong, in my view. Common sense *is* ultimately the only test for an ethical theory, and, despite appearances, ordinary morality is maximizing. As for the methodological primacy of common sense, appeal to it seems inappropriate only if one takes the aim of moral philosophy to be the discovery of prescriptive norms. As I view matters, this is not the aim of moral philosophy at all; moral philosophy is, rather, a curve-fitting problem whose data points are ordinary moral judgments. Moral philosophers seek to analyze the sprawling value systems that mankind has created, with special attention to the modes of reasoning by which positions within these systems are held to be justified. There is simply nothing else for moral philosophers to do. There are moral revisionists in philosophy busily defending infanticide and other deviant doctrines, but their attempts to transcend their culture resemble the contortions of cartoon characters who unwittingly run off a cliff, realize that they are suspended in mid-air, and then plummet to earth. The practice of revisionists themselves underlines the futility of defying prephilosophical morality, for they characteristically justify their heterodoxies by alleging them to follow from more general principles that their audience already accepts. Tooley (1984) has defended infanticide, and Singer (1975) has defended animal rights. Tooley's position rests on the factual thesis that a neonate cannot conceive its own future existence and on the moral principle that you cannot have a right to anything you cannot conceive. Plausibly or implausibly, Tooley defended his moral claim by attempting to show its consistency with ordinary judgments of rights. Singer's claim rests on the contention that pleasure and pain are the only parameters relevant in judging a course of action (i.e., Singer is a straight utilitarian) and on the factual premise that animals experience pleasure and pain. Singer expects reliance on pleasure and pain as the indices of morality to lie at the bottom of his reader's everyday moral reflection, and hence that his reader is already tacitly committed to equal treatment of animals. (For more on the nature of philosophical ethics, see Levin, 1986, 1987.)

If a philosophical theory like liberty-maximizing purports merely to describe, not prescribe, it cannot constitute the basis for a self-contained moral argument for torture or anything else. Like all moral arguments, my defense of torture is, ultimately, addressed to its reader's sense of consistency: You, reader, condemn aggression against innocents. You must therefore prefer less aggression to more. You must therefore be prepared to tolerate a little aggression to prevent a lot. If you could abstract yourself from your own deepest commitments, you could regard this argument as establishing no more than a hypothetical implication. But since you cannot disengage yourself from yourself, the argument is, so far as you are concerned, conclusive.

Is ordinary morality really maximizing? It certainly seems Kantian. The basic rules of moral systems are virtually all categorical commands to conform to rules of personal behavior. The Sixth Commandment tells *you* to honor *your* father and mother, not to strive to maximize filial piety in the general population. Children are taught a Kantian morality. They are told to be honest no matter what, not to maximize honesty overall. In addition, praise, blame, and responsibility are apportioned as if what counts is conformity to rules rather than promotion of good. When some unperformed act on the part of A would have forestalled the evil act of B, it remains B, not A, who is blamed for the evil. This remains so even if B's action if unforestalled was as predictable as any natural process. Thus, although the police who have the terrorist will have to live with their consciences if they do not torture the terrorist to discover the location of the bomb, it is the terrorist who commits murder should the bomb go off, and the terrorist rather than the police who must face justice if anyone does. Indeed, the commitment of maximization theory to sanctions against failure to prevent harm is one more damaging discrepancy between maximizing theory and common sense.

It is no defense of maximizing to observe that moral rules are frequently relaxed in emergencies. (Nozick, 1975, recognized "catastrophic moral horror" as a problem for Kantian morality, but he explicitly passed over it to preserve the simplicity of his own theory.) Such relaxation may be interpreted as showing the incoherence of human morality—Kantian in basic form but inconsistently maximizing in some of its applications. Maximizing must also be shown to account for the apparently Kantian character of the basic rules as well, and the Kantian character of assignments of responsibility. This is an onus that sophisticated maximizers have recognized, and there is indeed a plausible maximizing explanation of these phenomena (in both senses of *explanation* described earlier).

Suppose you wanted to maximize some value like honesty in a society you were designing, its inhabitants to have whatever moral system you wanted them to have. You would probably get more honesty out of them if you programmed them to tell themselves and each other "Never lie," to reinforce unconditionally their children's honesty, and always to punish lying, than you would if you programmed them to tell themselves and each other "Maximize honesty in society as a whole," to reinforce their children's tendency to maximize honesty in society as a whole, and to punish lying when and only when it fails to maximize honesty in society as a whole.

This oddity, sometimes called a "paradox" of utilitarianism, is easily explained. The typical member of a society is a private person acting within a relatively quite narrow private sphere, not a public figure whose decisions have far-reaching consequences. The only honesty over which a person has any influence is his own and his children's. Therefore, a person best contributes to overall honesty by being honest. Should he always be honest, he is unlikely ever to inhibit the honesty of anyone else. The average person is not a diplomat whose undue public candor might wreck secret frank negotiations between governments. The time the average person spends wondering about the possible remote honesty-adverse consequences of his own honesty is time wasted, and, given the average person's readiness to rationalize self-interested misbehavior, such wondering will merely weaken the tendency to be honest.

It is interesting to speculate whether modern technology's enhancement of the average person's informational resources will make us all more maximizing. We can all reach and therefore influence many more people than we could in past centuries, and we are better able to estimate at least some of the indirect consequences of our actions. If the future is when everyone will be famous for 15 minutes, as Andy Warhol assured us, will it also be when everyone will be a maximizer for 15 minutes?

Children for their part cannot grasp the impersonal rule "Usually be honest, but lie when lying will promote honesty elsewhere." They will interpret such instructions as meaning that their elders do not care about honesty. That is why you will give the children in your society a Kantian socialization. Children brought up as Kantians will develop into more efficient adult maximizers than will children brought up as maximizers. Thus a lemma: A society created for the purpose of maximizing some value will display a Kantian morality with respect to that value. The members of the society will deny that maximizing this value is the purpose of their morality, and believe that their Kantian morality has some other basis, which their resident philosophers will expend much effort seeking to identify.

This lemma opens the possibility that *our* Kantian morality has a maximizing basis. For, although actual human morality was not designed by anybody, it was produced by a process that mimics design. Human morality exists because of the function it performs, which means, in nonteleological language, that actual Kantian-appearing morality was selected during the course of social evolution because of (some of) its wholly unintended effects. The function of morality is that effect of morality that explains why human societies display morality, just as the function of the heart is that effect of the heart that explains why animals have hearts. And, just as there is no future for organic structures whose possession tends to kill off their possessors, there is no future for social institutions that tend to render societies unstable.

A society free of a destabilizing institution will, all things being equal, displace a society with that institution. Therefore, any enduring social institution exists because it at least does not destabilize a society, and in most cases because it positively enhances stability. As it seems unlikely that the presence of morality is neutral in its effects on social stability, it follows that moral rules almost certainly exist because the values they promote contribute to social stability.

Societies would disintegrate without some degree of noninterference, honesty, and filial piety, and they become more stable as these values become more pervasive. As I have shown, Kantian rules have the unintended effect of maximizing these values more efficiently than do maximizing rules. There will be less aggression in a society whose members are taught not to aggress, period, than in a society whose members are taught to minimize aggression. This is why, I conjecture, human society socializes its members, and especially its children, in Kantian morality. The superficially Kantian form of morality overlays a maximizing function.

I also suspect that the great advantageousness of nonaggression toward littermates, and similar behaviors, has by now gotten this nonaggression (and the associated tendency to reinforce it in others) selected into our genes. Genes stand the best change of copying themselves if they encode cooperation cued by observable correlates of littermatehood. This hypothesis is eminently compatible with the evidence of an innate developmental sequence in moral thinking, and moral instruction no doubt conforms itself to this sequence.

Mention of stages of moral development calls Kohlberg to mind. It might be suggested apropos of Kohlberg (1971), that unimpeded moral development culminates in rejection of Kantian rules, as in the cases of Martin Luther King's and Gandhi's disobedience to unjust positive laws. King and Gandhi, however, are too anomalous to exemplify any part of a normal developmental sequence. What is more, Kohlberg and his followers appear to conflate absoluteness with simplicity. "Never disobey the law" is absolute, but so is "Never disobey the law except when it countenances racial segregation"; so indeed is any rule with no more than finitely many exceptions. "Never disobey a law except when it countenances discrimination" enjoins obedience to all laws not countenancing discrimination. I have even encountered the incoherent suggestion that when one attains Kohlberg's sixth stage one simultaneously rejects all absolute rules *and* comes to reject torture as never permissible.

Kohlberg and the "values clarification" group would hasten children's natural moral development by presenting them with Socratic moral dilemmas, designed to elicit the need to hedge all moral rules. Even assuming that the last stage of moral development is the highest stage of moral development and is the stage reached by Martin Luther King, Jr., when breaking the law, this pedagogy is seriously confused. If the developmental sequence identified by Kohlberg is really innate, it can no more be speeded up than can puberty. Second, young children desire blanket prescriptions as part of a general desire for a stable environment, a point that one would have thought would be manifest to psychologists dealing with children. Until they are ready for it, children are merely confused by the suggestion (to take one of Kohlberg's) that theft is permissible when it is life-saving medicine that is stolen. All an unready child can learn from this suggestion is that his elders do not mind theft. And when a young person *is* ready for the message that morality is not simple, life itself will supply him with a sufficiency of illustrative instances.

So maximizers can explain why ordinary moral convictions are nonmaximizing everywhere but at the extremes. This explanation does not imply that everyday morality or the thought processes generating it are themselves tacitly maximizing. They are not. Our rules and thought processes really are Kantian in character, as maximizing theory predicts. But we follow and reinforce and teach Kantian rules because they lead to maximizing results—results that, according to the rules, are not those we should pursue. Only in extreme cases, like those warranting torture, where the form of morality is felt to frustrate its function, do people find Kantian morality intuitively inappropriate and begin thinking in maximizing terms.

So far as I can tell, this maximizing explanation of morality has no moral implications. That morality as a natural phenomenon arose because it minimizes aggression does not mean that aggression ought to be minimized, nor that minimizing aggression ought to beat out Kantian eschewal of aggression when the two conflict. No *is* implies an *ought*. But this view of morality may have a certain psychological impact. I noted earlier that choosing whether to aggress against the terrorist's family involves choosing between two platitudes: If aggression is wrong it is wrong to aggress, or if aggressing is bad, the less of it the better. It would, to repeat, be a non sequitur to accord the latter principle moral priority over the former because it enjoys a kind of explanatory priority. However, I suspect that it becomes psychologically more difficult to adhere to the former principle, and let justice be done though the heavens fall, once one realizes that justice evolved precisely because of its capacity to keep the heavens up.

REFERENCES

Berlin, I. (1969). *Four essays on liberty*. Oxford, England: Oxford University Press.

Hocutt, M. (1986). Must relativists tolerate evil? *Philosophical Forum, 17*, 188–200.

Kant, I. (1964). *Groundwork of the metaphysics of morals* (H. J. Paton, Trans.). New York: Harper & Row. (Original work published 1797)

Kohlberg, L. (1971). Stages of moral development as a basis for moral education. In C. Beck, B. Crittendon, & E. Sullivan (Eds.), *Moral education* (pp. 23–92). Toronto, Canada: University of Toronto Press.

Levin, M. (1982, June 17). The case for torture. *Newsweek*, p. 13.

Levin, M. (1984, Autumn). Negative liberty. *Social Philosophy and Policy, 2*, 84–100.

Levin, M. (1985, Fall). Introspection. *Behaviorism, 13*, 125–136.

Levin, M. (1986, Summer). [Review of *Life in the balance*]. *Constitutional Commentary, 3*, 500–512.

Levin, M. (1987, December 16). Philosophers discover the bomb. *National Review*, pp. 34–39.

Nozick, R. (1975). *Anarchy, state and utopia*. New York: Basic Books.

Perry, J. & Bratman, M. (Eds.) (1986). *Introduction to philosophy*. New York: Oxford University Press.

Singer, P. (1975). *Animal liberation*. New York: Ballantine Books.

Sorenson, R. (1988). *Blindspots*. Oxford, England: Oxford University Press.

Spieler, J. (1982, October). Penthouse interview. *Penthouse*, pp. 132–181.

Tooley, M. (1984). *Abortion and infanticide*. Oxford, England: Oxford University Press.

II

PSYCHOLOGY'S RESPONSE TO TORTURE

7

Psychologists as Victims, Administrators, and Designers of Torture

Peter Suedfeld

The goal of this chapter is to provide an overview of how psychologists, individually and in their professional organizations, have been involved in torture. *Involved* is interpreted not only in its invidious connotation of acceding to, cooperating with, or even contributing to torture, but also in the sense of being among the tortured. Next I take up the issue of whether theoretical or empirical knowledge generated by scientific and professional psychology has been used to increase the impact and potency of torture techniques. Some suggestions are made as to needed research and other contributions from psychology. In all of these areas, I have relied on the available documentation. Obviously, information may come to light after the publication of this book that would make it appropriate to amend or even drastically alter current conclusions; but our judgments at any given time must be based on the information we have at that time.

PSYCHOLOGISTS AS VICTIMS

Psychologists per se have not figured very prominently either as victims or perpetrators, the two most direct and active roles in the context of torture. Among professional groups, physicians are probably the most frequently cited single category in both capacities. They may be victims of torture for various reasons. Because the educated citizens of dictatorships are usually among the most vocal and visible dissenters, and because in many countries medical personnel form a large (and the most highly respected) portion of this group, they may be relatively highly involved in oppositional activism.

The high status accorded to physicians in many societies may result in their feeling an obligation to speak out against abuses. Medical education in many cases emphasizes a humanitarian orientation that may lead doctors to take an active part in opposing oppression. Their skills are sometimes called upon by political groups whose members need treatment, sometimes clandestinely, and the providing of such treatment may be interpreted by government officials as disloyalty. There may also be a reciprocal relation between the involvement of doctors in administering torture and in becoming victims of it—as in the case of Anatoly Koryagin, a psychiatrist imprisoned for criticizing the political abuse of psychiatry in the Soviet Union, members of the profession who are outraged by their colleagues' breach of medical ethics may express public criticism and lay themselves open to punishment. Incidentally, members of the clergy have also figured as both accomplices and victims, possibly for reasons similar to those cited for physicians.

By contrast, psychologists are much more on the periphery of state-administered torture. They can be victimized in situations where educated people are targeted either in the whole nation (e.g., the Khmer Rouge massacres in Cambodia) or within oppressed groups whose educated classes are viewed as potential leaders of resistance. But in many of the countries where torture is particularly well established, there are few if any psychologists; in others, the psychologist's role in society is subordinate and ancillary to that of psychiatrists and other physicians. When psychologists are subjected to torture, it is usually because of personal political activism or dissent rather than because of some professionally relevant activity. It is difficult to establish the prevalence of such experiences.

The Societé Française de Psychologie has tabulated 16 cases of psychologists who had been arrested, imprisoned, or "disappeared" (apparently kidnapped by military or paramilitary groups acting for the government) for political reasons between 1977 and 1984. An unknown number of others have gone into exile to avoid the possibility of such a fate (e.g., Mervis, 1985). The countries involved were Argentina, Chile, Czechoslovakia, El Salvador, Kenya, Paraguay, Poland, and Uruguay. No information concerning torture is given (M. Pages & R. Ghiglione, Letter to the President of the American Psychological Association, April 26, 1984). In a Salvadorean case, the victim (the name was not given) was killed, as was Mayra J. M. Soberanis, a Guatemalan psychologist, between October 1984 and 1985 (Guatemala Human Rights Commission/USA, personal communication to S. Kennedy, October 16, 1985). Ana L. Orellana Stormont, another Guatemalan psychologist, was reported to have died as a result of torture (Amnesty International, personal communication to F. E. Spaner, March 4, 1984). Psychologist Mykhaylo Horyn, a Ukrainian nationalist, has been reported to suffer eye damage from being held in a constantly illuminated cell. The political arrest or kidnapping of psychologists, with physical brutality but not necessarily torture under our definition, has been reported from Chile, Kenya, and Uruguay (Bales, 1986; Padilla & Comas-Diaz, 1986; Spaner, 1984).

PSYCHOLOGISTS AS TORTURERS

Medical personnel have often collaborated in torture. Among the most notorious occurrences were in Nazi Germany and in the Soviet Union, but similar reports have emerged from Uruguay, Chile, South Africa, Japan (torture of and experimentation on prisoners during World War II), Romania, and Iraq—where atrocities included the taking of lethal amounts of blood from prisoners (e.g., Bloche, 1987; British Medical Association, 1986; Goldstein & Breslin, 1986; Stover & Nightingale, 1985). Most physicians involved in torture perform chores such as certifying that a prisoner is or is not fit to undergo further interrogation or torture, signing false death certificates for those who die under mistreatment, and resuscitating and treating victims whose injuries are severe. Some take a more actively malignant role, prescribing and injecting pain-inducing or disorienting drugs, performing or attending at amputations, or affixing the electrodes used in administering shocks (Bloche, 1987; British Medical Association, 1986).

The involvement of physicians can be attributed to a number of factors. One is that their actual role can be somewhat anomalous. It is arguable, for example, whether administering a physical examination to a prisoner under torture is necessarily collaboration: Would it be more ethical to refuse and allow the prisoner to die? Second, physicians are members of their society and are subject to legal and extralegal retribution if they resist. Individuals who risk sacrificing themselves to uphold the ethical code of their profession are worthy of our utmost admiration; but, not having faced the dilemma, we have no right to condemn those who choose self-preservation. In many cases, doctors are members of the armed forces or police and are under even more stringent regulations than are ordinary civilians. Last, some medical personnel certainly share the ideological positions used to justify torture in the particular context—for example, that non-Aryan or non-Japanese prisoners are less than human, and therefore their pain is justified by the development of medical techniques that will help the higher race; that Communists (or anti-Communists) are a deadly menace that must be suppressed; or that torture is the only way to gain information from criminals or terrorists.

Even members of the clergy have been implicated in torture, for example, in Argentina ("Priests' Aid," 1985), and more pervasively in the systems of torture that exist in theocracies such as Iran. They experience the same pressures as do physicians, although it must be said that in the most notable episodes clergy collaborating in the mistreatment of prisoners seem to be motivated by the fervent belief that they are defending their faith—exactly as many clergy who have resisted and defied torture have done for the same reason.

In contrast, psychologists have not featured prominently as the targets of torture allegations (along with low victimization rates, this may explain why psychological organizations have been relatively uninterested in developing codes of ethics and other formal position statements related to torture). Uruguayan psychologists have been accused of working in Libertad prison "to bring about the depression and in many cases complete mental breakdowns" of prisoners (Stover & Nightingale, 1985, p. 17). Among the specific activities cited were inducing disorientation, for example, by ordering unpredictable changes in cell assignments and prison regulations; arousing dread, for example, by housing sane political prisoners with aggressive psychotic inmates; transforming prisoners into informers; keeping psychological records that would inform prison officials as to the weak points and vulnerabilities of the prisoners; and directing the administration of psychoactive drugs (Wilk, 1984).

Only one person, Dolcey Britos, was actually named as a psychologist involved in these practices (Cordes, 1984). In accordance with the guidelines of the American Psychological Association (APA), the staff of APA tried to obtain more specific information on this matter. Britos apparently is a qualified psychologist by Uruguayan criteria: He has a four-year undergraduate degree in psychology, with postgraduate work in clinical psychology. He has taught psychology and has been acting head of the psychology department at the Jesuit Instituto de Filosofia, Ciencias y Letras, but he is not a member of the Sociedad de Psicologia del Uruguay (Cordes, 1984). The charges leveled against him by a number of former prisoners have not been tested in court, and his association with the prison apparently ended in 1982. Under the new Uruguayan government, further information may become available. The Sociedad de Psicologia del Uruguay is investigating the case.

More recently, accusations have been brought against unnamed psychologists in Chile and Cuba. Former political prisoners from Chile have stated that psychologists were involved in administering torture there (Mercer, 1986), and it has been reported that the Chilean Colegio de Psicólogos is looking into the matter. According to Armando Valladares (1986), a refugee from Cuba who later represented the United States in the United Nations Commission on Human Rights, psychologists from the Department of Psychiatric Evaluation of the Political Police in Cuba designed torture techniques and conducted detailed interviews on the prisoners' feelings, thoughts, and dreams, and also performed extensive medical and psychological testing of prisoners.

ALLEGED ABUSES OF PSYCHOLOGICAL RESEARCH AND TECHNIQUES

Although technology has contributed new devices for torture, it seems clear that these are relatively peripheral additions to the techniques. For example, an electric cattle prod inflicts pain, but there is no reason to believe that this pain is very different in intensity or quality to that caused by older procedures. In fact, technology and science seem to have been quite unimportant in the repertoire of torture methods. In the case of the medical and behavioral sciences specifically, common accusations such as "The sophisticated malevolence of several modern torture techniques is incomprehensible without the involvement of medical expertise" (Kosteljanetz & Aalund, 1983, p. 323)—and its psychological counterparts—are hardly justifiable. They seem to reflect a kind of perverse professional egotism more than any neutral assessment of the evidence.

What should we make of accusations that torture is being systematically taught by agents of some countries to those that are less advanced? Among the countries accused of exporting torture technology and knowledge are Cuba, Great Britain, the Soviet Union, North Korea, the United States, and Uruguay. But hard facts are difficult to obtain. In the specific context of scientific and psychological torture, Valladares (1986) alleged that controlled experimentation occurred in the Cuban prison Boniato, with experts from the Soviet Union, Czechoslovakia, East Germany, and Hungary collaborating to design and assess procedures for breaking the prisoners' resistance. Although one innovation may have been a medically designed diet that induced scurvy and other deficiency diseases, the other techniques mentioned seem not to have been very different from torture techniques used elsewhere without such scientific consultation.

Even when instruction in interrogation techniques is provided, there is seldom clear evidence that either the acceptability or the methods of torture is part of the curriculum. Western agencies have consistently maintained that their training of Third World law enforcement personnel excludes and even opposes the use of torture. In any case, it is doubtful whether they would have much to teach. For example, although a Brazilian group was sent to learn "the English system of interrogation," the Brazilian security forces decided that the system was too slow and did not adopt it (cited in Amnesty International, 1984). In general, one is tempted to agree with an interviewee in a Canadian Broadcasting Corporation

program on torture (Taylor, 1982): Countries that have traditionally and systematically practiced torture have nothing to learn from even technologically more sophisticated "tutors."

The Role of Psychology

Leaving aside the torturer's intuitive or learned practical understanding of psychological factors that increase the suffering of the victim, psychology as a discipline appears to have played no verifiable role in the development of torture
techniques. Torturers, being fairly eclectic, would probably adopt any product of
professional psychology if they thought it to be more effective than their existing
repertoire. However, an examination of the techniques in use around the world
indicates that the transmitted knowledge derived from centuries of experience,
plus a recognition of the obvious effects of brute force, have been quite sufficient.
There does not seem to be much that psychologists could add, or have added, to
the tools already at hand.

Psychological principles have been invoked to explain some effects of traditional interrogation procedures: the arousal of cognitive dissonance, the discomfort induced by the violation of personal space, and the like. Other components of
police interrogation, such as guidelines for the proper interrogation of eyewitnesses, identification parade (line up) procedures, and polygraphy have been made
more informed by the work of psychologists. But torture is a different matter.
Among the effects of the techniques described elsewhere in this book may be the
sense that the victim is unable to control or predict crucial aspects of the environment; the result may be learned helplessness (see, e.g., Foster, 1987). Such formulations tend to be post hoc explanations of how particular practices have worked
rather than roads to the invention of new ones.

It is obvious that most of the methods summarized by Amnesty International
(see chapter 1, this volume) are not primarily psychological in nature or ancient in
origin and/or usually common-sense, and thus there is no need to hypothesize that
the torturer derived them from reading the psychological journals. Comments such
as "physical methods of torture are administered by physical means, but their
main impact is of a psychological nature" (Somnier & Genefke, 1986) are truisms
with no specific implications for contemporary torture techniques. Psychological
impact has always and obviously been one of the major (rational) reasons for
torturing people, whether the Inquisition was torturing heretics or the Red Guards
were torturing revisionists. None of these facts makes it possible to evaluate accusations of the misuse of systematic or scientific psychological knowledge, particularly because the accusations themselves tend to be vague or even demonstrably
distorted. An example of the former is a statement that in a special hospital wing of
a Portuguese prison "several psychiatrists oversaw the application of the most
refined methods of sensory and sleep deprivation. Many victims suffered hallucinations, anxiety, and nervous breakdowns" (Jonsen & Sagan, 1985, p. 32). In the
absence of further information about the grounds for this statement, or about what
these "refined" methods might be, the involvement of psychological research
remains unknown.

Some broad-ranging criticisms indict many areas of clinical and experimental
psychology as contributors to torture techniques. Among the methods listed are
drugs, conditioning, behavior modification, psychoanalysis, sensory deprivation,

encounter techniques, aversive conditioning, psychosurgery, sensory overstimulation, cognitive effects of fatigue, and electroshock. One wonders what to do with such allegations, particularly in the absence of evidence that there was any involvement of psychologists in the possible winnowing of psychological knowledge to find relevant bits that could be applied to torture—or in fact, that there was any such winnowing in the first place. We may turn to an analogy that has been used before: If torturers use dental drills on healthy teeth, this does not imply that researchers and practitioners who develop, improve, and use such drills in the course of ethical dental practice should feel guilty.

Sensory Deprivation

Because the treatment of detainees by British authorities in Ulster has been described as the most sophisticated example of psychological torture, we may posit that if any torture procedure were to be based on psychological research, this would be it. One critical psychologist wrote: "Clearly the only area of psychological research that could have helped in the development of these techniques is sensory deprivation research, since the general principles of anxiety-production and cognitive disorganisation are traditional interrogation methods" (Shallice, 1972, p. 399). Thus, even in the supposedly advanced case of Ulster, only one product of scientific psychology has been implicated. But three additional points must be noted.

First, sensory deprivation is hardly an invention of modern psychology, although sensory deprivation research may be. The use of lightless cells and dungeons appears in history long before psychologists do: In the 14th century, Dante Alighieri "was forced to remain in a sitting position, chained in his dark cell to a bench, unable to lie down or walk about for four years" (Sonnenfeld, 1977, p. 3). Second, no one has even claimed to have, much less shown, actual evidence that the designers of the Ulster intensive interrogation procedure had read or used any of the psychological literature in developing their system. Last, Shallice misrepresents the use of sensory deprivation in Ulster.

The melodramatic accusations concerning the use of sensory deprivation research as the foundation of some torture techniques are a prime example of allegations based on distortion (e.g., Shallice, 1972; Taylor, 1982; Watson, 1978; see also chapter 8, this volume). On examination, almost all torture procedures labeled by these sources as sensory deprivation turn out to involve either sensory overstimulation or alternation between high and low stimulation (Suedfeld, 1980), or to depend heavily on complex procedures in which the major components are unrelated to stimulus reduction (Watson, 1978). When stimulus reduction occurs, it tends to do so as part of techniques such as solitary confinement—standard procedures that owe nothing to science (Krivitsky, 1939; Smith, 1833). Although very long periods of solitary confinement, particularly in complete darkness and with restricted movement (certainly not invented by psychologists), can validly be considered a form of both psychological and physical torment (e.g., Kolff & Doan, 1985), shorter intervals of solitude and reduced stimulation present a chance for mental and physical recuperation from torture and intense interrogation (Popov, 1970).

Hoods are used to depersonalize the prisoner or to make the interrogator and possible informants unidentifiable: In Argentina, when prisoners took a shower "the guards removed our blindfolds and covered their own faces with black hoods" (Kolff & Doan, 1985, p. 48). They are used by kidnappers to avoid later identification ("Ordeal of Silence," 1989). They were used in some 19th-century prisons whenever a convict was in the presence of other people, and they have been mentioned in literature as far back as Alexandre Dumas's mid-19th century novel, *The Man in the Iron Mask* (which was based on a 17th-century historical episode). Even methods such as standing against the wall staring at a blank surface had been used before the first sensory deprivation experiments were conducted (e.g., on Popov, in 1948).

Extensive hearings before the European Commission of Human Rights identified the unacceptable aspects of the Ulster intensive interrogation procedure as hooding, wall-standing, subjection to continuous noise, deprivation of sleep, and deprivation of food and drink. The European Court of Human Rights held by a large majority that these techniques, although inhuman and degrading, did not in fact "occasion suffering of the *"particular intensity and cruelty implied by the word torture* as so understood" (cited in Amnesty International, 1984, p. 15; emphasis mine). Clearly, some aspects of the Ulster procedures had the effect of reducing the level of stimulation, whereas others increased that level. This seems to be typical of all episodes in which any sensory deprivation can be identified.

Thus, the overall picture is that severe and prolonged stimulus reduction and isolation, imposed through methods that antedate psychological research, can be a component in the mistreatment of prisoners and hostages. The parameters that define its role (e.g., in exacerbating the victim's suffering or in temporarily relieving it) are not well understood. One thing is certain: In the absence of even semi-accurate measures of total stimulus input, mixed techniques such as those used in Ulster should not be labeled simply as "sensory deprivation" (an excellent discussion of this issue can be found in Foster, 1987).

Deindividuation

One reviewer (Watson, 1978) suggested that the Ulster technique had more in common with the Stanford prison simulation (Haney, Banks, & Zimbardo, 1973) than with sensory deprivation. The surprise "arrest," forced depersonalization (deindividuation, to use Zimbardo's term), the roles played out by guards and prisoners, led to symptoms similar to those reported by Haney et al. These include the rapid appearance of overwhelming emotions, psychosomatic complaints, and the nonappearance of the deactivation (low arousal) reaction frequently found in isolated convicts imprisoned under "normal" circumstances. Watson presented no evidence that torturers anywhere or at any time actually drew upon psychological research, and, again, all of these procedures had been in use long before the Stanford study was conducted.

Group Pressure

Another relationship is raised by the intense group criticism, self-criticism, and mass trials used in the People's Republic of China (see, e.g., Amnesty International, 1978). These procedures frequently last for many hours or even days at a time and for many prisoners are repeated over a period of years. To a Western psychologist, they are reminiscent of intense marathon sensitivity sessions. The responses, too, are similar. The target in the fishbowl experiences defensiveness, fear, and shame, followed by strong emotional flooding, acceptance of the justice of the criticisms, and sometimes major reorganizations of self-concepts and attitudes. The physical arrangements also resemble some forms of group therapy, involving lack of privacy and sleep, restricted access to sanitary facilities, and the like. However, these techniques were common in China long before their development for treatment or self-improvement in the West (Lifton, 1961; Seybolt, 1986); some of the procedures have been used for centuries (Alldridge, 1984).

Psychic Driving

In the mid- to late 1950s, the well-known psychiatrist D. Ewen Cameron attempted to produce an effect akin to brainwashing in a therapeutic context. He argued that "depatterning" learned psychotic and neurotic thoughts could pave the way for "implanting" adaptive ideas. His technique, psychic driving, included weeks of induced sleep, frequent and severe electroconvulsive shocks, the administration of psychoactive drugs, prolonged monotonous stimulation, and thousands of repetitions of particular words or phrases. Some of these methods were exaggerated applications of then standard treatment techniques. We know now, after the fact, that the treatment proved to have no reliable therapeutic effects and apparently did have adverse ones on at least some patients. Two other things are clear: Cameron was genuinely trying to help patients, and there is no known evidence that any governmental agency anywhere has ever used a torture technique remotely similar to the intense multimethod approach of psychic driving (Cameron, 1957; Cooper, 1986; Gillmor, 1987). Incidentally, Cameron's work has resulted in a group of Canadian ex-patients suing the CIA (which had funded most or all of the research) and receiving an out-of-court settlement. It has also led to a minor publishing boom, with at least four books describing the project—usually from the patients' viewpoint—appearing in Canada in the span of less than two years.

Psychiatric Commitment and Treatment

The only salient exception to the general lack of evidence implicating the behavioral sciences in torture is the abuse of psychiatry in the Soviet Union. Here, the basis of torture is altered. First, the prisoner is diagnosed as psychotic, dissent being a prima facie diagnostic sign of "sluggish schizophrenia." Because the individual is considered to be ill, hospitalization follows—in one of several special psychiatric hospitals. It should be noted, incidentally, that even here the basic idea may not be all that novel: Political prisoners were sometimes diagnosed as insane and put in an asylum even during the Czarist regime (Bloch & Reddaway, 1977).

Being diagnosed as insane and confined with patients who really may be psychotic could itself be defined as torture. In fact, putting a political prisoner in a small cell with a potentially violent psychiatric patient has been alleged as a torture method in some other countries. But in addition, the Soviet Union also administers torture to such individuals under the guise of therapy. Again, however, psychology had little part in this: The "treatments" are chemical, not mental. Such treatments include disorienting, mood-altering, and pain-inducing drugs such as haloperidol, sulfizine, chlorpromazine, and trifluoperazine, frequently in excessive dosages and in disregard of contraindications. Insulin shock, immobilization, and beatings have also been reported (Bloch & Reddaway, 1985; Hannibal, 1985).

Soviet medical ethics apparently countenanced such proceedings; several of the most prominent members of the profession were implicated in rationalizing and administering the system, with some 50 others known to have participated in commissions whose judgments have led to the hospitalization of dissenters (Bloch & Reddaway, 1977). On the other hand, there have been psychiatrists and others who have had the courage to denounce the practice. Quite a few of these then also ended up in special psychiatric hospitals, and others have been sent to labor camps or prisons. One well-known victim is Dr. Anatoly Koryagin, a psychiatrist who after examining a number of dissident patients publicly pronounced them sane. Koryagin was only recently released from a labor camp. Several other members of the Soviet civil rights group, the Moscow Commission to Investigate the Use of Psychiatry for Political Purposes, were also jailed, hospitalized, or exiled (see, e.g., American Association for the Advancement of Science, 1985).

While this chapter was being written, the Soviet Union officially admitted that psychiatry had been misused (according to *Izvestia*, cited in Amnesty International, 1987; according to *Komsomolskaya Pravda*, cited in "Lid off Docs' Abuse," 1987). Although no specific mention of political persecution had been made, this first reform was followed by promulgation of a law to protect citizens against psychiatric "errors and malpractices" ("Soviets Pass Law," 1988 p. A-6). Most recently, it was announced that the "last remaining patients detained [in psychiatric hospitals] for anti-Soviet activity" had been recommended for release ("Soviets to Free Last Dissidents," 1989). Unfortunately, Dr. Robert Van Voren, the Secretary General of the International Association Against Political Abuse of Psychiatry, said in a radio interview (Canadian Broadcasting Corporation) on February 28, 1989 that all of these promises had so far been empty and that no change had occurred in the actual practice of psychiatric abuse of dissidents in the Soviet Union.

The Soviet Union has undoubtedly been by far the worst offender in this context, having thus committed hundreds of political "patients" in the past 10 years. Estimates range up to "about 6,000 inmates of Soviet mental hospitals . . . held on nonmedical grounds" (Bloch & Reddaway, 1985, p. 152). However, the Soviet Union is not the only country to use psychiatry as a tool of political control. The confinement of political dissenters in psychiatric hospitals has also been alleged in Czechoslovakia, Romania, Hungary, Yugoslavia, and the United States (here, the case of Ezra Pound is the most frequently cited example). In these latter instances no use of torture has been charged; in fact, Pound was apparently committed through the connivance of friends and admirers who saw this as the only way to save him from being convicted of and punished for treason.

WHAT CAN PSYCHOLOGISTS DO ABOUT TORTURE?

It appears that not many psychologists participate in the so-called torture network. Given that both of the major roles, either administering or receiving torture, are distasteful (to say the least), the psychological community can take comfort from this finding. In addition, there has been no evidence to support the accusation that psychology has contributed to torture indirectly by providing theoretical, empirical, or technical knowledge.

There are, however, other roles that psychology should be taking on more than it has—those that are the most compatible with the ethics and ideals of our discipline. One is the role of intervention agent. Individual psychologists, like individual physicians (see Nightingale & Stover, 1986), have long been engaged in opposing torture. Organized psychology has begun to combat torture by publicizing and condemning it. It is inspiring to see that in at least some countries where torture is widely practiced, leaders and members of psychological associations, at great risk to themselves, publicly oppose the practice and name its practitioners. The APA has actively stepped in on some occasions, particularly when psychologists were identified as the victims or perpetrators of torture, and several European associations have also taken action. It is in the best traditions of psychology that in such cases the first step has generally been to establish the facts of each case, so as to minimize the role of rumor and bias. Among other societies, the International Council of Psychologists has taken a public position condemning torture (Spaner, 1984). However, the response from many national bodies has been weak, and the International Union of Psychological Science, our major world-wide umbrella organization, has not been highly visible in this regard.

Another realm for appropriate intervention is on the individual treatment level. Again, psychologists in some countries have been providing therapy for torture victims released from confinement, and a number of countries have similar facilities for victims who find refuge abroad (for a summary, see Krajick, 1986, and chapter 11, this volume). But we need much better and more information exchange, specific training of therapists, referral networks, and treatment facilities. A number of articles have appeared in both professional and popular psychology publications in the past five years that could serve to inform colleagues as to the need, opportunity, and procedures for treatment of torture victims.

The psychological understanding of torture and its consequences also needs considerably more, and more systematic, research—some of which should involve investigations of several topics reviewed in this book. For example, the development of appropriate social policy would require a systematic way of assessing the number of torture victims within particular catchment areas and the proportion of those who are likely to need various kinds of help. Existing research from related areas, such as the aftermath of natural disasters, should be used as a model (see, e.g., Vitaliano, Maiuro, Bolton, & Armsden, 1987).

We must also learn how to make an accurate diagnosis of the problems encountered by victims. This can be problematic. For one thing, by the time the therapist sees the victim, the situation has been confounded by many experiences. The person may have managed to leave the country where torture has taken place, sometimes through very uncomfortable and dangerous routes (e.g., the Southeast Asian boat people); may have spent time in the unsettled and deprived circumstances of a refugee camp; or may have emigrated to a new country, with all of the adjustment problems that such resettlement involves. Survivors may be motivated both to minimize and to maximize claims of injury. The need to maintain a stoic self-image or the need for an illegal immigrant not to attract attention may deter someone from seeking help; conversely, a desire to publicize the evils of one's government or to qualify as a political refugee may lead to exaggerating the level of mistreatment experienced. Nor can ideological and political goals be ruled out when reading either condemnations or exonerations of particular regimes.

Psychologists have barely begun to consider the range of possible reactions to torture. In spite of the many well-known autobiographies of leaders whose thought had developed during periods of solitary imprisonment (in this century, including both Hitler and Gandhi, a fair enough range), we usually ignore reports that some victims have used even the torture experience to reach new levels of personality integration and understanding (e.g., Engdahl, 1987; Frankl, 1985; Segal, 1986). Many others may at least exhibit no obvious negative aftereffects. Who are these people, and what differentiates them from victims who suffer long-lasting symptoms? Do high-profile victims tend to be better copers? Is it part of their coping skill to become sufficiently well-known so that international support for their release is generated? Or can we expect similar proportions of hardy individuals among the "ordinary" victims of torture who, not being famous, nevertheless survive, put their lives in order again, and move forward? Supplementing psychology's traditional pathogenic perspective with a health-oriented "salutogenic" (Antonovsky, 1982, 1987) analysis of these groups would certainly be important and has not yet been systematically approached.

We also need a clearer idea of the negative sequelae of torture. At the experimental level, we can use existing knowledge (e.g., of the behavioral effects of certain types of brain trauma, the effects of parental separation on child development, and the like) and analogue studies (on sleep deprivation, stress experiments, etc.) to formulate hypotheses and explanations, test general assertions, and identify high-probability problems and possible solutions.

A basic question is whether torture is a main effect or part of an interaction with other stressors, and if the latter, how important is it compared to other factors in the victim's total experience? For example, how do reactions to torture vary as a function of the victim's previous history, personality, and cultural and demographic characteristics? Different responses may be evidenced (and accepted by themselves) by men and women; children, youths and adults; or members of various ethnic, occupational, and socioeconomic groups. And what differences result from different torture experiences? Does acute physical torture alone have the same effects as when it is combined with malnutrition, uncomfortable temperatures, immobilization, and untreated medical conditions? Or with humiliation, disorientation, and depersonalization? Is being tortured by a few "professionals" the same as being denounced and harangued by thousands of fellow citizens?

Indeed, is the "torture syndrome" really just an example of posttraumatic stress disorder (PTSD) (Boland & Rudmin, 1987)? Posttraumatic stress symptoms may vary as a function of whether pain is inflicted deliberately or accidentally, by human beings or by forces of nature, in anger or with deliberate coolness, predictably or randomly; whether the victim feels helpless or resistant, part of a group or psychologically isolated, hopeless or optimistic, and so forth (see, e.g., August & Gianola, 1987). Do all combinations of these factors yield one syndrome, or are there important variations?

If such variations exist, what implications do they have for treatment, and what may the optimal treatment approaches be? How important is the adage that treatment should be given as promptly and as close to the "front lines" as possible (McCaughey, 1985; Milgram, 1986), given that remaining in place may be dangerous to the victim (and sometimes the therapist)? On the other hand, how does living in a foreign country as an exile or refugee, sometimes illegally, complicate the symptomatology and the treatment? What difficulties is the therapist likely to encounter, both psychologically and culturally (e.g., language problems, ideals of stoicism and nondisclosure, or unfamiliarity with psychotherapist–client roles and expectations)? The patient may have a world view that does not recognize psychological explanations for the immediate and delayed reactions to torture, that denies the importance of events in a particular lifetime, or that attributes all experiences to transcendental powers so that no protagonist is viewed as responsible for any step along the way from the administration of torture to recovery from it. Such value systems may be difficult for Western-trained therapists to deal with. How can they be trained to do so? What is the relative importance and usefulness of medication, group and individual therapy, practical assistance with legal and financial problems, a holistic approach to health maintenance, reestablishing the feeling of control, meaningfulness, and predictability in the environment (Antonovsky, 1982, 1987), and other possible interventions (cf. Ochberg, 1988)?

Torture survivors do not live in a vacuum. Therapeutic attention may have to be directed to how the experience affects their adjustment at home, at work, and in society at large. For example, we know from work on Holocaust survivors that the children of parents who have survived horrendous experiences may be at increased risk. This possibility must be investigated in the case of the families of tortured refugees for timely intervention to be made available to family members. Conversely, with some education and training, the family or other social network may become a significant source of therapeutic help for the victim, particularly when the home culture emphasizes the extended family. How can such a role be optimally integrated with professional intervention?

In places with a large refugee community, treatment may involve support-group meetings among torture victims and the use of refugee professionals, paraprofessionals, and interpreters. Is this a good idea? It may be, if the participants are culturally and ideologically homogeneous, but there are obvious dangers if this is not the case (Bryden, 1989). These include not only the likelihood of conflict within the group, but also the revival of internalized anxiety. If another exile in the group is suspected of adhering to the enemy, the torture survivor may fear retribution for having survived, escaped, and revealed the truth.

Other questions are related to the psychology of torturers. Our knowledge of how they are selected and trained is fragmentary at best and leads to very few credible implications for how individuals could be "inoculated" against such training. Even the sparse data available are restricted in scope. For example, although torture suffered by hostages and other kidnap victims is documented only too well, there is little factual material on torturers who are not government agents. The experiences of people who are victimized by political fanatics, death squads, terrorists, and criminal gangs need to be studied independently of the general literature on torture. Presumably, a group of captors that is not legally responsible to any official hierarchy, that is itself in hiding from the superior forces of the government, that must reckon with the disaster that would follow from the victim's escape or rescue, is self-selected differently from police or military torture agents and interacts differently with its captives.

Moving beyond the ordinary torturer, we have speculations but few hard facts as to the conditions under which members of generally highly ethical professions such as medicine will accept or reject the role of collaborators in torture (cf. Bloche, 1987). More generally, how can an entire society be converted to accepting torture as a standard police procedure or, conversely, to rejecting it? Does psychology, in its studies of values, ideology, obedience to authority, diffusion of responsibility, and the like, have knowledge useful for explaining and perhaps combating society's toleration of torture?

The last issue brings up the matter of prevention. It may be too grandiose to think that psychology, organized or not, can prevent torture. But we can certainly recommend procedures that will make it less likely (or whose rejection by authority may be a warning sign). For example, Stover and Nightingale (1985) proposed some medical safeguards against torture, such as an examination when a prisoner first arrives at the detention center, with an offer of repeated examinations every subsequent 24 hours. There is no reason why such examinations should not be broadened to include the psychological aspects of the prisoner's condition.

Another aspect of prevention is to help the prisoner to minimize the adverse psychological consequences of torture. We know, for example, that it is crucial to fill empty time (e.g., during long periods of isolation) by instituting and maintaining a structured schedule of activities. These should include both physical exercise to the maximum degree possible and mental games (making up puzzles or recalling familiar objects or experiences). Cultivating a sense of humor and of commitment to one's preexisting framework of values helps the prisoner to resist persuasion and interrogation. Communication among prisoners and the development of a community of mutual help, camaraderie, and resistance can be crucial (e.g., Hunter, 1956; McConnell, 1985; Pawelczynska, 1973/1979). A realistic appraisal of the relationship between the prisoner and the captors can help to develop some degree of mutual consideration and respect (while avoiding the Stockholm syndrome, or identification with the aggressor, as well as potentially fatal outbursts of rage arising from reactance and frustration). It is important to retain control over some area of one's life, even if only internally, to fight off the feeling of learned helplessness; and to find some meaning and value in the experience, to decide how it will affect life after release, aids survival.

Psychologists and psychiatrists have produced some guidelines for people who are at risk of being kidnapped or held hostage (e.g., diplomats, high-level business executives, and foreigners living in turbulent areas), which may with some modifications also be applied to those at risk of governmental terror. Such manuals should prepare potential victims as to what they can expect in captivity. This may reduce the fatal acceptance of hopelessness and helplessness, which arises from uncertainty and the feeling that one has no control at all over one's fate. It helps to know that the behavior of one's captors, one's supporters on the outside, and oneself, are all within a "normal" pattern (given the abnormality of the situation). Thus, the captive will cope better and will also perceive that he or she is coping better. The efficacy of such guidelines can be tested to some extent by simulation techniques (Strentz & Auerbach, no date).

Equivalent preparation for people who have been recently released after torture should outline what to expect in terms of both short- and long-range effects. Some patients suffering from PTSD show strong feelings of guilt and shame about both their experiences and reactions during the period of torture and the symptoms that appear afterward. Again, knowing that all of these feelings and symptoms are common can be an aid in recovery.

The appropriate roles of psychology span a wide range. They involve not only the most salient direct treatment delivery specialties within the discipline, but many subareas that are no less relevant for being less obvious. As we accumulate knowledge with the goal of reducing the use and damage of torture, we may also gain important new insights into broader areas of human behavior.

REFERENCES

Alldridge, P. (1984, December). Brainwashing as a criminal defence. *Criminal Law Review*, pp. 726–737.

Amnesty International. (1978). *Political imprisonment in the People's Republic of China*. London: Author.

Amnesty International. (1984). *Torture in the eighties*. New York: Author.

Amnesty International. (1987, November 9). *Urgent Action Newsletter.*

Antonovsky, A. (1982). *Health, stress, and coping*. San Francisco: Jossey-Bass.

Antonovsky, A. (1987). *Unraveling the mystery of health: How people manage stress and stay well*. San Francisco: Jossey-Bass.

August, L. R., & Gianola, B. A. (1987). Symptoms of war trauma induced psychiatric disorders: Southeast Asian refugees and Vietnam veterans. *International Migration Review, 31*, 820–832.

Bales, J. (1986, February). U.S. delegation finds intimidation and fear uproot Chilean society. *APA Monitor*, pp. 4–5.

Bloch, S., & Reddaway, P. (1977). *Psychiatric terror: How Soviet psychiatry is used to suppress dissent*. New York: Basic Books.

Bloch, S., & Reddaway, P. (1985). Psychiatrists and dissenters in the Soviet Union. In E. Stover & E. O. Nightingale (Eds.), *The breaking of minds and bodies* (pp. 132–163). New York: Freeman.

Bloche, M. G. (1987). *Uruguay's military physicians: Cogs in a system of state terror*. Washington, DC: American Association for the Advancement of Science, Committee on Scientific Freedom and Responsibility.

Boland, F., & Rudmin, F. (1987, Spring). Victims of torture: Considerations for Canadian psychologists. *Canadian Psychological Association Highlights, 9*(2), Suppl. # 5, 16.

British Medical Association. (1986). *The torture report*. London: Author.

Bryden, J. (1989, March 18). Refugee status for executioner creates huge ethical headache. *Vancouver Sun*, p. B-2.

Cameron, D. E. (1957). Psychic driving: Dynamic implant. *Psychiatric Quarterly, 31*, 703–712.

Cooper, G. (1986). *Opinion of George Cooper, Q.C., regarding Canadian government funding of the Allan Memorial Institute in the 1950's and 1960's*. Ottawa: Department of Justice of Canada.

Cordes, C. (1984, December). Psychologist said to be architect of abuse. *APA Monitor*, pp. 6–7.

Engdahl, B. E. (1987, August). *Psychological consequences of the WWII prisoner of war experience*. Paper presented at the meeting of the American Psychological Association, New York, NY.

Foster, D. (with D. Davis & D. Sandler). (1987). *Detention and torture in South Africa: Psychological, legal, and historical studies*. New York: St. Martin's Press.

Frankl, V. E. (1959). *Man's search for meaning: An introduction to logotherapy*. New York: Pocket Books.

Gillmor, D. (1987). *I swear by Apollo: D. Ewen Cameron and the CIA-brainwashing experiments*. Montreal, Canada: Eden.

Goldstein, R. H., & Breslin, P. (1986, March/April). Technicians of torture: How physicians become agents of state terror. *The Sciences, 26*(2), 14–19.

Hannibal, K. (1985, December). Soviet psychiatric abuse: A view from within. *Clearinghouse Report on Science and Human Rights, 7*(3), 4–5.

Haney, C., Banks, C., & Zimbardo, P. (1973, September). A study of prisoners and guards in a simulated prison. *Naval Research Reviews, 26*(9), 1–17.

Hunter, E. (1956). *Brainwashing: The story of men who defied it*. New York: Farrar, Straus & Cudahy.

Jonsen, A. R., & Sagan, L. A. (1985). Torture and the ethics of medicine. In E. Stover & E. O. Nightingale (Eds.), *The breaking of minds and bodies* (pp. 30–44). New York: Freeman.

Kolff, C. A., & Doan, R. N. (1985). Victims of torture: Two testimonies. In E. Stover & E. O. Nightingale (Eds.), *The breaking of minds and bodies* (pp. 45–57). New York: Freeman.

Kosteljanetz, M., & Aalund, O. (1983). Torture: A challenge to medical science. *Interdisciplinary Science Reviews, 8*, 320–327.

Krajick, K. (1986, November). Healing broken minds. *Psychology Today, 20*(11), 66–69.

Krivitsky, W. G. (1939). *In Stalin's secret service*. New York: Harper.

Lid off docs' abuse. (1987, November 12). *Vancouver Province*, p. 43.

Lifton, R. J. (1961) *Thought reform and the psychology of totalism*. New York: Norton.

McCaughey, B. G. (1985). *U.S. Navy special psychiatric rapid intervention team (SPRINT)* (Rep. No. 85-41). San Diego, CA: Naval Health Research Center.

McConnell, M. (1985). *Into the mouth of the cat*. Scarborough: New American Library of Canada.

Mercer, E. (1986, August). Professional associations and their response to human rights violations in Chile. In A. Padilla (Chair), *Fear and repression in Chile: Report on a human rights fact-finding mission*. Symposium conducted at the meeting of the American Psychological Association, Washington, DC.

Mervis, J. (1985, October). Salvadoran psychologist flees after right-wing death threat. *APA Monitor*, p. 5.

Milgram, N. A. (Ed.) (1986). *Stress and coping in time of war: Generalizations from the Israeli experience*. New York: Brunner/Mazel.

Nightingale, E. O., & Stover, E. (1986). A question of conscience: Physicians in defense of human rights. *Journal of the American Medical Association, 255*, 2794–2797.

Ochberg, F. M. (Ed.). (1988). *Post-traumatic therapy and victims of violence*. New York: Brunner/Mazel.

Ordeal of silence. (1989, February 16). *Vancouver Province*, p. 8.

Padilla, A., & Comas-Diaz, L. (1986, November). A state of fear. *Psychology Today, 20*(11), 60–65.

Pawelczynska, A. (1979). *Values and violence in Auschwitz: A sociological analysis*. Berkeley, CA: University of California Press. (Original work published 1973)

Priests' aid to terror. (1985, May 12). *Vancouver Province*, p. 25.

Popov, H. (1970). *Tortured for his faith*. Grand Rapids, MI: Zondervan.

Segal, J. (1986). *Winning life's toughest battles: Roots of human resilience*. New York: Ivy.

Seybolt, P. J. (1986). Terror and conformity: Counterespionage campaigns, rectification, and mass movements, 1942–1943. *Modern China, 12*, 39–73.

Shallice, T. (1972). The Ulster depth interrogation techniques and their relation to sensory deprivation research. *Cognition, 1*, 385–405.

Smith, G. W. (1833). *A defence of a system of solitary confinement of prisoners adopted by the State of Pennsylvania*. Philadelphia: Philadelphia Society for Alleviating the Miseries of Public Prisons.

Somnier, F., & Genefke, I. K. (1986). Psychotherapy for victims of torture. *British Journal of Psychiatry, 148*.

Sonnenfeld, J. (1977, October). Prisoners of conscience, famous and forgotten. *Canadian Association of University Teachers Bulletin, 25*(5), 3.

Soviets pass law against psychiatric-care abuse. (1988, January 5). *Vancouver Sun*, p. A-6.

Soviets to free last dissidents held in mental institutions. (1989, January 6). *Vancouver Sun*, p. B-1.

Spaner, F. E. (1984, August). *Human rights policies and procedures for psychologists*. Paper presented at the meeting of the American Psychological Association, Toronto, Canada.

Stover, E., & Nightingale, E. O. (1985). Introduction. In E. Stover & E. O. Nightingale (Eds.), *The breaking of minds and bodies* (pp. 1–26). New York: Freeman.

Strentz, T., & Auerbach, S. M. (no date). *Adjustment to the stress of simulated captivity: Effects of emotion-focused vs. problem-focused preparation on hostages differing in locus of control*. Unpublished manuscript, Federal Bureau of Investigation and Virginia Commonwealth University.

Suedfeld, P. (1980). *Restricted environmental stimulation: Research and clinical applications*. New York: Wiley.

Taylor, R. (Executive Producer). (1982). *The hooded men* [Television program]. Ottawa: Canadian Broadcasting Corporation.

The prisoners have to be annihilated (Translation of an article in *La Voz de la Mayoria*, Montevideo, Uruguay). Circulated by Uruguay Coordination Group, Amnesty International, USA.

Valladares, A. (1986). *Against all hope*. New York: Knopf.

Vitaliano, P. P., Maiuro, R. D., Bolton, P. A., & Armsden, G. C. (1987). A psychoepidemiologic approach to the study of disaster. *Journal of Community Psychology, 15*, 99–122.

Watson, P. (1978). *War on the mind: The military uses and abuses of psychology*. London, England: Hutchinson.

Wilk, V. A. (1984). Translation of an article in *La Voz de la Mayoria*; circulated by Uruguay Coordination Group, Amnesty International USA.

8

"The Hooded Men": Victims
of Psychological Research?

Steven B. Kennedy

For intellectual and emotional reasons, the causes underlying acts of torture resist our efforts at assimilation and understanding. Indeed, our indignant bewilderment at what Amnesty International has termed the worldwide "epidemic of torture" easily outpaces or occludes our comprehension of the phenomenon and may have the unfortunate consequence of leading us into hasty and erroneous conclusions concerning the causes of torture. To the extent that this occurs and the true causes remain concealed, the effort to chase torture from our planet is ill-served. For these reasons, it is clear that Amnesty International (AI), the leader of the campaign to abolish torture, should wish to discourage and correct misapprehensions about its causes.

This chapter recounts the efforts of Canadian and American psychologists to mitigate the destructive consequences of a televised film that inaccurately and irresponsibly implicates the sensory-deprivation research of the late John P. Zubek of the University of Manitoba in the design of the procedures used by the British government in Northern Ireland in 1971. The article also details the successful efforts of the American and Canadian Psychological Associations (APA, CPA) to convince AI to join the psychological community in rejecting the film's dramatic but erroneous conclusions.

THE CONTROVERSY OVER "THE HOODED MEN"

On March 23, 1982, the Canadian Broadcasting Corporation (CBC) aired a program entitled "The Hooded Men" (McKenna, 1982). This documentary film, produced by Brian McKenna and narrated by Eric Malling as part of CBC's "fifth estate" series, explored various aspects of the worldwide phenomenon of torture, including the detention and interrogation of 14 suspects in Northern Ireland in 1971, the abductions and disappearances that terrorized Argentina throughout most of the 1970s, and the systematic training of torturers in Greece during the 1960s and 1970s. The purpose of these varied depictions was to demonstrate that torture was not an isolated product of a few deranged minds, but rather a deliberately and systematically applied instrument of state power subject to the exercise of political will on the part of government authorities. After launching its Campaign for the Abolition of Torture, AI acquired rights to the film and began to distribute it internationally as part of the organization's Human Rights Film Library.

The film's original producers chose to reinforce their thesis concerning the systematic nature of torture through reference to the work of psychologists Stanley Milgram at Yale and the late John Zubek at the University of Manitoba, work that was cited in the record of the British government commission formed to investigate the 1971 interrogations (Parker, 1972). As a Canadian scientist working at a Canadian institution with funds provided by the Canadian Defence Research Board, Zubek must have appeared to the producers to be an ideal character around which to build "Canadian content" for the program. The apparently exotic nature of Zubek's research in sensory deprivation, the suggestiveness of such research to the popular imagination, and Zubek's death in 1974 under circumstances suggesting the possibility of suicide all added to Zubek's usefulness as a dramatic subject, a tragic embodiment of the harm that can come from seemingly disinterested scientific research. Unfortunately, the drama was created at the expense of veracity. Exploiting popular confusion over the meaning of the term *sensory deprivation*, the film very strongly implies that Zubek's research, and that of Milgram and others, was and may still be appropriated by governments for the purpose of designing torture methods.

If true, this would be a serious matter indeed, one implicating the social and political role of psychological research and the ethical obligations of individual psychologists. Psychologists and their professional societies would be required, if they were to retain the confidence of the public, to examine whether their ethical codes and related guidelines and practices could be changed so as to prevent further misapplications. If, as APA and CPA believe, "The Hooded Men" paints a misleading portrait of the links between psychological research and the practice of torture, then an equally weighty obligation rests upon those who control the film to ensure that inaccurate misperceptions of psychology and its practitioners are not perpetuated to the detriment of psychology and of effective prosecution of the Campaign for the Abolition of Torture. It should be noted that appeals to the CBC and Amnesty International to correct the problem were endorsed by the chairs of Canadian departments of psychology, the International Union of Psychological Science, and the Mental Health Coordinator of Amnesty International USA's Health Professionals Network.

The CPA and APA have argued (M. S. Pallak, personal communication, June 13, 1985; R. Perloff, personal communication, January 28, 1986) that the implications of abuses of academic sensory deprivation research by the British government, implications unproved in the film because probably unfounded in fact, trade on confusion over the meaning of sensory deprivation and on the readiness of many members of the public to explain various evils, in this case the frightful epidemic of torture around the world, as the work of "mad scientists." Accordingly, in 1985 APA urged AI to withdraw the film from distribution, which it declined to do, arguing that "the sequences referring to Dr. Zubek, though used in creating a narrative line, do not in our view outweigh the central emphasis which we believe highlights the international phenomenon of torture and addresses it as a question of the abuse of state power" (R. Reoch, personal communication, October 10, 1986). As a compromise, AI proposed, after consulting with the organization's medical advisers, to issue a disclaimer that would accompany all copies of the film leased out for showing. The disclaimer was to read as follows:

The film you are about to see was made by the Canadian Broadcasting Corporation in 1982. It deals with the phenomenon of torture and the use of psychological stress in the torture process. The film is not without flaws. For example, it focuses at points on what it calls "sensory deprivation," although many of the techniques shown, for example loud noises, involve sensory overstimulation.

Amnesty International does not oppose ethical research in the field of psychology, and does not support the implication in the film that the sensory deprivation research of the psychologist John Zubek was widely appropriated for abuses of human rights.

Amnesty International is showing this film to increase people's awareness of the responsibility of governments to ensure that no detention or interrogation procedure permits the cruel, inhuman or degrading treatment of any prisoner. What the film makes clear is that torture has become an issue transcending ideological barriers and that ultimately it is governments themselves which must be the focus of pressure if we are to generate the political will to eradicate torture once and for all. (R. Reoch, personal communication, October 10, 1986)

Pleased that AI appeared willing to distance itself from those aspects of the film that APA and CPA found objectionable, and eager not to hinder AI's Campaign for the Abolition of Torture, APA in 1986 dropped its insistence on withdrawal of the film and endorsed the concept of a disclaimer, with the proviso that the disclaimer be filmed and spliced into all copies of "The Hooded Men" under AI's control.

Between October 1986 and August 1987, APA and AI exchanged views on the wording of the disclaimer. After the committee charged with reviewing and advising on AI's medical work apparently reversed its earlier finding and concluded that it would be wrong for AI to agree that the term sensory deprivation was misused in the film or that sensory deprivation techniques had not been used in torture, as APA had asserted, APA added to its proposed disclaimer words that distinguished between the psychological and lay acceptances of the term. The text APA proposed to AI, intended to effect a compromise between the concerns of the two organizations, read as follows:

The film you are about to see was made by the Canadian Broadcasting Corporation in 1982. It deals with the phenomenon of torture and the use of psychological stress in the torture process. However, the American and Canadian Psychological Associations have drawn attention to references made in the film to psychological research and theory that are to various degrees inaccurate. For example, at several points the film focuses on what it calls "sensory deprivation," although the techniques shown under this heading—such as prolonged loud noise, standing in uncomfortable positions, hanging by manacles for long periods of time—involve sensory overstimulation. In fact, the term sensory deprivation is used in many different ways by many different people. As it is used in psychological research, however, sensory deprivation (or as it is now commonly referred to, restricted environmental stimulation or REST) is not a technique used in torture and according to researchers actually has beneficial effects including being an effective tool in various kinds of therapy.

Amnesty International does not oppose ethical research in the field of psychology, and does not support the unsubstantiated implication in the film that the sensory deprivation research of the psychologist Dr. John Zubek was appropriated for abuses of human rights. Furthermore, no evidence is presented that psychological research on this topic was in fact used in the design of any torture method. Amnesty International also acknowledges the role of psychologists and psychological research, including that of Dr. Stanley Milgram which is shown in the film, in alerting people to the dangers of torture, combatting its use, and treating its victims. (S. B. Kennedy, personal communication, August 7, 1987)

The third and final paragraph of the text remained unchanged from the version first proposed by AI.

In response to the APA text, AI cited a need to consult once again with its medical advisers over the correct usage of the term sensory deprivation and to obtain permission to insert a disclaimer from the CBC. On January 15, 1988, AI transmitted to APA the latest recommendations of its medical advisers, arguing as follows:

> While it is certainly true that . . . as defined and used by psychologists [emphasis in original], SD is not a technique used as torture, we are persuaded that . . . lowering of sensory stimuli does occur when, for example, prisoners are kept isolated in a cell with low sound and light levels. . . . While it is clear that the use of, for example, an SD water tank, has not been documented as a torture technique, there are documented cases of individuals who, while in detention, have been subjected to lowered sensory stimulation (light, sound), monotonous sensory stimulation (white noise), isolation, physical pain (painful positions, beatings) and psychological stress (threats). While it is clearly inaccurate to label these collectively as SD, we believe that it would be equally misleading to suggest that the SD component was not there. . . . Finally, it is difficult to rule out anything a priori as being a technique used in torture; the best we can say is that we have no reports of the use of a given procedure as a torture technique or that its use would seem to be extremely unlikely. (R. Reoch, personal communication, January 15, 1988)

Taking these points into account, AI proposed the following wording, which was accepted by APA with but one insertion (which appears in roman).

> The film you are about to see was made by the Canadian Broadcasting Corporation in 1982. It is an investigation of torture and the use of psychological stress in the torture process.
>
> The American and Canadian Psychological Associations have kindly drawn our attention to references in the film which can be misleading, such as the use of the term "sensory deprivation" to cover techniques using "sensory overstimulation."
>
> Since some scenes depict research into sensory deprivation, we wish to make clear that Amnesty International does not oppose ethical research in this topic or other aspects of human psychology. Nor are we able to confirm the role attributed in the film to Dr. John Zubek's research.
>
> Amnesty International welcomes the many positive steps being taken by psychologists today to oppose human rights abuses and help torture victims.
>
> This is an issue transcending ideological boundaries. Responsibility for torture rests with governments. Ultimately it is governments which must be the focus of pressure if we are to generate the political will to eradicate torture once and for all. (R. Reoch, personal communication, January 15, 1988)

As this chapter was going to press, a letter from the International Secretariat of AI (May 23, 1989) indicated that the previously circulated prints of the program have been withdrawn. They have been replaced with new copies, all of which contain the disclaimer. This has been done in both the English and Spanish versions, the two languages in which the prints had been made available. Thus, the long negotiations aimed at giving a fairer picture of the involvement of psychological research and of John P. Zubek have had the desired outcome.

What are the issues that lie beneath the wording of the disclaimer? As APA's version of the disclaimer shows, APA believes that the issues are (a) the use and abuse of term sensory deprivation and (b) the use and abuse of sensory deprivation research and techniques. The specific case of Zubek and his research will be clarified through a discussion of these superordinate issues.

USE AND ABUSE OF THE TERM *SENSORY DEPRIVATION*

Although the term *sensory deprivation* has become part of the popular lexicon, where it carries a vaguely sinister connotation, it means something much more specific and value-free to the psychological researchers who coined the term. The resulting bifurcation of meaning accounts for much of the misunderstanding that has long accompanied uses of the term. The retention of a single term, and its use in "The Hooded Men" to denote diametrically opposed sets of practices, lies at the root of the misapprehensions encouraged by the film. According to Andreassi (1987, p. 1020),

> *sensory deprivation is an experimental procedure in which an attempt is made to remove or restrict sensory stimuli with human subjects. . . . Studies of sensory deprivation suggest that a changing sensory environment is essential for normal human perceptual functioning. Monotonous situations, with their repetitions of the same stimuli, are not conducive to efficient performance, and severe sensory restrictions have serious psychological and physical effects.*

The sensory deprivation studies initiated in the late 1950s by Donald Hebb, Zubek, and others provided scientific backing for the universally recognized human need for stimulation. In classic studies (Zubek, 1969, 1972), volunteers were subjected to physically comfortable conditions that nevertheless limited sensory stimulation to varying degrees. Subjects might see no more than diffused, low-intensity light and hear only low "white noise," a humming sound calculated to mask other auditory stimuli. The early studies had obvious relevance to task performance in a variety of settings characterized by long periods of monotony such as those faced by astronauts, submarine crews, weather station teams, and so forth, which explains the support offered to sensory deprivation researchers by the Defence Research Board of Canada and military agencies in the United States. Of perhaps less obvious relevance were the findings on the precise sorts of mental and physical disturbance that may be engendered by various forms and degrees of isolation.

Depending on experimental conditions and on the instructions and information provided prior to the experiment, varying proportions of the participants in early studies found sensory deprivation, social isolation, or simple confinement to be intolerable after a short time (see, e.g, Schultz, 1965; Smith & Lewty, 1959). In such cases, experimental subjects were known to request that the experiment be discontinued, particularly if a specific duration had not been set at the outset. Many subjects experienced boredom, anxiety, or visual or auditory hallucinations. Others, however, found the procedures to be relaxing or refreshing, and it was not uncommon for subjects to request that an experiment be prolonged or continued. A common interpretation of the results of early sensory deprivation studies was that humans require a certain level of stimulation in order to function normally; when the necessary inputs are not provided by the environment, they are manufactured by the brain.

In the years since its origination, however, sensory deprivation research, or, as it is now commonly known, the restricted environmental stimulation technique (REST), has spawned forms of therapy based on the clinically validated principle that many individuals—tense, troubled, or normal—benefit from the lessening or elimination of daily stimulation (Suedfeld, 1980, 1983; Suedfeld, Ballard, Baker-Brown, & Borrie, 1985–1986; Suedfeld & Clarke, 1981). Roughly the same principle lay behind earlier prescriptions of extended periods of bed rest and sleep, which, as the pace of life has quickened, have given way to shorter periods of total sensory deprivation in commercial flotation tanks or other isolating devices.

Sensory deprivation research and REST therapy, as understood and practiced by psychologists, do not involve invasive, coercive, or harmful procedures, as is evidenced by the fact that they have never occasioned a complaint leading to an ethics investigation by APA or, as far as we know, to any sort of legal complaint. Research subjects in all cases have been volunteers and have retained the right at all times to terminate the experiment in which they are engaged. Such safeguards, strongly held by vast consensus within the psychological community, are codified in APA's *Ethical Principles for Research with Human Participants* (APA, 1982). In no case on record has a subject suffered permanent psychological or physiological damage through participation in a sensory deprivation study.

The circumstances of the Irish prisoners whose treatment was examined in "The Hooded Men" is obviously quite different and shared no commonalities with the benign surroundings of sensory deprivation experiments and REST therapies. In Ulster, the 14 detainees interrogated by the British authorities were subjected to the following procedures (Parker, 1972):

1. They were kept hooded except when being interrogated or when alone in confinement and were forced to wear a baggy "boiler suit."
2. They were forced to endure continuous and monotonous noise at the level of 90 decibels, very close to the pain threshold and far above the soft masking noise used by psychologists in sensory deprivation experiments.
3. They were forced for long periods of time to maintain a painful standing position against a wall.
4. They were forcibly prevented from sleeping.
5. Their diet was inadequate.

With the possible exception of exposure to continuous noise, all of these abusive procedures have long figured among the repertory of jailers, interrogators, and torturers and appear repeatedly in the literature devoted to the mistreatment of POWs in World War II and the Korean War (e.g., Hinkle & Wolff, 1956). Conversely, these procedures are emphatically not among the conditions of any sensory deprivation experiment, again with the partial exception of continuous noise and the masking of normal visual stimulation. In the face of such potent dissimilarities in conditions (e.g., the status of a volunteer as against that of a prisoner) it is far-fetched indeed to suggest that meaningful conclusions can be inferred from the common restriction of vision or exposure to continuous sound of unspecified intensity.

Nevertheless, through the use of various dramatic devices, frankly employed for dramatic effect, "The Hooded Men" attempts to establish a logical and causal connection between Zubek's experiments in Manitoba and the harsh interrogation of Irish prisoners in Ulster. In this, unfortunately, it succeeds, if only on a purely dramatic level. When the film was first shown under AI's auspices, at the 1985 annual general meeting (AGM) of Amnesty International USA (AIUSA) in Boston, it was followed by the reading of a mild disclaimer prepared in response to APA's initial protests. This reading brought one AIUSA member in attendance to his feet, objecting angrily to what he saw as an unnecessary defense of a profession that the film had demonstrated to be scientifically irresponsible and unconcerned with human rights. The incident prompted the mental health coordinator of AIUSA's Health Professionals Network to write to the AI International Secretariat in the following terms:

> The AGM statement did not clearly indicate that the film distorts the nature of sensory deprivation research by incorrectly equating sensory deprivation with torture. Such a statement should assert this, unequivocally and without reservation. It is of course awkward to make this assertion and show the film given AI's concern and deserved reputation for accuracy. Any statement, such as that at the AGM, that merely attempts to placate psychologists is not suitable. (S. V. Faraone, personal communication, September 19, 1985)

How does the film manage to create the impression of a connection between sensory deprivation research and torture without actually establishing the fact? First, it works through images. The film opens dramatically with a camera tracking ominously down a sinister corridor in what the narrator informs us is a psychological laboratory at the University of Manitoba, where Zubek conducted much of his famous research. A contrast is drawn between the innocence of the setting ("In the middle of the wheatfields of the Canadian prairie") and the horror of events far away in Northern Ireland. Thereafter, images of Manitoba are juxtaposed with scenes of abuse in order to reinforce the connection between Zubek's research and the British practices in Ulster. The laboratory scenes are accompanied by an ominous background noise purporting to be the infamous sensory-deprivation "hum." This is tacitly equated with the much louder noise used on the Ulster prisoners.

Second, the film works by confounding the scientific and nonscientific acceptations of the term sensory deprivation. Although most nonpsychologists are unaware of the precise content of sensory-deprivation research in the laboratory setting, the term is unfortunately composed of two common words having opposing emotional connotations. Because the subject's, or the victim's, senses (which are "good") are being deprived (which is "bad"), the procedure as a whole takes on a negative connotation. At the same time, the term retains in the ear of the listener a certain scientistic aura or mystique that implies a hidden content fully available only to the scientist and to those who sponsor his or her research. This linguistic effect played an important role in propelling the wave of criticism that engulfed the study of sensory deprivation in the 1960s and in leading current researchers to drop the term in favor of the less loaded term, restricted environmental stimulation technique (REST), which implies a sheltering from, rather than deprivation of, external stimuli. In any event, the broad recognition and shallow understanding of the term sensory deprivation have permitted it to be grossly misapplied to abusive techniques such as those depicted in "The Hooded Men," most of which combine periods of isolation or confinement (not invented by psychologists) with various forms of sensory overloading that are totally foreign to scientific sensory deprivation research.

Third, the dramatic structure of the film, its plot, works to establish the connection between the experimental and prison-based conditions. Accounts of Zubek's research, and of his death by drowning, provide the major narrative throughline and most readily identifiable theme of the film, with the result that the revulsion engendered in the viewer by the appalling practices (in Ulster and elsewhere) described and depicted in the film tends to become focused on the "villain" of the piece, Zubek. Although it was never firmly established that Zubek's death was a suicide (he was taking heavy doses of antidepressants at the time of his death and was at times quite disoriented), the film uses word and image to imply very strongly not only that Zubek drowned himself, but also that he did so as a response to the controversies surrounding the purported abuses of his military-sponsored research (none of which was classified and all of which was published in the general psychological literature).

Through two brief comments from Pressey, a former colleague and research subject of Zubek's, comments lifted from their proper content in a 45-minute interview, the film misleadingly informs us that Zubek was "devastated" by the publicity he received as a result of the alleged connection between his research and the interrogation procedures used in Northern Ireland. However, the film does not clearly establish that Zubek in fact believed the allegations to be true or even plausible. In view of the inconclusivity of the legal record and of the recollections of Zubek's colleagues (J. S. McIntyre, personal communication, December 3, 1982), the film's account of his death is irresponsibly and almost willfully factitious.

Fourth, the connection between research and application is made through the words of interviewees, one of whom, Pressey, was mentioned earlier. The comments of two other individuals interviewed in the film are equally inconclusive. Psychologist Timothy Shallice, a specialist on aphasia, dyslexia, and related problems and the author of a discursive paper aimed at establishing the relation of sensory deprivation research to the interrogation techniques used in Northern Ireland (1972), declared in the film that the techniques used by the British forces "were clearly derived from a detailed knowledge of the literature on brainwashing [to which Zubek made no contribution] and *probably also* on the science of sensory deprivation" (emphasis added). He offers no firm evidence for the counterintuitive proposition that the British authorities required specialized scientific guidance for the elaboration of the specific interrogation methods used in Northern Ireland. Returning to the 1972 article that led the CBC to use Shallice in the film, one finds that the author does not prove, or even assert, that Zubek's work was in fact read, or had to have been read, by the authorities.

Another interviewee was Lord Gardiner, author of the minority report submitted as part of the British government's investigation of the Ulster abuses (Parker, 1972). In a defense of "The Hooded Men," Robin Taylor (1982), Executive Producer of the CBC program that carried the show, stated that Lord Gardiner was interviewed for the film on the strength of the following reference in his official report: "Sensory isolation is one method of inducing an artificial psychosis or episode of insanity. . . . There is a considerable bibliography of experiments in this field, particularly in Canada" (p. 5). Asked about this in the film, Lord Gardiner stated: "I don't remember the details of it now. We certainly had the results of research works that had been done in Canada."

These assertions are in themselves plainly inconclusive, establishing only that the British investigators were among those aware of certain published psychological research performed in Canada. What is nowhere established, but what is plainly implied in the film, is that the British military authorities not only had access to, but actually used, Zubek's research in the design and application of their interrogation methods. The fact that those methods, as depicted in the film, are so radically unlike the conditions of academic sensory deprivation experiments places a heavy burden of proof on anyone asserting the existence of a connection between the two phenomena. Although that burden is not squarely met in the film, the implied links, seemingly confirmed by putative experts, serve to create the desired effect in the mind of a viewer unfamiliar with the nature of sensory deprivation research.

THE USE AND ABUSE OF SENSORY DEPRIVATION RESEARCH AND TECHNIQUES

In its 1975 *Report on Torture*, AI concludes a long chapter entitled "Medical and Psychological Aspects of Torture" by urging that

> *No research into torture or such subjects as sensory deprivation should be undertaken without consideration of the motives of the sponsoring organization or individual, so that at least some estimation can be made of the eventual use to which the results of the work will be put. (p. 69)*

Because the chapter provides no evidence that research in sensory deprivation has in fact been consulted by torturers, psychologists may be excused for finding this policy recommendation unwarranted and gratuitous. Nevertheless, the quotation serves to introduce the broader question of the actual and potential abuses of sensory deprivation research.

With respect to actual abuses, I must be brief because there is no conclusive material with which to illustrate the point. The arguments advanced by CBC to substantiate the implications of abuses of Zubek's research are sorely deficient. Taylor (1982) attempted to prove the point by arguing, circularly, that if the research had not been useful for the design of interrogation techniques, it would not have been funded by the Canadian Defence Research Board:

> *The Defence Research Board . . . was clearly motivated, as its very name implies, by a desire to develop defences, if any are possible, against the machinations of "agencies of torture." Unfortunately, to develop defences, one must replicate the offensive tactics. It was this replication by Zubek of the techniques of isolation and monotonous and constant noise that was of such immeasurable assistance to the "agencies of torture" in Northern Ireland—all the leading juridical, academic and political sources of the United Kingdom and Europe are in agreement on this point. [No citation provided.] Shallice, indeed, is quite explicit. He argues that sensory deprivation "probably has" aided in the development of interrogation techniques. (p. 7; emphasis added; quotation marks in original)*

Contrary to this reasoning, the fact that Zubek's research was funded by the Defence Research Board (which has since been absorbed into other branches of the Canadian defense establishment) tells us nothing very specific about the actual or potential applications, military or otherwise, of that research. Over the years, the Board, like its counterpart agencies in the United States, funded a great deal of basic research in sensory processes, motor skills, perception, and learning, most of which had a very remote connection to defense issues generally, and even less so to torture in particular. Zubek himself stated that he would not perform classified research or accept research funds unless the product of the research could be published in the general psychological literature. The readily available published accounts of Zubek's research, and the open public record of Defence Research Board grant applications and reports, do not support Taylor's thesis concerning the replication of "offensive tactics" (B. H. Sabiston, Canadian National Defence Headquarters, personal communication, August 23, 1982).

But what about the *potential* for abuse of research in sensory deprivation? Although all of the coercive interrogation procedures used in "The Hooded Men" were known long before Hebb and Zubek commenced their research in sensory deprivation, it is perhaps conceivable that individuals or institutions bent on inflicting torture *might* be able to derive certain refinements of technique if they were to delve into the psychological literature. That a torturer would choose to do this is highly implausible, because (a) sensory deprivation has very little to teach the torturer or "coercive interrogator," and (b) as AI has made clear (1975), the primary purpose of most instances of torture—to humiliate and dehumanize the victim and to spread terror in his or her social milieu—can be achieved by very crude methods not requiring forays into academic research.

In its *Report on Torture* (1975), Amnesty International concluded that

> Even if the revelation that less violent forms of treatment may be the most efficient means of interrogation were advanced in all the Ministries of Interior in all the countries of the world, this scientific reality would pale before the political reality of a torture state. Obtaining information is only one purpose of torture; in most states it is one of relatively little significance. (p. 69)

Instead, psychological research into sensory deprivation investigates the effects of stimulus reduction in producing alterations in visual, auditory, and tactile perception, motor coordination, and cognition (including greater openness to factual messages concerning the effects of harmful behaviors such as cigarette smoking), all of which alterations are of rather finer magnitude than the dramatic "confessions" produced by Stalin's interrogators, or by the Chinese military, a half-century ago.

Suedfeld (1980) pointed out that isolation and stimulus reduction have long been applied in situations of interrogation and indoctrination. The most thoroughly documented instances of such use were in the Soviet Union and Eastern Europe during the purge trials of the 1930s and 1940s. Isolation was used to magnify the effects of periodic intense interrogation sessions. This application was the extension of traditional police practices in Russia, and it antedates scientific research into the effects of sensory deprivation.

To illustrate the distinction between crude forms of torture and tangentially related scientific or medical research, Suedfeld (1980) has drawn an analogy to the field of dentistry. One of the more excruciating tortures known is drilling into the unanesthetized tooth, yet many dentists regularly repair teeth without an anesthetic. Aided by psychologists, some dentists even do research on music, white noise, and other distractions as alternatives to the use of anesthetic. Such research is no more connected to dental torture than is sensory deprivation research to psychological torture.

It is interesting to guess at what might have been the reaction of the general public (let alone of the dental profession) if CBC had chosen to use a Canadian dental researcher to build the dramatic throughline to a story on torture. The difference between the two cases, and the element that makes the psychologist so much more susceptible than the dentist to misleading associations of the sort suggested by the film, lies in the fact that the activities of the dentist and of the dental researcher are not surrounded by the same mystique as that which shrouds the work of academic and professional psychologists.

Another analogy may be drawn to pharmacological psychiatry. In its *Report on Torture*, AI (1975) explicated and condemned the use of psychotropic drugs in torture but took pains to highlight the beneficial effects of such drugs when used properly (pp. 55–58), going so far as to warn the reader against credulous acceptance of claims of pharmacological torture and to note that "any drug if misused can be harmful" (p. 57). In a related passage, AI noted that:

> It is all too easy to want to believe a distressed man who claims he is being tortured or persecuted by the police and to regard as further torture what may be an attempt to reduce his distress with phenothiazine, especially if you believe that the police of his country torture people. Normal people believe what they want to believe; it is important that they should want to believe the truth. (1975, p. 57)

Despite widespread actual and potential abuse of common dental techniques and dozens of common pharmacological agents, AI has not called for restrictions on dental or pharmacological research, and rightly so. The organization has long recognized that the prevention of torture lies in political and legal remedies and has conducted its campaign for the abolition of torture on this basis. In this context, it is clear that the tendency of "The Hooded Men" to deflect attention from the necessary political and legal remedies, and to focus it, for no better purpose than melodramatic effect, on the research work of psychologists, is harmful, not just to the image of psychology, but to the cause of abolishing torture. The mad scientist motif that makes for such good drama in "The Hooded Men" must, by reason of its deviation from reality, be less effective in motivating social and political action against torture.

From the perspective of the psychological community, meanwhile, the fact that CBC was able to exploit public misunderstanding of what it is psychologists do in order to fashion compelling drama from flimsy evidence constitutes a serious challenge to the psychological community. To meet this challenge, psychologists must continue, through their professional associations, to "banalize" their discipline, so they will be less appealing as models for the mad scientist role. This is not to excuse the producers of a film that sullies the memory of Zubek and his research. Unfortunately, the CBC was unswayed by the facts presented to it by the CPA in 1982. Let us hope that it will not now oppose addition to the film of a disclaimer designed to disassociate AI from the inaccurate Canadian content of "The Hooded Men."

REFERENCES

American Psychological Association. (1982). *Ethical principles in the conduct of research with human participants*. Washington, DC: Author.

Amnesty International. (1975). *Report on torture*. New York: Farrar, Straus & Giroux.

Andreassi, J. L. (1987). Sensory deprivation. In Corsini, R. J. (Ed.), *Concise encyclopedia of psychology* (p. 1020). New York: Wiley.

Hinkle, L. E., Jr., & Wolff, H. G. (1956). Communist interrogation and indoctrination of the enemies of the state. *Archives of Neurological Psychiatry, 76*, 115–174.

McKenna, B. (1982). *The hooded men* [Film]. Canadian Broadcasting Corporation, Toronto. (Available from Facets Multimedia, Inc., 1517 W. Fullerton, Chicago, IL 60614; 312-281-9075)

Parker, Lord of Waddington. (Chairman). (1972, March). *Report of the Committee of Privy Councillors appointed to consider authorised procedures for the interrogation of persons suspected of terrorism.* London, England: Her Majesty's Stationers Office.

Schultz, D. P. (1965). *Sensory restriction: Effects on behavior.* New York: Academic Press.

Shallice, T. (1972). The Ulster depth interrogation techniques and their relation to sensory deprivation research. *Cognition, 1*(4), 385–405.

Smith, S., & Lewty, W. (1959). Perceptual isolation using a silent room. *Lancet,* 342–345.

Suedfeld, P. (1980). *Restricted environmental stimulation: Research and clinical applications.* New York: Wiley.

Suedfeld, P. (1983). The restricted environmental stimulation technique in the modification of addictive behaviors: Through the centuries to frontiers for the eighties. *Bulletin of the Society of Psychologists in Addictive Behaviors, 2*(4), 231–237.

Suedfeld, P., Ballard, E. J., Baker-Brown, G., & Borrie, R. A. (1985–1986). Flow of consciousness in restricted environmental stimulation. *Imagination, Cognition and Personality, 5*(3), 219–230.

Suedfeld, P., & Clarke, J. C. (1981). Specific food aversion acquired during restricted environmental stimulation. *Journal of Applied Social Psychology, 11*(6), 538–547.

Taylor, R. (1982). *The hooded men.* Unpublished report, Canadian Broadcasting Corporation, Toronto.

Zubek, J. P. (Ed.). (1969). *Sensory deprivation: Fifteen years of research.* New York: Appleton-Century-Crofts.

Zubek, J. P. (1972). Behavioral and physiological effects of prolonged sensory-perceptual deprivation. *Revista Interamericana de Psicologia, 6*(3–4), 151–200.

9

Treating Victims of Torture: Psychology's Challenge

Jacqueline C. Bouhoutsos

WHO ARE THE VICTIMS OF TORTURE?

According to Amnesty International, 98 nations currently practice torture, more than 30 of them systematically. Among the leading offenders are Iran, Chile, Libya, Pakistan, and Turkey. The number of victims affected has been reported to be in the tens of thousands annually. There are reportedly 15 million refugees in the world today (Allodi & Rojas, 1985). How many of these individuals have been subjected to torture in their native lands is difficult to ascertain, but the most frequent estimates are between 30% and 60% of the refugees (Chester, 1987). Nightingale (1987), one of the best known authors on the topic, estimated the number of torture victims to be between hundreds of thousands and millions. The number of refugees currently living in the United States is unknown because many of them have entered this country illegally. Figures for arriving refugees in four states for the year 1984 are available (see Table 1).

According to the U.S. Immigration and Naturalization Service Yearbook (1985), 37,500 South Americans, 57,600 Mexicans, and 15,000 Central Americans came to the United States in 1984. Yet, information from the *Los Angeles Times* (1983) indicated that 300,000 Central American refugees arrived in Los Angeles during the years 1982 and 1983. Approximately 500,000 lived in Los Angeles in 1986, and the current figure approaches three quarters of a million. How many of these are victims of torture we have no way of knowing. We do know that many of these people who immigrated to California began their journey from El Salvador or Guatemala. There is documentation from the Legal Aid Office of the Archdiocese of San Salvador that 4,113 civilians were murdered by "security forces," the army, and right-wing death squads, and 67 were killed by guerillas in the first 10 months of 1983 (Griffin, 1984). Similarly, in Guatemala, the leadership of the San Carlos University student government was kidnapped in May 1984, and only 1 of the 11 students reappeared, severely tortured and close to death (Manuel, 1984). Because the United States government has not recognized people from these countries as political refugees, they were not given official status and therefore were "illegals." Before the amnesty program was instituted

Table 1 Refugees arriving in the United States in 1984[a]

Destination	Arriving from			
	Southeast Asia	Eastern Europe and the Soviet Union	Afghanistan, Iran Ethiopia, Iraq	Cuba (1982)
California	16,718	2,150	2,435	5,700
Florida	896	266	166	86,600
Texas	4,510	498	603	2,000
New York	2,130	2,292	764	6,400

[a]From the U.S. Department of Health and Human Services' Office of Refugee Resettlement Services' Report to Congress (1985).

they had no legal access to any medical or other assistance. They lived in fear of being picked up and deported to the countries from which they escaped and where many had experienced torture.

Although there was no official help available, a sanctuary movement and underground railroad assisted several thousand Central American political refugees with border crossings, resettlement, jobs, medical care, and other services. Volunteer social workers and members of other professions banded together to help these refugees (Anonymous, 1985). There was a great deal of risk involved with this activity. Harboring or aiding undocumented aliens carries a penalty of $2,000 and five years in prison for each count. Nonetheless, many humanitarians helped this population. People who work in the sanctuary movement point out that the U.S. Refugee Act of 1980, the United Nations Protocol on Refugees, and the Geneva Convention have explicit statements protecting political refugees and prohibiting sending them back to their homelands if they are in danger. However, this has not prevented such incidents from occurring, even when these refugees were knowingly returned to certain torture and death. The sanctuary movement continues to call public attention to the plight of the refugees and seeks to create a public demand to effect a change in our national policy.

Some members of that public have argued that it is not our responsibility to care for illegal aliens, whether or not they have been tortured. The counterargument is that costs for physical and emotional care are lower when early diagnosis is available, that schools and other public services are utilized by the children of refugees or refugees themselves when emergencies arise, and that refugees are heavily employed in many industries,such as food service and child care, where their untreated health problems may pose a potential risk to others. In many instances refugees suffer from long-term physical and emotional illnesses, which, if not treated, hamper their adjustment and keep them from becoming contributing members of our society.

A problem unique to those refugees who have been tortured is their exquisite sensitivity to stimuli that would present no problem to the average refugee. This sensitivity makes it possible, therefore, for professionals or paraprofessionals who have not been specifically trained to work with this population to unintentionally retraumatize them without even realizing that they are doing so. For example, *Time* (Leo, 1985) vividly described a Latin American refugee who froze in terror when a well-wisher brought him a gift basket that included two pineapples. In the refugee's native country, he had been forced to watch as his military captor hacked several prisoners to death, then carved up a ripe pineapple with the bloodstained machete and calmly ate the slices.

For victims of torture, the world is an inchoate mass of horrifying memories. The *Time* article also described a woman who panics whenever she sees a dark Ford like the one that hauled her away to severe beatings and a gang rape. Some survivors have trouble entering bathrooms, because the tile, lighting, and smell summon up images of their torture chambers. A knock at the door during an interview might elicit a startle response and an anxiety reaction. Most of the victims are hypervigilant and fearful. Many recount episodes of death squads and brutality. For example, one told of finding a family member shot and burned with genitals stuffed into his mouth and another family member hacked to pieces and placed in a plastic garbage bag.

TREATMENT APPROACHES FOR VICTIMS OF TORTURE

Unfortunately, there are currently more descriptions of the consequences of torture than information about the effectiveness of various types of treatment for the victims. Many questions arise specific to this population. Special training is necessary to treat the victims, and few mental health professionals have received such training. For example, if victims of torture present by requesting medical services when there are obvious emotional problems, when should psychotherapy be provided? Even if the problem is psychologically based, the likelihood is that if there is no medical response the patients will leave. Experience has shown that psychological intervention should be started right away. But how can this be done if the demand is for medical care?

The reverse of this problem is to consider all complaints to be psychosomatic and not respond to actual physical damage, which many of these victims of torture have sustained. Yet, it is important for mental health professionals to recognize the presence of physical injury and to refer patients to physicians for treatment. If victims were hanged by extremities for days, they usually mention joint and muscle pains; if they were hit on the head, they frequently mention headaches; if they were beaten on the soles of their feet, they describe pain in walking; if they had electrodes placed in their ears, their hearing is usually affected.

If the torture was mainly psychological, there is a strong likelihood that there will be depression, anxiety, loss of memory and concentration, nightmares, sexual problems, fatigue, headaches, and feelings of being a changed, different person. But it is also likely that the victims will not mention any of these psychological symptoms. Differential diagnosis is difficult when working with victims of torture and demands careful and complete history-taking and collaboration between medical and mental health professionals. A related dilemma confronts psychologists. If medical care is given initially, when should assessment be done? A possible compromise might be to do evaluation when patients come in for follow-up. However, that does not allow for baseline data collection.

Another unresolved issue is whether traditional intakes should be done in which the patient fills out forms or the interviewer asks routine questions. Many patients find it difficult to talk about their ordeals. Treatment of patients who have posttraumatic stress disorder (PTSD) is best initiated by facilitating their talking about their experiences. It is inadvisable to go into the trauma story in the first few sessions with certain patients. Torture victims frequently deny or pass over their experiences. A basic admonition is that the patient should never be coerced to deal with material for which he or she is not ready. "Such coercion may lead to a psychotic break, the emergence of uncontrollable suicidal impulses, or other destructive consequences" (Pope & Bouhoutsos, 1986, p. 106). Repressed aspects of the trauma must be gradually acknowledged and worked through so that patients will not experience nightmares, flashbacks, and obsessive repetitions. The basic purpose of treatment is to help these victims gain some control over their lives. As Horowitz (1984) stated: "Psychotherapy should begin with reconstruction and review of the past, move on to present difficulties, and conclude when adaptive mechanisms for future use are in adequate state of recovery" (pp. 374–375).

Working through the trauma is a painfully slow process for both the therapist and the recovering victim. Even after substantial gain, there may be recurrence of symptomatology after a particular event triggers recall of earlier experiences. Role-playing has been found to be very effective when patients are ready, as have painting and drawing, which help them to depict their experiences in creative form. Therapists have found it useful to discuss the drawings about the torture with patients, helping them to gradually begin talking about their experiences and abreacting to break through the fear. In some particularly difficult instances, in which historical material is not accessible, antidepressant medication may help elicit the history of the trauma. However, many experts working in this area feel that psychopharmacological treatment should not be used, because some of the torture experiences included the administration of drugs. Because victims who come for help are not generally suffering from mental disorders as such, and normal psychological states will return gradually, in most instances, medication should be avoided, if at all possible. Unfortunately, some cultures see medication as being sine qua non for treatment. Obviously, decisions must be made case by case. Another caveat is that the therapist must be particularly careful with sexual matters. For example, when rape has occurred, the questioning of a female patient, particularly by a male therapist, may result in retraumatization and will probably ensure that she will not return. A careful, sensitive diagnostic interview by a female therapist can assist the therapy process.

More information is needed about the effectiveness of the various treatment modalities that have been used with victims of torture. There is a growing body of literature on the treatment of various subcategories of PTSD and some of the approaches appear to have applicability to this population of victims. For example, the treatment of Vietnam veterans by hypnosis in the context of brief psychotherapy (MacHovec, 1985) has been used as a treatment stratagem. The use of group therapy for victims of Therapist–Patient Sex Syndrome, has been described as being helpful (Pope & Bouhoutsos, 1986; Sonne, Meyer, Borys, & Marshall, 1985). In each of the subcategories of PTSD, the importance of a support network is emphasized, particularly when the victim is in an environment where he or she is neither believed nor understood. Peer counseling or peer support groups of other survivors who successfully made it through similar torture experiences have also been described as being helpful. Historically, identification with others who have been able to restructure their lives and adapt has been helpful to patients. For victims of torture, it is particularly important not to separate them from their families, because fear for the life and safety of a spouse and children or parents has usually been a part of the trauma (Svendsen, 1985).

The following are some cautions that have particular relevance to torture victims.

1. Service providers should dress in street clothes and be addressed by their names rather than by title. Frequently the victims have perceived physicians or other professionals as enemies because many torturers dressed as white-coated specialists, and some insisted that victims call them "doctor" to help legitimize the physical abuse they meted out to their victims.

2. Professionals dealing with victims should be sensitive to the fact that the anxiety of the victims is easily evoked by sensory, auditory, or visual signals or experiences symbolizing torture and persecution.

3. No matter what the etiology of their victimization, winning the trust of victims who have been abused can be painfully slow because of the burdens of their past. Survivors experience guilt or feelings of complicity. Depression, sleeplessness, and recurrent nightmares are almost universally present. Fear of authority is so frequent that almost any kind of dependency feelings can panic a survivor.

4. It is crucial for the therapist not to promise something that cannot be fulfilled. The victim's trust is so fragile that any lapse on the part of the therapist is seen as betrayal.

5. One of the most problematic treatment issues in working with PTSD patients is caused by their neediness and vulnerability. It is often important for them to be able to speak with someone at the moment that there is a recurrence of the flashbacks, when they tend to panic and, in some instances, become suicidal. Therapists working with this population have found that it is not possible to have contact with the victims only once a week and to expect progress or even maintenance. Their intense need for support and understanding requires that they receive longer and more frequent sessions and, ideally, other indications that they are not alone, such as phone calls. Assigned substitute behavioral procedures may assist them in tolerating the time between sessions (e.g., talking into tape recorders or keeping journals). Another possibility is a self-help group. This model has been found to be very helpful in working with patients who have been sexually involved with their therapists (Pope & Bouhoutsos, 1986; Sonne et al., 1985). The process of reexperiencing the pain of the loss and the sharing of feelings with others facilitates recovery. In fact, some therapists who treat victims of torture consider sharing as quintessential and maintain that if feelings are not shared the pain will remain locked in as an individual experience in profoundly destructive ways: depression, anguish, despair, and, sometimes, an inability to go on living.

6. With most victims of torture, there are additional problems of political proclivities, language, culture, educational level, and socioeconomic factors that complicate sharing with others outside their family. Victims are widely disparate in their backgrounds, and compatible group composition is crucial. For example, those from Latin cultures are frequently more able to address their feelings than those from Asian cultures, which do not look with favor on admitting psychological difficulties. In working with Asian cultures, therefore, the therapist would, of necessity, describe the symptoms as something other than psychological and would expect the patient to do likewise. Depression is frequently presented by this population as "pressure" or "sluggishness."

THE NEED FOR BILINGUAL SERVICE PROVIDERS

Through this abbreviated recitation of the complex and conflicting factors that must be considered in working with this population, it is obvious that either intensive training of professionals is necessary or an alternative solution must be sought. Irreparable harm can be done to these patients, just as it is done to patients who are sexually abused by their therapists when a subsequent therapist places blame on an already guilt-ridden patient. Harm can be done to victims of torture by a service provider's insensitivity to, or ignorance of, the cultural backgrounds from which victims come and the experiences they have had.

One alternative that is often suggested is the use of interpreters, co-clinicians, paraprofessionals, or various professional individuals who are from the same cultural background as the victims. The use of interpreters (used here as a generic term not descriptive of their activities) in the therapeutic setting is a controversial subject. Concerns have been voiced about the breach of confidentiality that occurs when a third party, not a therapist, is introduced into the therapeutic session. Further problems mentioned are the dilution of the transference that occurs, the linguistic and conceptual difficulties in interpreting affect across cultures, and the possibility that patients feel less understood and are less satisfied when interpreters are used. This latter concern was researched and found not to be pertinent (Kline et al., 1980), and Egli (1987) interpreted the concern as indicating the therapist's discomfort with interpreters rather than the patient's. Some of the therapist's discomfort may stem from the use of interpreters in clinics where relatives or clinic personnel such as janitors are called in to translate rather than people with clinical experience (Westermeyer, 1987).

The reverse of this situation is found when agency directors do not allow their bilinguals to be called interpreters, translators, or even paraprofessionals, because they consider these titles demeaning. Some of these directors view bilinguals as competent to intervene in crisis situations, perform therapeutic interventions, administer tests, make referrals, and do case management. Yet, they are not accredited, are not licensed, and are performing functions frequently limited to professionals in many states. Few refugee mental health workers have had previous mental health-related experience in their home countries. Few have advanced degrees (Egli, 1987). Agencies use bilinguals in a number of ways, as is clear from their various titles: clinician, social worker, co-therapist, interpreter, counselor, social adjustment worker, mental health assistant, and mental health worker.

Bilinguals face some of the same issues that American paraprofessionals face: obtaining adequate training, refusing to perform services beyond their areas of competence, and gaining recognition for the considerable skills they do have. For example, many advocates applaud the use of paraprofessionals in alcohol and drug counseling. Advocates feel that experience, empathy, and supportiveness, along with sufficient in-service training, can compensate for the lack of education (Mollica, 1987). Certainly, having a linguistic and cultural connection between therapist and patients is advantageous; but can paraprofessionals deal with the severe pathology of the victims of torture?

Egli (1987) revealed that 60%–70% of the caseloads in refugee clinics visited are chronic patients with seriously disabling psychiatric diagnoses. American paraprofessionals would be unlikely to see this patient population and, if they did, would undoubtedly have close supervision after intensive training, such as is the case with psychiatric technicians. But necessary supervision and training is not available for bilinguals in most settings, given the inability of teachers and supervisors to understand the recorded tapes or notes of their students or supervisees, which is the material that is usually most crucial to the supervision process. There is also a lack of quality assurance, because supervisory-level personnel are almost nonexistent in most small clinics.

Nonetheless, there is an important role for bilinguals to play. With adequate funding, training could be provided and certification for bilinguals could be modeled after the "mental health worker" category popular in the late 1960s and early 1970s, when many county departments of mental health were hiring minority workers for community outreach. An alternative suggestion is the development of psychiatric technician programs for cross-cultural and cross-lingual service. Whichever model proves to be feasible, the services of these caregivers are crucial for adequate treatment of victims of torture, and efforts are needed to provide the training, supervision, and career path for bilinguals entering the mental health field.

TREATING THE FAMILY AND THE INDIVIDUAL

In addition to language and culture, yet another variable should be taken under consideration in providing treatment for victims of torture: the large percentage of victims who are members of families, and the need of those families for family therapy. For example, the rehabilitation of children should optimally take place largely within the family structure, and their progress would therefore be dependent on that family's ability to retain its structure and its protective and nurturing qualities. Children and adults undergo the same process of reparation and therapy, and, although the language used and the levels of personality integration are different, their basic needs are the same. As families begin to explore being together again and leading productive lives, a restructuring of personality can take place for both adults and children (Svendsen, 1985).

Most problems of the victims manifest themselves in familial relationships, and spouses and children need to be treated as well as the individual who was the direct recipient of the torture. For example, in many instances the wife was left alone in charge of the family. When the spouse returned from his torture experience, he was expected to take over as head of the household. But the returning victim is frequently not the same kind of person, and adjustment is necessary on the part of both spouses and children (Lunde, 1982). One stratagem found to be helpful to spouses of victims was group process. Those who have been in similar positions with their spouses can assist one another. Again, in constituting such a group, considerations of political, cultural, socioeconomic, educational, and language compatibility must be observed.

When no family or social network is available, the individual who has been a victim of torture faces other problems: loneliness, depression, isolation, and despair—particularly if the victim is older. In such instances, it is necessary for the therapist to devise a different treatment plan. As has been emphasized, the main purpose of torture is to destroy the personality of the individual, to dehumanize, denigrate, humiliate, and debase the victim (Somnier & Genefke, 1986). An antidote to such experiences might be to design a treatment program for the victim that would reframe the torture experience, thus assisting the victim to reconceptualize the suffering that he or she has undergone.

For example, in the history of some American Indian tribes, the rites of passage for young males included being dragged along the ground behind horses by hooks passed through the breast area, without anaesthetic. "Braves" who were able to tolerate such torture were idealized and took pride in their achievement. Recasting the victims of torture as heroes and survivors might assist them to regain their self-respect and counteract the degradation and humiliation they suffered at the hands of their torturers. Recent literature on victimology, recognizing the benefits of such an emphasis, suggests using the term *survivor* rather than *victim* (Walker, 1984).

SERVICE DELIVERY FOR VICTIMS OF TORTURE

Federally–Funded Refugee Mental Health Programs

There has been, until recently, a paucity of information about services for refugees generally, and victims of torture in particular. Refugees are defined as "people who have left their home country and are unable to return because of persecution or a well-founded fear of persecution" in the Immigration and Nationality Act (1980). In 1987, the Refugee Mental Health Resource Development and Technical Assistance Center was established under a three-year contract with the National Institute of Mental Health, to provide technical assistance and consultation to state mental health agencies.[1]

Twelve states were awarded funds for refugee mental health programs: California, Colorado, Hawaii, Illinois, Massachusetts, Minnesota, New York, Rhode Island, Texas, Virginia, Washington, and Wisconsin. The objectives of this program are as follows.

1. To develop a refugee planning, program development, advocacy, and coordination capacity within each of the funded state mental health agencies.
2. To establish a nationwide refugee mental health resource development and technical assistance capacity.
3. To increase the number of trained refugee mental health professionals to provide clinical services to refugees.
4. To ensure more effective placement, utilization, and career development of trained refugee paraprofessionals within agencies providing mental health services to refugees.
5. To develop needs assessment and ongoing epidemiologic studies regarding refugee mental health (Deinard, 1987, personal communication).

In 1987, the first year of the project, the Technical Assistance Center focused on a review of the literature, needs assessment, and models of diagnosis, prevention, and treatment of refugee mental health problems. In the second year, the focus was on training, with assistance given to various existing agencies to help

---

[1]For more information about the Refugee Mental Health Resource Development and Technical Assistance Center, write to Box 85, 420 Delaware St., S.E., University of Minnesota Hospitals, Minneapolis, MN 55455.

them in treating the refugee population. In the third year (1989), development of a source book and videotapes for providers will assist them in providing the identified necessary services.

The initial needs assessment determined that acute services were in highest demand; in fact, six times as great among this population as among the national average of patients (Shon, 1988, personal communication). Concerns about the availability of personnel to meet the needs of the refugees resulted in an effort to enlist mental health professionals with the ability and interest to work with this population. The overall plan is that such services to refugees will be integrated into the mainstream and that local agencies will be able to offer adequate services to this special population.

Forms have been sent out by the Technical Assistance Center to licensed professionals and paraprofessionals in the 12 states, requesting information regarding prior experience working with refugees, willingness to be listed in a directory of professionals and paraprofessionals, and availability to move to other cities or states to work with refugees. Work groups will facilitate the sharing of knowledge among the states and other interested organizations through national workshops, particularly in identifying and providing culturally sensitive models for the prevention, diagnosis, and treatment of mental health problems of refugees. These programs are not specifically designed to treat victims of torture. Nonetheless, the heightened sensitivity to cultural issues and the readiness to work with a refugee population, can provide baseline experience for working with victims of torture, provided that additional training specific to torture victims is added.

Centers for Torture Victims

In 1973 Amnesty International turned to the medical professions worldwide to fight against torture. Out of this effort came a recognition that treatment and rehabilitation for the victims of torture were needed. The Danish physicians who were part of the first medical group of Amnesty International recommended the establishment of a special institution for treating victims. In 1982 the first Research Centre for Torture Victims (RCT) was established in Copenhagen, with voluntary staff augmented by a secretary, a neurologist–medical director, and a lawyer who served as legal director. Interpreters and paraprofessionals also became an integral part of the services offered.

With the increase in immigrants, the need for such a treatment center in North America became obvious. More than 300,000 refugees had entered Canada since the end of World War II. Many of these were from Latin America and sought political asylum after having been tortured in their own countries. Thus, a second center was established, this time in Toronto, in 1983. Currently, the Toronto Center has 50 physicians and 20 other volunteers on call.

An unprecedented influx of refugees to the United States, as described in the introduction to this chapter, made it imperative to find help for those among them who needed medical and psychological assistance. In 1985, Minnesota appointed a task force to look into the possibility of establishing a center for treating victims of torture and in October, 1986, the Minnesota Center for Victims of Torture was opened, the third such center.

The Indo-Chinese Psychiatry Clinic

A different model from these three centers is provided by the Indo-Chinese Psychiatry Clinic (ICPC), established in Boston as an outgrowth of the federal government's six national mental health projects for Southeast Asia. Established in 1982, the program merits particular attention because of its unique approach to treatment of torture victims.

After the initial evaluation of the presenting symptoms of the patient, a thorough history is taken. Weekly clinic contact by a co-therapy team is then begun. Integration of folk healers and folk treatment systems is also attempted, although few such healers are available in the Boston area. At first, most of the patients present medical problems, and only later do psychological problems surface. Most clients treat emotional symptoms as secondary to their somatic complaints; as pointed out earlier, Southeast Asians feel more comfortable with the medical model. The expectation is that pills or injections will be given by a physician; unless this happens, the patients feel that they have not received treatment. Most of these refugees do not wish to talk about trauma or torture experiences initially. On both coasts, more than 50% of a group of Indo-Chinese patients scored high on screening instruments assessing Western depressive symptoms, although none of these patients had sought treatment for emotional distress.

When the patients are able to acknowledge such difficulties, interpreters become crucial in the treatment pattern. At the ICPC, bicultural workers are given ongoing clinical training and consistent, supportive clinical supervision. They are already knowledgeable and empathic with their clients because they are close to the trauma of the patient, having experienced similar incidents themselves. The issues of transference surface regularly in supervision, and the bicultural clinicians have the prerogative of not accepting cases too evocative of personal experiences.

Most of the ICPC patients are seen for two or more years, weekly or bimonthly. Many of them are very poor and need assistance from welfare agencies to obtain services. Often their need is so great that clinical issues are subordinate to requirements for assistance. It is necessary, therefore, for staff to be trained in information and referral skills so that other social services can be made available. Yet another innovation in this clinic is the utilization of self-evaluation. Patients are encouraged to use the Hopkins Symptom checklist and to chart their own progress, a fine antidote to authoritarianism and a boost for self-empowerment, so necessary for victims of torture.

Other Resources in the United States

There are efforts being made by individuals through small, local clinics, staffed primarily by volunteers and supported by private individuals and groups. Most of these clinics specialize in assisting people of particular nationalities or religious groups. One example, in Los Angeles, is the Clinica Monsenor Oscar A. Romero (Oscar Romero, Archbishop of San Salvador, was slain while celebrating mass on March 24, 1980), which offers free care to refugees from Central America, most of whom are undocumented aliens. A nurse, a physician, and a psychologist, all unpaid, work to help the victims of torture. Some monies given by religious groups pay for supplies and medication, but the 200 persons seen in the first month of this clinic's existence soon exhausted these funds (Beyette, 1983). Survival of such independent clinics is tenuous at best without government subvention.

A question that emerges from a discussion of the various models of care for victims of torture is whether there should be torture centers distinctive from other centers, or whether treatment should be integrated into other more general service delivery systems such as hospitals, community mental health clinics, and so forth. Nightingale (1987) hypothesized that isolating victims of torture might stigmatize them. She cautioned against over-medicalizing torture or creating a "science of torturology." The sequelae of torture are not medical illnesses, caused by a germ or genetic condition, but an injury purposefully inflicted on a victim. According to Nightingale, treatment at a special center might suggest to victims that they are people who are labeled and somehow not a part of the mainstream.

Other experts have supported the importance of creating a separate torture center as a symbol, which raises the issue of human rights beyond the clinical issues. Because one of the hypothesized causes for the ubiquity of torture in the world has been the silence enveloping torture activities, these experts agree that founding and supporting a center for the treatment of victims brings the reality of the existence of torture to the consciousness of the communities that establish them. A more telling, if pragmatic, argument has been made by Suedfeld (1988, personal communication), who pointed out that if special rules are necessary for this population (e.g., no white coats or "doctor" titles, inclusion of families, treatment by bilingual co-therapists, self-help groups, and more frequent access to therapists by telephone), mainstreaming this population would appear to pose significant problems.

Treating victims of torture in local small clinics is a third and apparently viable alternative. The Boston ICPC previously described has developed an excellent training, treatment, and research program. A Cambodian Women's Center in New York treats women who have experienced various types of victimization, among them torture and sexual crimes, and has been sufficiently successful to motivate a group of dynamic refugee clinicians and leaders to advocate opening a similar center in Boston. There are some difficulties with smaller clinics, however, for a variety of reasons: uncertainties in funding, finding sufficient supervisory personnel, providing adequate training for bilinguals to enable them to provide services to clients, establishing relationships with traditional community institutions to facilitate referrals of victims in need of services, enlisting community support, and creating an awareness of the clinics and the patient population they serve.

PSYCHOLOGY'S ROLE IN TREATING VICTIMS OF TORTURE

Medicine has been the discipline most often associated with treating victims of torture, but physicians have also been in the role of perpetrators. Psychiatry, specifically, has been implicated in participating in torture activities such as prescribing drugs, committing prisoners to mental wards, and engaging in more subtle forms of mind games. Conversely, psychiatrists have also been active in providing shelters on mental wards for prisoners or escapees who would have been killed in Germany during World War II. More recently, psychiatrists have been active in the treatment of victims of torture. The World Psychiatric Association currently runs treatment centers in Sweden, France, Norway, the Philippines, and Latin America. In Denmark, medical students learn about torture in their medical–legal curriculum. In 1986, the World Health Organization meeting in Holland supported the introduction of material about torture in the curricula for health personnel, which subsequently has been communicated to all the governments in Europe.

Psychologists have been notably absent from the torture arena, both as perpetrators and as treaters (see chapter 7, this volume). Although there have been a few recent investigations of torture (e.g., Gibson & Haritos-Fatouros, 1986; Padilla & Comas-Diaz, 1986), organized psychology has been silent on issues of treatment. Psychologists are absent from the Stover and Nightingale's (1985) list of 34 "Organizations Concerned with Torture and/or Psychiatric Abuse," with the exception of the British Psychological Society, which is listed. In 1976, that Society set up a working group to study abuses of psychology for political purposes, particularly in the Soviet Union and Northern Ireland (Stover & Nightingale, 1985, pp. 284–285).

Psychology has much to offer in addition to a formal declaration on its disapproval of torture. If there is to be a treatment network formed by the Technical Assistance Center, training and supervision must be available to physicians, nurses, social workers, and other professionals as well as bilinguals or cotherapists. Consultation is needed on diagnostic evaluations and research design. Empirical studies comparing the various existing settings that provide assistance to victims of torture would be desirable before decisions are made about funding. Research, training, supervision, consultation, and program evaluation are within the scope of practice of many psychologists. Psychologists could also assist in designing interdisciplinary service delivery systems to provide adequate physical and psychological assistance to victims, and they could systematize the collection of data to assess the effectiveness of the services offered.

REFERENCES

Allodi, F., & Rojas, A. (1985). The health and adaptation of victims of political violence in Latin America. In P. Pichot, P. Berner, R. Wolf, & K. Thau (Eds.), *Psychiatry: The state of the art* (pp. 58–78). New York: Plenum Press.

Anonymous. (1985). Social work in the sanctuary movement for Central American refugees. *Social Work, 30*, 74–76.

Beyette, B. (1983, August 9). A free health clinic for Latino refugees. *Los Angeles Times*, pp. 1, 4, 5.

Chester, B. (1987, Winter). Center for victims of torture: Salvaging lives. *Northwest Report*, 24–26.

Egli, E. (1987). *The role of bilingual workers without professional mental health training for refugee services in mental health*. Unpublished manuscript, University of Minnesota, Minneapolis,

Gibson, J., & Haritos-Fatouros, M. (1986, November). The education of a torturer. *Psychology Today*, pp. 50–52, 56–58.

Griffin, E., (1984, April). Reagan runs into the religious left. *These Times*, pp. 11–17.

Horowitz, M. (1984). Stress and the mechanisms of defense. In H. Goldman (Ed.), *Review of general psychiatry*. Los Altos, CA: Lange Medical Publications.

Immigration and Nationality Act, §010(a) (42), as amended by the Refugee Act of 1980.

Kline, F., Acosta, F., Austin, W., & Johnson, R. (1980). The misunderstood Spanish-speaking patient. *American Journal of Psychiatry, 137*, 1530–1533.

Leo, J. (1985, February 13). Salvaging victims of torture. *Time*, p. 34.

Lunde, I. (1982, August). Mental sequelae to torture. [*Manedschrift for praktish laegegerning*], 1–14.

MacHovec, F. (1985). Treatment variables and the use of hypnosis in the brief therapy of post-traumatic stress disorders. *International Journal of Clinical and Experimental Hypnosis, 33*, 6–14.

Manuel, A. (1984, July 15). Don't help Guatemala. *New York Times News Service*.

Mollica, R. (1987, June 2). *Indo-Chinese Psychiatry Clinic*. Paper presented at the meeting of the Conference on Treating Victims of Torture. Minneapolis, MN.

Nightingale, E. (1987, June 2). *Recognition of the problems of torture*. Paper presented at the meeting of the Conference on Treating Victims of Torture. Minneapolis, MN.

Padilla, A., & Comas-Diaz, L. (1986, November). A state of fear. *Psychology Today*, pp. 60–65.

Pope, K., & Bouhoutsos, J. (1986). *Sexual intimacy between therapists and patients*. New York: Praeger-Greenwood.

Somnier, F., & Genefke, K. (1986). Psychotherapy for victims of torture. *British Journal of Psychiatry, 149*, 323–329.

Sonne, J., Meyer, C., Borys, D., & Marshall, V. (1985). Clients' reactions to sexual intimacy in therapy. *American Journal of Orthopsychiatry, 55*, 183–189.

Stover, E., & Nightingale, E. O. (Eds.) (1985). *The breaking of minds and bodies*. New York: Freeman.

Svendsen, G. (1985, November). When dealing with torture victims, social work involves the entire family. *Socialraedgiveren*, pp. 1–6.

U.S. Department of Health and Human Services, Office of Refugee Resettlement Services. (January 31, 1985). Report to Congress.

U.S. Immigration and Naturalization Service. (1985). *U.S. Immigration and Naturalization Yearbook* (Document no. 164-513/50787). Washington, DC: U.S. Government Printing Office.

Walker, L. (1984). Violence against women: Implications for mental health policy. In L. Walker (Ed.), *Women and mental health policy* (pp. 197–206). Beverly Hills: Sage.

Westermeyer, J. (1987). Clinical considerations in cross cultural diagnosis. *Hospital and Community Psychiatry, 38*, 160–168.

10

Dealing with the Unbearable: Reactions of Therapists and Therapeutic Institutions to Survivors of Torture

---

Enrique Bustos

During the last several decades there has been a perceived increase in the use of torture in the world because of greater publicity. New forms of mass communication, with their increasing immediacy, distribution, and internationalization, have led to wider awareness and more immediate contact with the occurrence and consequences of torture. There may also have been a real increase in the use of torture, as a result of dictatorial governments and the sharpening of the contradictions inherent in societies in crisis. International and civil wars and occupations by foreign troops have led to many acts of persecution committed against civilian populations.

In the face of constantly recurring evidence, it is difficult to deny the contemporary fact of torture or to relegate it to the past such as can be done with Nazi atrocities or the medieval Inquisition. Any such evasion is contradicted by the presence of living beings marked by extreme traumatization, by physical and psychological scars, and by memories of persecution, imprisonment, and torture. These people live with the permanent intrusion of painful memories; their emotional world is indelibly marked by the torture and imprisonment they have suffered.

Scientific and clinical study has led to a more profound understanding of the torture phenomenon. Intense professional discussions have been generated as to the definition of torture, its nosological classification, and its effects on the individual, the family, and society. There is consensus that contemporary torture is part of a strategy of domination by an apparatus that uses it systematically to enhance control in the face of crisis. Torture is used to obtain information, to punish, and to physically and psychologically annihilate. Opposition in the rest of society is intimidated, terrorized, and paralyzed. In political terms, torture is the

I am grateful for the help of Carmen E. Ramirez, Department of Psychiatry, University of British Columbia Health Sciences Centre Hospital (Shaughnessy Site), in translating some of the quotations in this chapter from their original Spanish.

most acutely repressive stage of social confrontation, and it demonstrates at a microsocial level the drama and profundity of the relationship between those who hold power and those who are oppressed.

This institutionalized phenomenon corrodes the whole society. It intensifies the disjointedness of daily social interaction to such a degree that because of fear, silence, the breaking of bonds of solidarity, and the distortion of reality, human relationships come to reflect the values of totalitarian power. All of these complex elements become internalized within tortured people, and will be critical determinants of the character of the institutional atmosphere and the problems of treating such people.

The purpose of this chapter is to encourage the discussion of aspects of therapeutic work with tortured people that until now have not been deeply analyzed. These include the risks involved for the institution, as well as the emotional consequences for therapists who confront what Jean Paul Sartre called "the plague of our era." In order to do this, I present examples from my own professional experience. The supervision of therapists and the interchange and cooperation with other institutions and groups working with tortured refugees in the Scandinavian countries have given me the opportunity to observe parallel or alternative processes to those I have experienced myself. The possibility of sharing and interchanging opinions with professionals from Europe, Latin America, and North America has also made possible the comparison of my analysis with different realities.

THE ROLE OF THERAPEUTIC INSTITUTIONS

The need to help tortured people has resulted in the formation of various forms of therapeutic attention. A variety of initiatives, working for both preventive and curative action, have emerged in affected countries (including countries of refuge). Specialized assistance is not generally obtainable from the traditional health system, but there are a small number of institutions that specifically offer medical, psychological, or psychosocial assistance to the tortured. It is important to understand that the great majority of these institutions—many of which exist under precarious conditions—are shaped by circumstances specific to each country. They are further influenced by the nature of the groups whose activity and support make possible the formation and starting out of such institutions. Generally, the initiative necessary for the sustenance of these institutions is provided by a leader or small group of leaders. This leadership takes various forms, according to the focus and origin of the work. In some cases it is political, in other professional; but it always possesses an immanent force attracting other forces and interests that allow the establishment and functioning of the institution.

Conflicts and functional problems within psychiatric institutions have been studied in relation to group processes (including leadership) as well as to the intrapsychic processes of individuals within institutions. Menzies (1970) has written a classic work about a health organizational system. In that system, the development of social structures served the staff as a defense against anxiety stemming from stress and dissatisfaction that, in turn, derived from certain work routines and forms of decision making. Jorstad (1984) has shown how problems related to authority and leadership influence all the members of an institution. He postulated that psychiatric institutions may suffer unusually high rates of group regression and pathological phenomena at the leadership level because of daily contact with psychic pathologies. Group regression, a group's acting out that uses its capacity and energies in the pursuit of repetitive, regressive goals instead of verbalizing the conflicts and pursuing the appropriate group task makes the organizational problems of this type of institution especially acute. Kernberg (1980) has pointed out how important leadership is for the organizational problems that derive from institutional regression. The presence of latent or manifest pathological structures among administrative leaders or those who are responsible for the organization poses specific problems at both organizational and group levels.

Torture involves bodily and psychic suffering induced by means of brutal or refined techniques. This produces a series of immediate psychic reactions and physical consequences in the individual. Many psychological (and in many cases, physical) problems arise subsequently. These problems frequently preclude the development of a normal life and will in many cases require that survivors receive specialized assistance. By means of psychological and psychotherapeutic intervention it is possible to handle these traumatic experiences, to support adaptive mechanisms, and to remove the obstacles that hamper good functioning. Variables that determine the success of the intervention include the following: the psychic and physical aftereffects directly related to torture (among them the degree of psychosomatization and brain damage), the type of trauma experienced, the degree of psychopathology developed, the degree of motivation to adapt, the personality structure, and the repertoire of defensive maneuvers. All of this provides the framework for therapeutic intervention. This framework should be complemented by the analysis of family dynamics, the social network (especially pertaining to work or study), the degree of political awareness, and the occurrence of other traumatic experiences. If the treatment takes place in exile, one must also consider its different phases and complications and the importance of the eventual return as an existential moment.

PROBLEMS ENCOUNTERED BY THERAPISTS AND INSTITUTIONS

Professionals who deal with survivors of torture come into constant and intense contact with some of the most primitive elements of human behavior. They may encounter absolute power, maximum aberration, unbearable pain, uncontrollable sorrow, bottomless helplessness, and atavistic rage daily. They must deal with profound depression, anxiety, and aggressiveness far beyond classical syndromes (Barudy & Vieytes, 1985; Bustos, 1987; Mollica, 1987; Roche, 1987; Schlapobersky & Bamber, 1987). The intensity and extreme demands of institutional work with tortured people may easily lead one to feel isolated from reality.

Such demands may also create an institutional climate of anxiety and threat and, in response, the emergence of defensive reactions. The pathological reactions of the patient, transmitted through the individual therapist, are projected onto the organization. Thus, parallel situations arise at the personal, group, and institutional levels. The development of conflict within the institution leads to the use of identificatory and regressive processes. The patients' intrapsychic conflicts, interacting with tensions among the staff and within the social system of the institution, result in the distortion of interpersonal relations. This activates primitive defensive maneuvers, in the context of internalized object relations as well as in the existing social system. The need to establish a defense against anxiety and the search for security may stimulate easily detectable forms of group regression. Regression then leads to conflicts over work and power and to the development of bureau- cratic systems that help to express and ward off group anxiety.

Control and Power

The leader's role and the group's sense of loyalty and belonging attain vital importance in institutions that treat tortured people. Institutional dynamics develop a dominant ideology. The development of a social system of defense (Menzies, 1970) will determine the structure, culture, and manner of functioning of the institution, also creating the scope for specific dynamic group processes. These group processes shape the search for solutions within the parameters of the team's functions, available resources, administrative structure, and leadership capacity.

Power, a fundamental element in any understanding of the relationship between the torturer and the tortured, is a central aspect of all institutions. So is the possi- bility that it will be abused. The majority of conflicts have shown that attributing to oneself an absolute truth, and then using this truth to justify one's actions, is a phenomenon that is present not only in the torture chamber. Pathological tenden- cies can easily find expression within this pattern. For example, depending on the nature of the leadership—autocratic, democratic, or laissez faire (Lewin, 1939/ 1948, 1943/1948)—coercive, punitive, or rewarding forms may appear in the guise of humanitarian and scientific concerns. This disguise is accepted by a pro- cess of collective rationalization. At this point, the institution may be only a step away from starting to coerce its members into submission. A study of the function- ing of a European institution revealed that, ironically, a large part of the institu- tion's psychological resources and a far from negligible part of its economic re- sources are invested in disputes about power within the institution and vis-à-vis its governing body.

Bion (1958), in his classic work on groups, postulated that every human group constantly shows two states, with one dominating the other at any given time. One is the work group state, when the group is working toward its explicit goals. The other is the state called basic assumptions. Within the latter there are three possi- bilities (dependence, pairing, and fight or flight), determined by emotional ten- sions among the group members. The work group state may be relegated to a secondary position, pushed by the basic assumptions that allow the weakening of primary organizational goals and their displacement by other (secondary) goals. These secondary goals do not focus on the success, stability, or growth of the institution but on resolving emotional tensions experienced by the group. Empha- sis on security measures (security checks upon entering the institution, alarm sys- tems, or people responsible for keys); an obsessive insistence on rules and rigid ways of functioning; manipulation and control of information; covert and overt persecution of dissidents and favoring loyal staff members; fear that intellectual contributions might be appropriated or used improperly; and so forth, are some examples of goals that are recognizable in other environments, such as prisons, concentration camps, and life in a dictatorship.

A clear demonstration of this was a conflict that occurred at the end of 1986 at a famous international center for the treatment of torture victims—an institution with which I was especially familiar. The original goals of the institution were ignored during the adoption of rigid treatment forms and the development of an authoritarian structure. An authoritarian and contemptuous manner replaced constructive debate and led to the use of Machiavellian techniques to allay criticism among the staff. Conflicts concerning the care offered to tortured people appeared at all levels. Emotional tensions that had accumulated over a long period came to light, astonishing the protagonists themselves by the intensity and strength with which they were expressed. Accusations of unethical and even criminal misbehavior were made, which eventually led the majority of professionals involved in treatment and documentation to leave the institution.

To my knowledge, conflict with governing boards and disillusionment with the operational aspects of the work have occurred in several institutions working with survivors of torture and repression in different parts of the world and operating under quite different circumstances. For example, in the single year 1987 a large number of the individuals fundamental to clinical and theoretical work left a renowned Latin American institution. The reasons for this were the lack of channels for constructive debate and a climate of oppression and control by the leadership over the medical and psychiatric personnel.

Different forms of these problems flourish, exacerbated by countertransference. When these phenomena are brought to light, they are explained away by elaborated intellectualization or rationalization. The institution's conflict-reduction objectives acquire greater importance than the primary objective of treating tortured people. This change can lead to neglect, exploitation, and abuse of the patients. The intensification of individual psychopathologies and the existence of real conflicts with the surrounding reality (other individuals or institutions) endanger the search for collective action to overcome problems. Human diversity and complexity are interpreted in absolute terms. The internalization of the relation between tormentor and tortured leads to the perception of the world in terms of Good and Evil, They and We. This dichotomization is encouraged by regression, which stimulates a paralyzing depression or splitting and paranoid ways of analyzing reality.

Splitting and Paranoia

A clear example of splitting appears in one of the few published reports on one of these institutions. Westin (1988, p. 52) wrote:

> *The Center has as its counterpart, ideologically, politically and as concerns treatment, the torture centers which . . . exist almost everywhere in the world. It is adverse that the Center only enters into indirect contact—by means of the patients—but an adversary against which the identity of the Center must be contrasted. I am of the opinion that one must speak of the* bad *clinic and the* good *clinic. In both, people are "treated," in both, one looks for knowledge about the effects of the treatment. But they are necessarily opposites.*

Paranoid attitudes may be found in a kind of conspiratorial functioning by individuals and by institutions facing other individuals and institutions. Participants in various international and European meetings on torture and political oppression have observed the primitiveness and intensity of the dissensions and debates at these meetings. They originate not only in ideological, professional, or personal disagreements but also in conspiratory attitudes and behaviors. Some contributions are designed to isolate, silence, or eliminate opponents from legitimacy in this social universe. The arguments used to justify these actions are generally based on differences in the ideological-human conceptions represented in the debate, and they deny the possibility of pathologically regressive, paranoid, or dissociative origins of the conflict.

Concrete examples are difficult to document because the phenomenon involves a large number of subtle factors. However, I may be able to illustrate by describing what occurred at one of the most recent European conferences, sponsored by an international organization in 1988. In preparation for the conference, one institution took steps that led to its almost total control over the program, choice of participants, and evaluation of papers at the meeting. By presenting an overwhelming number of papers, this group attempted to decrease the time available for other contributions, discussion, and debate during the two days dedicated to the principal theme of the conference. This was justified by the controlling group's claim to possess the "correct line" as to the form and meaning of therapeutic work with torture victims.

Institutional Breakdown

Ultimately, institutional psychopathology can lead to the abandonment of primary goals, nonfulfillment of functions, and demoralization. Deterioration of the work situation mobilizes what Bion called "basic assumptions," aggravating the latent pathologies of the leader and staff. Members of the staff become disillusioned, often because of unrealistic expectations of oneself and the patient. A gap between the idealized and the actual interventions leads to more conflicts with the system.

Of course, not every conflict involving human relations implies a worsening of social relations and structures. Internal conflict concerning the institution's goals and interests can be functional if it does not contradict the institution's basic premises. However, even productive conflicts tend to be suppressed in groups that have a high level of interaction and personal involvement (Coser, 1956; Janis, 1972), like the organizations discussed in this chapter. The direct consequence of such suppression is a demand for group unity, with no tolerance for internal struggles deriving from external conflicts (latent or evident). Internal conflict leads to the dissident's expulsion or withdrawal or to a (spiritual or actual) breaking up of the group. This situation is easily recognizable to people inside institutions who work with tortured people.

PATHOLOGICAL REACTIONS AMONG THERAPISTS

The power relationship (dominant–dominated), the leadership function (direction), regressive characteristics, and estrangement from reality lead to forms of functioning that violate common sense and reasonableness. The experience of being imprisoned and tortured is characterized by rules and restrictions and the agonizing wait for voices and footsteps that can culminate in the metallic sound of the key in the lock that may mean release or relief, but most often signals the start of a new episode of stress and real anxiety concerning an immediate threat to personal integrity. This experience is internalized and projected onto the therapist through identification. As identification progresses, the therapist in turn internalizes this material, taking on the roles of both the tortured person (in submission) and the torturer (in holding power). Regressive and pathological introjections lead to global changes in the representation of the self of the psychotherapist. If the therapist cannot go back to the former representation, a distorted internal world is thus reelaborated in which character structure influences the individual's interpersonal field. The pathological introject is further projected onto the institution and its personnel. Intensifying the latent psychopathologies of the staff, interpersonal and intrapsychic processes aroused during torture are reproduced symbolically.

One way of analyzing these phenomena is to assume that the high level of anxiety involved in working with tortured refugees may stimulate repression, splitting, projection, and denial. These defense mechanisms, useful during the traumatic experiences of torture and imprisonment, become manifested again during the course of therapy. Transference and countertransference, along with the projective identification that takes place during therapy, lead to the projection of torture-related problems onto the institutional frame, transforming the intrapsychic perspective into an interpersonal one.

Burnout

Somatization and stress among the staff are intensified by the demands of the system. The often intense work leads to emotional strain, and the repetition of this strain leads to emotional exhaustion. The relation between these pathogenic aspects of the work and the nature of how power is exercised will be decisive for the occurrence of burnout. *Burnout* is a term used by Freudenberger (1974, 1975) to denote a state of physical and emotional depletion resulting from conditions of work. The burnout syndrome is characterized by attitudinal, emotional, and physical components. Some of the major symptoms are depression, anxiety, irritability, inflexibility, stubbornness, lack of self-esteem, and feelings of powerlessness, combined with physical manifestations such as general fatigue, lack of appetite, sleeping disorders, and persistent colds.

Many studies of the phenomenon have focused on the psychological capabilities and vulnerabilities of individuals in stressful work situations. This clinical approach to burnout has been supplemented by the empirical approach (Maslach, 1976, 1978; Pines & Maslach, 1978), a social psychological perspective with a focus on the relation between environmental and individual factors. Many researchers use the term burnout only to refer to people working in the helping professions. Farber (1983) argued that such a limitation acknowledges the unique pressures of using oneself as the tool in face-to-face work with needy, demanding, and often troubled clients.

Breakdown

Farber (1983) contended that in a psychotherapeutic career, personality traits such as grandiosity or emotional distancing and personality breakdowns such as psychosis and suicide can be attributed primarily to the stresses of therapeutic role. A more psychoanalytic point of view is that many therapists are very sensitive or neurotic individuals to begin with. This sensitivity to inner states and feelings can be enlightening and fulfilling, but it can also lead to unbearable personal stress in the therapeutic encounter with profound human suffering.

A related viewpoint is found in Bennet's (1979) discussion of the "wounded healer." Woundedness implies vulnerability, the possibility of being wounded, and the experience of suffering. Bozzolo wrote: "A psychic pain appears, generated by empathy in the face of the knowledge of the suffering to which other human beings have found themselves subjected" (1983, p. 75, my translation). From this perspective, Comas-Diaz and Padilla (1988) have recently analyzed the case of Chilean therapists working at the depths of human abjection, through denial, helplessness, and despair. The authors postulated that by experiencing suffering and being wounded as they face the terror and trauma of their patients, the therapists achieve new insights into the human condition. The experience of helplessness and despair should develop genuine empathy between the wounded healer and the patient and should therefore facilitate the process of helping patients deal with their own helplessness and despair.

Misperceptions of Torture and the Tortured

The political framework of torture, in which the dialectic of domination and defenselessness reflects the relationship between the holders of power and those who are repressed by it, should not veil the fundamental goal of psychotherapeutic intervention. That goal is to establish an atmosphere that makes possible psychic repair, reduction of symptomatology, and the ability to revive existential projects. As two Chilean therapists said:

> The therapist does not fear the establishment of a personal and close relationship. It is inappropriate here to be the receptacle or the screen for projections and childhood anxieties. On the contrary, only by being a real person is one capable of empathizing with so much pain and thus, it becomes possible to offer the help necessary to reconstruct life and overcome defeat. (Pollarolo & Morales, 1984, p. 191, my translation)

Similarly,

> One of the fundamental elements which determines the character of the therapeutic process in persons who have been subjected to torture is exactly the fact that the therapist does not fight against the horror which the patient withholds. . . . This does not have to do with the therapeutic statement being transformed into a political statement, it has to do with a relationship in which the psychotherapist imposes neither a solution nor an orientation. Instead, a dialogue of active listening is established in which the therapist accompanies the patient in discovery and reflection. It is of course true that the therapist reflects and influences the progress of the patient, but he will nonetheless maintain therapeutic neutrality and accept the patient's words. (Vieytes & Barudy, 1985, p. 69, my translation)

In certain sectors of the psychotherapeutic field, there is a tendency to overpoliticize the torture phenomenon. Individuals who have been subjected to torture are seen as heroes who fought in the torture chamber without yielding even in the face of overwhelming power and accepted the risk of death. Such a death is perceived as liberating the prisoner and ultimately defeating the torturer. Conversely, any yielding is interpreted as conscious submission to and collaboration with the repressive apparatus. For example, at a Latin American conference that I attended in

1985, some participants asserted that political prisoners come out of the torture chamber strengthened. The move from political language and analysis to the psychotherapeutic arena may also be formulated in remarks such as "Those who were broken, were weak" (meaning those who did not withstand torture and who gave information to or collaborated with the captors). Another version of this perspective is the dogmatic insistence on the part of certain European professionals that every tortured person has a strong personality and can, with help, come to function again with all the energy and strength that was available prior to the torture experience.

Such statements should be seen as an attempt to deny the horror, wretchedness, and intolerability of torture. Denial may be necessary to preserve intact an image that people can withstand inhumane practices aimed at this annihilation. Any observer, including the therapist, suffers feelings of impotence and limited ability to consider such an emotional hell. In defense, the observer may place too much importance on the political dimensions of the conflict that takes place in the torture chamber. But one must try to understand the emotional and experiential world of the patient, with his or her own individual present and past psychological and physical answers.

The stress-inducing knowledge that the torturers are omnipotent and the tortured are physically and psychologically defenseless leads to the assertion of a role reversal, endowing the tortured with omnipotence and demanding total resistance consistent with an internal moral code. This occurs at the same time as the human condition of the torturer is deprecated. Disguising the situation in this way leads paradoxically to the negation of the political content of torture as a conscious, systematic practice with defined goals, carried out and suffered by human beings who participate in a value system whereby extreme means are used in defense of its interests. The psychotherapeutic relationship is converted into a political one, a relationship of solidarity and combative partnership with no room for reparative processes.

Some workers in the field are well aware of this point. Bozzolo, in describing the activities of the Team for Psychological Aid to the Mothers of Plaza de Mayo in Argentina, wrote:

> Feelings of another kind sometimes appear, ones that may impair our effectiveness and that must be handled very cautiously. An example is the profound admiration generated in us therapists by the strength and valor of some of the family members [of the disappeared] and the way in which they continually enriched themselves psychologically during their struggle. In order to be able to function and to help us think, we had to protect our capacity for reflection from the "idealization" that the mothers, by their capacity for struggle, may generate in us. (Bozzolo, 1983, p. 76, my translation)

At the opposite end from the idealization of resistant, and rejection of defeated torture victims is the isolation of torture as a phenomenon, separating it from its political and social context in supposed professional neutrality. The individual is reified, transformed into a diagnostic entity recognizable by syndromes and illnesses. Allodi (1982) and Allodi et al. (1985) have advocated the use of the term *torture syndrome* to refer to the cluster of symptoms and signs that tortured people exhibit. Rasmussen and Lunde (1980) have suggested that future research may establish a basis for doing so (see also chapter 2, this volume). Once more, a new syndrome. This permits the incorporation of the reified individual into theoretical schemes that will determine what attention he or she will receive in the future. The presumed syndrome becomes an important tool for research and clinical work.

Experience thus becomes a diagnosis, and the mere fact of having lived through the experience of torture suggests the necessity of an established model of treatment (and with it, stigmatization). The subject is deprived of substantive interiority and is stripped of the purposefulness, reflection, and intentionality demonstrated by his or her conflicts, problems, and sorrows that call for psychotherapeutic aid. A purely symptom-oriented solution, based on a syndromic classification or nosology, ignores the humanity of the patient.

The psychodynamics of trauma must be seen to be, as they are, directly related to the individual's capacity to organize and integrate intrapsychic processes in relation to the external traumatic event (Krystal, 1971). Unconscious thoughts, wishes, and needs, together with a reactivation of conflicts and a mobilization of primitive defense mechanisms, play important roles in the emergence of symptomatology. Predisposition and vulnerability are also significant. Symptomatology should be interpreted in relation to this background, and particularly in relation to changes in psychological functioning. When evaluating what is traumatic for a specific individual, it is of the utmost importance to take into account that person's affective tolerance and affective maturity (desomatization, verbalization, and differentiation) in relation to various conditions of pain, depression, and anxiety (Krystal, 1977, 1978).

Transference and Identification

Transferential and countertransferential aspects of therapeutic contact should be strongly emphasized in working with tortured people, as they are vital to the progress of the treatment. The experience of torture leads to an extreme use of defensive forms elicited by the subject's need to avoid awareness of the intolerable affects, principally depression, guilt, shame, and helplessness. The internal world is defended against a traumatically experienced relationship, transformed into a pathological introject. Splitting or denial prevents the formation of accurate representational memories. The tortured need to deny a part of their self; they use amnesia and numbing to prevent the repetitive and intrusive flooding of painful memories and to block affects related to the introjected object.

Because of the intensity of the trauma, the understanding of regression as a therapeutic tool is also important. In the therapeutic setting, regressive experiences arising from contact with painful internal objects stimulate intense affective transferences and projective identifications. My professional experience in therapy and supervision is that these transferences and identifications are commonly returned to the patient as projective counteridentification (Grindberg, 1962) or lead to mutual projective identification (Langs, 1978).

In *projective counteridentification*, the therapist avoids fighting against the already incorporated introjects, externalizing them by means of projection and thus creating new pathological introjects in the internal world of the subject. As an example, the therapist refuses to accept what is already incorporated (commonly a nonverbal transference containing affect that is unbearable to the patient), and verbalizes his or her own affect inadequately by means of a premature and inadequate interpretation of the transferential situation. In this way the therapist reestablishes the unity of a terrifying and dangerous internal world for the patient, satisfying in turn the narcissistic necessity to preserve interpretive ability.

Psychotherapist *A* illustrated this type of functioning. At the time of the consultation, she had been working for more than a year with several patients who had been tortured. During this time she treated seven patients; five of these contacts were abruptly broken off. In the other two, she felt that the communication was incomplete and that the therapy was not progressing. In consultation, the model of functioning used by *A* came to light.

In therapy, she verbalized her own fantasies as to the consequences of the type of torture used and the possible emotions awakened in the patient. This is something that she appreciated and stimulated because it produced in her a feeling of professional satisfaction to have established a deep empathic contact with the patient. Symptomatically, *A* consulted on cases that were continuing, but not on those that were interrupted. The two patients who continued with her lacked the symbolic and associative capacity for an interpretive interchange and were therefore able to keep themselves intact when faced with the threats caused by transferential, nonverbal situations internalized by the therapist. *A* said that she felt the pain of the torture in her own body and that her resulting interpretations were modeled by her empathic capacity. The combination of physical problems caused by the inability to make progress in the two ongoing therapies and the bodily and emotional reactions of the patients who have stopped coming made it possible for *A* to overcome a dissociative process, integrating her therapeutic experiences with the needs of her internal world.

Most therapeutic transactions should be conceptualized in terms of introjective-projective regressive relatedness, fostering the development of intense affective transferences. Therapists' denial of the effective action of their own unconscious defense maneuvers against unpleasurable affects and perceptions is an ever-present risk in this area. The satisfaction of sadistic or masochistic needs, the Florence Nightingale syndrome, sharing the distress with the patient, and so forth, are typical problems arising from such denial.

A more elaborate form of projective counteridentification, used in at least one institution, is the use of illustrations containing torture scenes. The stated purpose is to attain a cognitive elaboration of the trauma by means of a supposed verbalization of its objective aspects. Therapist *B*'s enthusiasm and energy when using this type of psychotherapeutic instrument may be understood by looking at her reason for using it: "Thus they cannot avoid speaking of the torture, they must confront the fact that they were tortured and cry about it." This reasoning avoids the development of unverbalizable transferential situations. However, there is a failure to appreciate the importance of a maternal transference (Krystal, 1988) that refers to the primary object-representation with the capacity to incorporate and hold what for the patient is unbearable. Instead of accepting the projective demand with its burden of preverbalized anxiety, both *A* and *B* return it, reloaded with therapist's specific affects (and the penetrating verbal attack or the brutal scenes shown to the patient, evoking a flood of intrusive images), through a polarized communication that recreates the relationship of victim and oppressor.

Mutual projective identification stimulates pathological modes of relatedness and communication on the part of the therapist. These can be at the self-object or symbiotic level, where each party supports and sustains the defensive activity of the other. Fears of being alone, of being abandoned and motherless in the regressive situation, are fostered by the fear of helplessness and annihilation experienced during torture. Separation anxiety in turn stimulates infantile symbiotic fantasies as an aid against the fear of the all-aloneness, of being solitary in the universe. Depending on the interpersonal situation, complementary modes of communication develop. These usually have a sadistic–masochistic or passive–dependent content.

This is commonly found during diagnosis, when the necessity of establishing the specific characteristics of the trauma hinders the rejection of the communication that is offered. The sadistic penetration of the therapist into the internal world of the subject is justified by the need to know about the forms of torture applied against the patient, in the most explicit way and including the most recondite details. Mutual projective identification is stimulated by the extremely detailed descriptions that satisfy the patient's masochism. This situation (and the inverse, with the roles reversed) requires complementary emotional manifestations in the therapist and the patient, as cathartic reactions in the patient or sharing the distress with the patient in the therapist.

Therapist C told me of the disagreeable sensation of working with a colleague for whom the main interest in conducting and presenting diagnostic interviews was to scrutinize and describe in detail the most violent, shocking, and inhuman aspects of the tortured individual's experiences. The most essential aspect of the initial contact became the extraction of complete descriptions of this type of material from the patient. In general, there seems to be a tendency during the diagnostic process to establish parallels between the form, duration, and refinement or brutality of the torture that was used and the presenting symptomatology. This link in turn determines the form of treatment offered. There appears to be no recognition that the way in which the individual interprets his or her experiences is what determines emotional reactions to events.

The "conspiracy of silence" (Danieli, 1980; Krystal, 1971) can be viewed as a contrasting example of miscommunication. This phenomenon has been studied in depth in relation to Holocaust survivors. The therapist and the patient, symbiotically attached, either completely or to a great extent avoid discussing material connected to the experienced trauma. This may occur because of the incomprehensible, unbelievable, or unbearable nature of the traumatic situation. An interactive process of emotional numbing takes place. The reprojected objects, carrying also the dread and horror of the internal world of the therapist, serve the goal of reinforcing a very factual, affectless manner of relating in the patient.

X, a man in his 30s, initiated treatment because of back pains that had tormented him daily for seven years. The first sessions developed information about how X was brutally tortured for six months and then imprisoned for five years. X suffered from terrible backaches and headaches, but several examinations had found no physical causes. The problems that X presented during the early sessions were directly related to the physical pain and the practical problems that this posed for him. Parallel to sessions with me, X also had physiotherapy twice a week; during the entire first year of therapy I found myself involved in the implications of the physiotherapy: the assessment of his pain, how severe it was compared to earlier sessions, and so forth. Emotions and psychological content emerge only in relation to being in exile. Incapable of confronting the psychological content of X's horrifying experiences, I was for a long time a prisoner of this mutual projective identification. A discussion with a colleague finally led to working through the countertransference during supervision, which liberated the therapy from the fixation on somatic factors.

The indiscriminate use of *testimony*, a therapeutic procedure developed in Chile to confront the consequences of repression at the level of the general population, may also be categorized as mutual projective identification. This technique involves using the first consultations to record in detail what happened to the patient in connection with arrest, torture, or suffering brought about by political repression. "Afterward when the tape is put into writing, the testimony acts as a sort of 'memory' that can be shared, reviewed, rewritten, and analyzed at any time by therapist and patient" (Cienfuegos & Monelli, 1983, p. 49). Lira and Weinstein recognized the importance of the tape recorder as an inanimate object that offers the patient the certainty that what is told is faithfully preserved. The suffering can thus be communicated time and time again. "This intermediary, technologically efficient as a tape recorder is, contributes to the containment of both the patient's and the therapist's feelings, permitting the development of a countertransference that can be evaluated" (Lira & Weinstein, 1984, p. 34, my translation). However, the same authors remind us that "the possibility of tolerating this brutal and persecutory internal world is initiated by the fact that someone else has been able to contain it" (p. 31, my translation). The use of testimony in the therapeutic process may easily be transformed into a countertransferential reaction if the underlying reasons are "the therapist's own resistances linked to the fantasy of letting oneself be invaded by the patient's anxiety and to losing control in strife over what is experienced and expressed" (Lira, Weinstein, & Kovalskys, 1987, p. 331, my translation).

Countertransference

Interventions that tend to satisfy the psychotherapist's unconscious needs lead to countertransference, a situation in which the therapist is incapable of maintaining the limits of the therapy and of working with the projections of the patient's psychic world. Racker (1968) differentiated between *direct countertransference* (directed toward the patient) and *indirect countertransference* (toward colleagues, supervisors, etc.). Direct countertransference can include *concordant identification* (with liked aspects of the patient's psyche) and *complementary identification* (with unwanted aspects). Multiple forms of countertransference may be encountered in therapeutic work with tortured people. Some of them have a more iatrogenic character than others and are therefore emphasized in this chapter.

Being overwhelmed by the incomparably gruesome experiences of the tortured provokes a reaction. The therapist sees the therapeutic setting as an arena of defiance that fosters the use of warding off or disarming techniques. In the supervision session, the therapist rationalizes about how difficult it is to achieve an optimal combination of empathy for and distance from the patient. These countertransferential reactions lead to manipulative attitudes on the part of the therapist, attitudes that renew a feeling of emotional abuse in the tortured person.

For example, *Y* initiated her therapy with me after a short (2-month) period of therapy with another therapist, who was forced to interrupt treatment for personal reasons. Because this occurred within an institutional setting, I had access to the patient's file. The first sessions served to establish contact and obtain more information. *Y* had many worries concerning the therapeutic situation, which, added to the information previously obtained about her experiences, created discomfort as each appointment approached. Faced with the consequent tale of refined forms of psychological and sexual torture to which she had been subjected, I began to anticipate prior to each session the uncomfortable and threatening situations that *Y* might bring with her. Her excessive demands, system of values, and manipulative interactions made it difficult for me to achieve a warm and accepting atmosphere. At the same time, the way in which I tried to liberate myself from the pressure exerted by the countertransferential relationship can be seen clearly in my supporting *Y*'s pleas that I would intervene to help her in dealing with social and medical institutions.

Clearly, the importance of the physical aftereffects and the degree of psychosomatization in tortured people is high; but a form of direct concordant countertransference overemphasizes these somatic complaints. This permits the blocking of the central goal of the therapeutic intervention, the elaboration of the psychic trauma. The fact that the use of torture inflicts bodily pain and is itself language-destroying (Scarry, 1985) leads one to see statements concerning somatic aftereffects as a priority.

The physical act of torture, with the two components of infliction and suffering, has a counterpart in the verbal acts of question and answer. Intense physical pain destroys a person's self and world and hampers verbal communication on psychological topics. The patient binds him- or herself to physical pain to be able to relate psychologically to the therapist. Communication in the therapeutic setting must therefore follow a model whereby the consequences of the verbal act in torture and its psychological and existential consequences return to the subject's self and world. The therapist may react with superficiality and open or hidden hostility against the difficulty of expressing the psychic content of the internalized traumatic experience. This emphasis conceals the therapist's fear of becoming immersed in an intolerably anxiety-provoking psychic world where distress has obliterated all other psychological content.

Dealing with the sequelae of sexual torture evokes strong possibilities of countertransference. Agger (1986, in press) distinguished between sexual and other forms of torture. In sexual torture, physical and verbal violence interweave dynamically with the psychosexuality of the tortured and the torturer. This unleashes an ambiguity, containing libidinous and aggressive elements both in the torturer and in the tortured. In subsequent therapy, psychological voyeurism may be induced by the dramatic sexually and aggressively charged nature of sexual torture. The satisfaction obtained from the communication of a traumatic sexual experience, with its libidinous or aggressive content, may unleash in the therapist a repetitive necessity to hear. Primitive elements of perverse sexuality are reactivated countertransferentially by the socially determined, the abnormal, and the forbidden in the traumatic sexual experience (Bustos, in press).

The humiliating, degrading, abnormal, and forbidden aspects of traumatic sexual experiences may be illustrated in the following sadistic variation of sexual torture.

> *At one point, he feels them lifting him, carrying him down the hall to another place. They order him to undress and throw him on an old cot and one says: "Hey, I'm 'The German.'" The prisoner hears men and women yelling. "The German" tries to push a tube into his anus. Another voice says to leave him alone, and addressing the prisoner, says: "You see, I'm 'The Galician' and I saved you from having this guy tear you apart by putting the pipe into you."*

They then spreadeagle him, naked, and tie him down with pieces of leather. "The Galician" orders him to talk, while proceeding to apply electric shock to his armpits, damaging the muscles where he even now has a scar. There is also a woman interrogator. "The Galician" laughs and says to the women, "You like this part, you take over." [The prisoner] feels the woman taking his member and putting it into a liquid, something caustic from which he still has problems urinating." (CONADEP, 1985, p. 48, my translation)

Needless recounting of such events activates ambiguity and strengthens feelings of shame in the patient. The elaboration of the trauma nonetheless demands the transferential repetition of the unique relationship that is established in sexual torture. The ego's loss of control over the patient's libidinous or aggressive impulses follows. The trauma is relived by the patient's acting out. This creates extreme tensions within the therapeutic framework and in the therapist's psychic world. The therapist may then be seen by the patient as a threat to the moral norms of the superego. Faced with this threat, the patient unleashes archaic defensive forms or may be seen as satisfying the perverse tendencies of the id, concealed under the mask of a libidinous, affective, and reparatory acceptance of the self. Resistance takes on enormous gravity as a result of the affects and representations that threaten the self-structure.

In a clinical meeting, therapist *D* expressed her desire to concentrate on treating sexually tortured women, which might have been understood as countertransferential reaction. The consequent use of sexological techniques in *D*'s treatments justified psychic access (and physical access on the part of the patient) to the erogenous zones, allowing the therapist to observe psychological reactions to the use of such techniques. The implicit threat to the patient's self was revealed by the number of reactions of a prepsychotic character.

In working with tortured people, there are three important forms of countertransference: (a) culturally determined countertransferential reaction, (b) countertransferential reaction in the supervision process, and (c) anomic countertransferential reaction.

Culturally determined countertransferential reactions appear primarily in work with tortured refugees and exiles. In addition to the drama of torture, persecution, imprisonment, and so forth, refugees must confront the challenge of a society generally different from their own in culture, politics, religion, and economy. The fact of belonging to a minority, with a real possibility of downward social mobility, leads to constant uncertainty about the present and the future. This situation can lead to serious emotional problems (Baker, 1983; Berner, 1965; COLAT, 1983; Eitinger, 1960; Miserez, 1987; Pedersen, 1949; World University Service, 1981).

In the therapeutic setting, the therapist's values and forms of cultural socialization, which are different from those of the patient, generate culturally determined countertransferential reactions that are strengthened by stereotypes about ethnic groups. The therapist's curiosity about the exotic aspects of the patient's culture hinders confrontation with the traumatic content of the patient's psychic world. The disproportionate amount of attention paid to cultural influences on the patient's emotional reaction keeps the therapist from seeing the universality of the patient's reactions and emotional needs. This can lead to serious misjudgments. For example, physical aggressiveness may be attributed to a different cultural norm, blocking the adoption of necessary measures such as hospitalization and medication.

The fact that I belong to a South American group in a Nordic area has permitted me to experience multiple forms of this type of countertransference as a patient and therapist, while supervising or being supervised. The overreaction of a Swedish therapist when I arrived ten minutes late for a session (a lateness caused by a power failure in the underground transportation system) can be explained by an anticipatory prejudice based on the generic myth of Latin irresponsibility. This unmetabolized countertransference was projected in the guise of a lecture, intellectual but at the same time angry, about the terms of the therapeutic contract. Internalized by me, this in turn led to a concordant identification giving rise to a discussion about the Swedish obsession with the time factor, thus preventing the progress of therapy. This exchange was a good example of culturally determined countertransference as mutual projective identification.

Language problems may also lead to the rejection of a subject who is deemed to be not sophisticated enough for insight therapies. The therapist condescendingly excuses the patient's acting out and other unproductive behavior by a countertransferential rationalization that the patient is unable to understand or follow the rules of the therapeutic or analytic game. In this context, it is necessary to mention, at least briefly, the problems that arise with the use of interpreters, bicultural workers, cultural transmitters, and so forth. One must consider the implications of introducing a third person into the therapeutic dyad, because this addition stimulates triangulation processes and multidirectionality in transferential and countertransferential reactions. The impact of this situation on communication in the therapeutic setting has been recognized only recently (Dahl, 1989; Lindbom-Jacobson, 1988; Marcos & Alpert, 1976; Marcos & Urcuyo, 1979).

Countertransference in the supervision process has special characteristics. The primary objective of supervision is to provide the therapist an opportunity for affective release and to clarify, by means of greater experience or more objective insight, difficulties encountered in the therapeutic process. Searles (1955/1965) suggested that in the supervisory relationship a "reflection process" is created by the therapist's identificatory projection, evoking in the supervisor emotions that may reflect what had previously been evoked in the therapist during therapy. The phenomenon is widely recognized in therapeutic circles, and is better known as parallel process (Ekstein & Wallerstein, 1958).

Identificatory projections, whose burden of horror is unbearable to the therapist, can be avoided by the supervisor by means of an intellectualized metatheoretical explanation of the technical difficulties of the treatment. Some of the torture-related material may already have been internalized by the supervisor, who is incapable either of metabolizing it or of understanding, through parallel process, the patient's need for a self-caring attitude. Instead, the supervisor chooses a nonselective way to disclose countertransference. The dramatic burden of even more threatening introjects derived from eternally new examples of horror leads him or her to reject the study of new cases. The therapist justifies this rejection by concentrating on cases that have already been initiated and internalized.

Therapist *E* confided to me how annoyed he felt at having to leave a supervision group that he had been attending. The supervisor adduced that the constant presentation of new cases had disturbed him in his function as a supervisor, and he therefore preferred to concentrate on a smaller number of therapists and therapeutic processes. *E* became isolated from the group and experienced an ever greater increase in the feelings of impotence, anxiety, and desperation that he had previously been able to bring to the supervision sessions.

Therapeutic work with tortured people provides a clinical reality that leads to even more specific countertransference phenomena in the supervisor. This occurs particularly in settings where the supervisor is removed from the therapist's daily clinical reality. Working in this unique and dramatic field may paradoxically lead the supervisor to feel envy. The theoretical and clinical challenges of work with tortured people encourage the therapist in the incessant search for a greater understanding of his or her labor. The task involves the clarification of formulations and proposals concerning problems of diagnosis, therapeutic techniques, and interpretive ability.

Daily confrontation with this reality leads the therapist (perhaps unconsciously) to question the authority of the supervisor, who represents the power- and knowledge-transmitting apparatus of psychoanalytic and psychotherapeutic schools and societies. This questioning in turn leads to conflict between the therapist and the supervisor. One of many ways of responding to this situation is the assumption of supervisory omniscience, with the supervisor expressing indifferent and superior attitudes such as absentmindedness and negligence and making use of clinical experience or theoretical argumentation in a suppressive way.

One consequence of this reaction may be seen in the difficulties I and other colleagues have encountered in obtaining supervision and assistance. A series of rebuffs on the part of supervisors was justified by the argument that they had no experience in treating tortured people. Therapist *F*, who has broad personal and professional experience in this area, described in an informal conversation his experiences with his supervisor. The supervisor did not accept *F*'s theoretical explication and, relying on supervisory omniscience, developed a highly abstract argument concerning the functions of a certain behavior in one of *F*'s patients. *F* was given no space to reflect, consider the subjective and intrapsychic determinants of his original interpretations, and perhaps revise his conclusions.

Anomic countertransferential reactions can occur when, as is common, tortured people have unclear, conflicting, or unintegrated internal norms. Brutal and savage techniques meant to produce physical and psychological pain sometimes lead to the disintegration of the contents of consciousness and the dissolution of the world of the tortured person. This is a direct deconstruction (Scarry, 1985), whereby the smallest, primary basic unit (human caretaking) of human civilization is destroyed. This "uncreating" of the created internal world leads to a condition in which internal norms are unable to combine the fragments into an integrated and nonconflicting internal system. The psychic world is chaotic, shaped by a fragmented self with pathological introjections that cannot be differentiated from the objects that had been previously internalized into a coherent and integrated psychic world. Meaningfulness has been destroyed, and with it, trust in humanity.

The consequences are varied. There may be a withdrawal from the real world because the person cannot relate to it in coherent terms. This brings about an absence of social ties, because of the threat implied by being the bearer of horrifying introjects in the self or the necessity of shielding the remaining, fragmented positive pieces of the self from the attack. Another possibility is the development of psychopathology because of the absence of integrating norms, social ties, and the internalization of new significant others. The therapeutic meeting with this set of reactions may result in anomic countertransference characterized by despair and helplessness. The norms governing the therapeutic relationship are unclear and unintegrated. The absence of basic trust creates immense difficulties that prevent the establishment of a therapeutic alliance. The therapist internalizes the chaotic and unstructured character of the patient's psychic world, giving rise to an internalization of the introject by means of anomic reactions. Therapeutic actions lack clear goals and norms, and attempts to achieve gratification fail to consider whether the methods used are compatible with treatment norms.

Z consulted me after having been in contact with a psychiatric clinic for a short period. Z said she was depressed, suffered from stress, felt powerless, had fears, and was insecure. Later, she said that she felt like an empty sack; the Nazis had experimented and by surgical means removed her whole insides. After a series of diagnostic sessions, I determined that Z had a schizoid personality disorder with paranoid tendencies. Having been subjected over six years ago to merciless sexual torture, involving the use of animals and tools, Z had developed a manner of functioning that had led to isolation and a break with society. In the course of therapy, it appeared that Z simulated insight into her symptoms, but that in reality it was her paranoid world view that dominated her. This situation was reinforced by Z's dependence on the public welfare office. The enormous difficulties of establishing a therapeutic alliance were complicated by Z's incapacity to integrate and function within the therapeutic contract. Soon, I began to react, functioning in ways and showing emotional reactions that were completely different from those with other patients. For one reason or another, notes of the session were not taken; I forgot the appointment; I found activities that required changes in the schedule; I accepted that she failed to keep an appointment, because my pay was guaranteed; I was sexually attracted by Z's description of a girlfriend and was tempted to use Z to establish contact with her friend; constantly feeling tired, I occasionally broke off the session before the allotted time was up. In an episode of transferential psychosis, I consciously gave in to the chaos, intellectualizing what had happened within the framework of supportive psychotherapy. The chaos of the therapy increased and after some months, Z ended the therapy by phone.

CONCLUSIONS

Because of the requirements for certain kinds of organizational and group characteristics determined by the unique nature of the work, organizations assisting tortured people face the risk of internal as well as external social conflict. The primary institutional goals are endangered by the development of social defenses against anxiety and by the reinforcement of latent pathologies within the leadership and the staff. Different pathological forms of functioning within the staff depend on the degree of regression and internalization of the events that take place during therapeutic contact. The degree of motivation for this kind of work and the earlier relationship between individual and institution will direct the search for solutions. Political dimensions and ideological commitment (conscious and unconscious) will influence the definition of power, the limits of the social system, and the primary goals of the institution. The reactivation of primitive levels of functioning in an inadequate social structure leads to confrontations and changes in work motivation.

The use of external consultants in organizational matters can be vital in gaining an understanding of interactions among the leadership, the institutional goals and each individual's functions, duties, and rights. The availability of consultants on a permanent basis makes it possible for personnel to be confronted with certain needs or failures that have been or may become catalysts of conflict. The degree of knowledge, professional experience, and self-esteem about one's own professional work all affect whether staff members can function in accordance with their primary goals and ideals. The same is true of problems of regression directly related to therapeutic contact, such as projective counteridentification, mutual projective identification, and the various forms of countertransference.

Consultations among colleagues and ongoing supervision are requirements relevant to every health institution. In the case of institutions concerned with tortured people, consultation and supervision also imply a set of group or individual routines that stimulates the reactivation of ego functioning and blocks regression. In cases of severe characterological disorders or borderline pathologies, the institutional social system must have the ability to suspend the usual roles and to look for therapeutic approaches. These approaches should facilitate the working through of these reactivated primitive object relations.

Institutional, group, and individual problems that arise in connection with the treatment of tortured people can be minimized if attention is focused on the variables that may generate conflict in the individual or in the group. This applies especially to problems derived from the different types of countertransferential reactions that directly affect the primary goal of the treatment and, in consequence, the institution. In working with tortured people, therapists should intensively analyze the unconscious transactions of the therapist–patient relationship.

A creative use of countertransference permits access to the patient's inner world and to the recognition of primitive internalized object relations that contribute to the genesis of somatic and psychic disorders. The therapist must also seek to know the realities of the relationship between torturer and tortured, in order to achieve a better understanding of the nature of relevant regressive processes and projective identifications. Even with a systematic in-depth study of our countertransferential reactions, we still may not fully understand the process, but at least we will come into contact with the experiential terror of a self faced with the chaotic, horrifying, and terrifying aspects of pathological introjects.

REFERENCES

Agger, I. (1986). Seksuel tortur af kvindelige, politiske fanger [Sexual torture of female political prisoners]. *Nordisk Sexologi, 4*, 147–161.

Agger, I. (1989). Sexual torture of political prisoners: An overview. *Journal of Traumatic Stress.*

Allodi, F. (1982). Psychiatric sequelae of torture and implications for treatment. *World Medical Journal, 29*, 71–75.

Allodi, F., Randall, G., Lutz, E. L., Quiroga, J., Zunzunegui, M. V., Kolff, C. A., Deutsch, A., & Doan, R. (1985). Physical and psychiatric effects of torture: Two medical studies. In E. Stover & E. O. Nightingale (Eds.), *The breaking of minds and bodies* (pp. 58–78). New York: Freeman.

Baker, R. (Ed.). (1983). *The psychosocial problems of refugees.* London: The British Refugee Council and European Consultations on Refugees and Exiles.

Barudy, J., & Vieytes, C. (1985). *El dolor invisible de la tortura [The invisible pain of torture].* Brussels: Franja.

Bennet, G. (1979). *Patients and their doctors: The journey through medical care.* London: Bailliere Tindall.

Berner, P. (1965). La psychopathologie sociales des refugies [The social psychopathology of refugees]. *Evolution Psychiatrique, 30*, 633–655.

Bion, W. R. (1958). *Experiences in groups and other papers.* London: Tavistock.

Bozzolo, R. C. (1983). Algunos aspectos de la contratransferencia en la asistencia a familiares de desaparecidos [Some aspects of countertransference in assisting relatives of the disappeared]. In

D. Kordon & L. Edelman (Eds.), *Efectos psicologicos de la represion politica* (pp. 73–86). Buenos Aires: Sudamericana/Planeta.

Bustos, E. (1987). Psykisk traumatisering hos flyktingar [Psychic traumatization in refugees]. *Psykisk Halsa, 1*, 24–34.

Bustos, E. (in press). Identidad, exile y sexualidad [Identity, exile, and sexuality]. In H. Riquelme (Ed.), *Identidad y contexto psicocultural*. Caracas: Nueva Sociedad.

Cienfuegos, A. J., & Monelli, C. (1983). The testimony of political repression as a therapeutic instrument. *American Journal of Orthopsychiatry, 53*(1), 43–51.

COLAT (Colectivo Latinoamericano de Trabajo Psicosocial [Latin American Collective of Psychosocial Work]. (Ed.). (1983). *Psicopatologia de la tortura y el exilio [The psychopathology of torture and exile]*. Madrid: Fundamentos.

Comas-Diaz, L., & Padilla, A. M. (1988). *Wounded healers: The case of Chilean therapists*. Unpublished manuscript, Transcultural Mental Health Institute, Washington, DC.

CONADEP [Comision Nacional sobre la Desaparicion de Personas [National Commission on the Disappeared]). (1985). *Nunca mas [Never again]*. Buenos Aires: EUDEBA.

Coser, L. (1956). *The functions of social conflict*. New York: Free Press.

Dahl, C.-L. (1989). Some problems of crosscultural psychotherapy with refugees seeking treatment. *American Journal of Psychoanalysis, 49*, 19–32.

Danieli, Y. (1980). Countertransference in the treatment and study of Nazi Holocaust survivors and their children. *Victimology, 5*, 355–367.

Eitinger, L. (1960). The symptomatology of mental disease among refugees in Norway. *Journal of Mental Science, 106*, 947–966.

Ekstein, R., & Wallerstein, R. S. 1958). *The teaching and learning of psychotherapy*. New York: International Universities Press.

Farber, B. A. (1983). Introduction: A critical perspective on burnout. In B. A. Farber (Ed.), *Stress and burnout in the human service professions* (pp. 1–20). New York: Pergamon Press.

Freudenberger, H. J. (1974). Staff burn-out. *Journal of Social Issues, 30*, 159–165.

Freudenberger, H. J. (1975). The staff burnout syndrome in alternative institutions. *Psychotherapy: Therapy, Research and Practice, 12*, 73–82.

Grindberg, L. (1962). On a specific aspect of counter-transference due to the patient's projective identification. *International Journal of Psychoanalysis, 43*, 436–440.

Janis, I. L. (1972). *Victims of groupthink*. Boston: Houghton Mifflin.

Jorstad, J. (1984). Gruppeprocesser som influerer pa teamsamarbeid og lederskap i vare psykiatriske institutsjoner [Group processes that influence teamwork and leadership in our psychiatric institutions]. *Nordisk Psykiatrisk Tidsskrift, 38*, 227–288.

Kernberg, O. (1980). *Internal world and external reality*. New York: Aronson.

Krystal, H. (1971). Trauma: Considerations of its intensity and chronicity. In H. Krystal & W. G. Niederland (Eds.), *Psychic traumatization* (pp. 11–28). Boston: Little, Brown.

Krystal, H. (1977). Aspects of affect theory. *Bulletin of the Menninger Clinic, 41*, 1–26.

Krystal, H. (1978). Trauma and affects. *Psychoanalytic Study of the Child, 33*, 81–116.

Krystal, H. (1988). *Integration and self-healing. Affect, trauma, alexithymia*. Hillsdale, NJ: Analytic Press.

Langs, R. (1978). *The listening process*. New York: Aronson.

Lewin, K. (1948). Experiments in social space. In G. W. Lewin (Ed.), *Resolving social conflict* (pp. 71–83). New York: Harper. (Original work published 1939)

Lewin, K. (1948). The special case of Germany. In G. W. Lewin (Ed.). *Resolving social conflict* (pp. 43–55). New York: Harper. (Original work published 1943)

Lindbom-Jacobson, M. (1988, August). *Working with interpreters in treating tortured refugees*. Paper presented at the First European Conference on Traumatic Stress, sponsored by the British Psychological Society, Lincolnshire, England.

Lira, E., & Weinstein, E. (1984). El testimonio de experiencias politicas traumaticas como instrumento terapeutico [The testimony of traumatic political experiences as a therapeutic instrument]. In E. Lira & E. Weinstein (Eds.), *Psicoterapia y represion politica* (pp. 17–36). Mexico City: Siglo Veintiuno.

Lira, E., Weinstein, E., & Kovalskys, J. (1987). Subjetividad y represion politica: Intervenciones terapeuticas [Subjectivity and political repression: Therapeutic interventions]. In M. Montero (Ed.), *Psicologia politica latinoamericana* (pp. 317–346). Caracas, Venezuela: Panapo.

Marcos, L. R., & Alpert, M. (1976). Strategies and risks in psychotherapy with bilingual patients: The phenomenon of language independence. *American Journal of Psychiatry, 133*, 1275–1278.

Marcos, L. R., & Urcuyo, L. (1979). Dynamic psychotherapy with the bilingual patient. *American Journal of Psychotherapy, 33*, 331–338.

Maslach, C. (1976). Burned out. *Human Behavior, 5*, 16–22.

Maslach, C. (1978). Job burnout: How people cope. *Public Welfare, 36*, 56–58.

Menzies, I. E. P. (1970). *The functioning of social systems as a defence against anxiety*. London: Tavistock.

Miserez, D. (Ed.). (1987). *Refugees: The trauma of exile*. Vitznau, The Netherlands: Martinus Nijhoff Publishers.

Mollica, R. (1987). The trauma story: The psychiatric care of refugee survivors of violence and torture. In F. M. Ochberg (Ed.), *Post-traumatic therapy and the victim of violence* (pp. 295–314). New York: Brunner/Mazel.

Pedersen, S. (1949). Psychopathological reactions to extreme social displacement. *Psychoanalytic Review, 63*, 344–354.

Pines, A., & Maslach, C. (1978). Characteristics of staff burnout in mental health settings. *Hospital and Community Psychiatry, 29*, 233–237.

Pollarolo, F., & Morales, E. (1984). Claustrofobia, paralizacion y participación. Psicoterapia de un militante politico [Claustrophobia, paralization, and participation: Psychotherapy of a political militant]. In E. Lira & E. Weinstein (Eds.), *Psicoterapia y represion politica* (pp. 180–192). Mexico City: Siglo Veintiuno.

Racker, H. (1968). *Transference and countertransference*. London: Maresfield Reprints.

Rasmussen, O. V., & Lunde, I. (1980). Evaluation of investigation of 200 torture victims. *Danish Medical Bulletin, 27*, 241–243.

Roche, J.-L. (1987). Multidimensional approach to exiles: Persecution experiences. In D. Miserez (Ed.), *Refugees: The trauma of exile* (pp. 223–235). Vitznau, The Netherlands: Martinus Nijhoff Publishers.

Scarry, E. (1985). *The body in pain: The making and unmaking of the world*. New York: Oxford University Press.

Schlapobersky, J., & Bamber, H. (1987). Rehabilitation work with victims of torture. In D. Miserez (Ed.), *Refugees: The trauma of exile* (pp. 206–222). Vitznau, The Netherlands: Martinus Nijhoff Publishers.

Searles, H. F. (1965). The informational value of the supervisor's emotional experiences. In H. F. Searles (Ed.), *Collected papers on schizophrenia and related subjects* (pp. 157–176). New York: International Universities Press. (Original work published 1955)

Vieytes, C., & Barudy, J. (1985). El proceso terapeutico [The therapeutic process]. In J. Barudy & C. Vieytes (Eds.), *El dolor invisible de la tortura*. Brussels: Franja.

Westin, C. (1988). *Roda korsets center for torterade flyktingar: Ett bidrag till utvarderingen [Red Cross center for tortured refugees: A contribution to evaluation]* (Rep. No. 19). Sweden: University of Stockholm, Centrum for Invandringsforskning.

World University Service. (1981, May). *Mental health and exile*. Paper presented at a Seminar on Mental Health and Latin American Exiles, London.

11

Because Mercy Has a Human Heart: Centers for Victims of Torture

Barbara Chester

A GROWING AWARENESS OF NEED

In May of 1984, representatives of the Chilean Medical Association (CMA) appeared before the United States House of Representatives Committee on Foreign Affairs. Two physicians testified about their association's efforts to discipline members of their profession who were known to collaborate with the military in the practice of torture (Stover, 1987). In the Committee's written report, a number of conclusions and recommendations were presented. Among these recommendations were three that called for creating programs of treatment and rehabilitation for victims of torture, educating the public as to how societal structures are created and maintained that enable torture to take place, and providing prevention campaigns so that the practice of torture would not only be eradicated, but also be prevented in the future. There was also a call for clinical physicians to develop objective techniques for diagnosing the effects of torture, as well as to provide physical and psychological remedies for victims of torture and other forms of oppression (Committee on Foreign Affairs, 1984).

Since 1948, the use of torture by governments has been prohibited on the international level. The World Medical Association (1975) defined torture as "the deliberate, systematic, or wanton infliction of physical or mental suffering by one or more persons, acting alone or on the orders of any authority to force another person to yield information, to make a confession, or for any other reason." The United Nations took steps to oblige member nations to make torture a punishable offense and to provide for the extradition of torturers and the compensation of victims. In adopting the Convention Against Torture and Other Cruel, Inhuman, or Degrading Treatment or Punishment, the United Nations also outlined the deliberate and systematic nature of torture, the severity of its physical and emotional consequences, and its oppressive intent (United Nations General Assembly, 1984).

These definitions, adopted for the legal purposes of treaty and convention, can hardly convey the intensity of human suffering that torture engenders. Torture has been described as "the methodological diminishing of a man" (Liwski, 1983), "psychological murder," and the complete "unmaking" of an individual's world in order to destroy the person's humanity (Scarry, 1985). The transformation of the victim's world occurs at all levels and involves all relationships. Language itself is violated. Words, symbols, and objects that generally denote comfort, care, and nurturing, are transformed into symbols of pain and terror. For example, individuals are often tortured in medical settings or in the presence of medical personnel, as was so eloquently conveyed by the leaders of the CMA. The room in which torture takes place is often given a euphemism, such as "the guest house" or "the tea party." Close relationships are often exploited and destroyed when family members and friends are tortured in front of one another. Even spiritual values can be used for purposes of torture. Women from Iran have stated that because the Muslim religion prohibits the execution of virgins, many of them are forced into speedy mock marriages and sexually assaulted in order to permit their eventual execution within the tenets of religious law.

The consequences of such cruel treatment are pervasive and affect every area of functioning. Lingering terror, humiliation, shame, nightmares, loss of memory and concentration, isolation, depression, and extreme physical pain plague survivors for many years. Cognitive problems, such as the loss of short-term memory and concentration, are frequent sequelae of the torture experience, making learning a new language, maintaining employment, or succeeding in school very difficult, if not impossible. In general, most people surviving the insult of torture feel its impact in the intrapsychic, cognitive, spiritual, and social realm. The effects span a continuum in terms of both severity and chronicity (Allodi, 1982; Allodi & Cowgill, 1982; Allodi et al., 1985; Amnesty International Danish Medical Group, 1980; Eitinger, 1971; Petersen et al., 1985).

These reactions do not decrease if left untreated. Primo Levi, a noted writer and survivor of the Nazi Holocaust, committed suicide 40 years after his ordeal. He was unable to contend with the severe nightmares that plagued his sleeping hours, the perceived indifference of others who were unwilling to listen to accounts of his suffering, and the belief that "each of us survivors is in more than one way an exception" (Levi, 1986, 1988). Philosopher and survivor Jean Améry stated:

> *Anyone who has been tortured remains tortured. . . . Anyone who has suffered torture never again will be able to be at ease in the world, the abomination of the annihilation is never extinguished. Faith in humanity, already cracked by the first slap in the face, then demolished by torture is never acquired again. (Cited in Levi, 1988, p. 25)*

THE IMPETUS: SERVICES UNDER REPRESSION AND IN EXILE

Although the existence of centers specifically treating victims of torture is a recent phenomenon, the work of providing medical documentation of torture and care to survivors on an individual level has been ongoing. This work was established under different circumstances and with different strategies in the first world and in areas of repression. One major impetus behind the creation of centers is the work of the Nobel Prize-winning human rights organization, Amnesty International, founded in 1961 by English attorney, Peter Berenson. Twenty-six years later, Amnesty International has supporters in more than 150 countries. The organization is nonpolitical. Its goals are to work for the release of prisoners who have been detained for their beliefs, color, sex, ethnic origin, language, or religion, provided they have neither used nor advocated violence; to ensure fair and prompt trials for all political prisoners; and to work for the abolition of torture and executions in all cases.

Medical work within Amnesty International began in 1973 after a conference in Paris that was devoted to the issue of combatting torture. Dr. Inge Kemp Genefke organized a group of Danish physicians to document the occurrence of torture by examining people who claimed to have been subjected to it. In 1974, the Danish Medical Group was established (Marcussen, Rasmussen, & Pedersen, 1983). Confrontation with the horrible realities of torture on a human and medical level revealed the necessity to establish programs that would treat victims of these abuses. Because the mandate of Amnesty International is to investigate and document torture—not to treat victims—the need to establish treatment programs had to be answered in other ways. In 1980, four members of the International Rehabilitation Group in Denmark started treating victims of torture at the Department of Neurology, University of Copenhagen. On October 30, 1982, the Rehabilitation Center for Torture Victims was established, and Genefke became its first director (Genefke & Aalund, 1983). Other centers soon followed.

In 1979, members of the Canadian Medical Group of Amnesty International organized a seminar for physicians that focused on the issue of torture. The work of those physicians eventually culminated in the Canadian Center for Investigation and Prevention of Torture, directed by Toronto psychiatrist, Dr. Frederico Allodi. Dr. Genevieve Cowgill, a former co-director of the Center, established Survivors International in Toronto to assist victims of torture and their families to become active members of their communities.

In 1985, the Center for Victims of Torture became the first center in the United States to provide treatment specifically for torture victims and their families. It was established by a multidisciplinary task force created by the governor of Minnesota. Since opening the doors of its separate facility in May of 1987, the Center has provided service to more than 200 people from approximately 20 countries around the world. The Marjorie Kovler Center, operating within the Travellers and Immigrants Aid organization recently began providing services to survivors in the Chicago area.

As a young physician, Dr. Helene Jaffé, worked with Algerian exiles in France. Her experiences led her to participate in groups connected with missions in French Guinea, Morocco , and Turkey and eventually led to the formation of the Association for Victims of Repression in Exile (AVRE), a center treating victims of torture located in Paris (AVRE, 1986). The Medical Foundation for the Care of Victims of Torture aids victims of torture through a referral network that extends throughout the United Kingdom. The Red Cross also sponsors two treatment programs, one in Sweden and one in Norway.

In addition to these centers, medical and other health-related services have been provided to more broadly defined groups, such as refugees, exiles, immigrants, and asylees. Often, services to torture victims are provided within these other contexts. Organizations providing these services include the Indo-Chinese Psychiatry Clinic in Boston, Center for Psycho-Social Assistance for Refugees (CEPAS) in Copenhagen, the Coalition to Aid Refugee Survivors of Torture and War Trauma in San Francisco, the Colectivo Latino-americano de Trabajo Psicosocial (COLAT) in Belgium, the Comité Médical Pour Les Exiles (COMEDE) in France, and the Centrum Gezondheidszorg Vluchtelingen (CVG) in the Netherlands. A unique program directed toward Holocaust survivors and their children now operates in New York under the direction of psychologist Yael Danieli.

Unfortunately, many worthy attempts to create programs have failed or are floundering because of lack of community support and resources, skepticism, and lack of funding (e.g., the Center for Rehabilitation of Torture Victims in New Jersey). Other practitioners are providing services on an individual basis, often in addition to a full-time practice (e.g., José Quiroga, Ana Deutsch, and Glen Randall in Los Angeles; Tato Torres, Yael Fishman, and Holbrook Teter in San Francisco). Still other groups are preparing to begin the rigorous endeavor of providing centralized services (e.g., Survivors International in the San Francisco area and the Walter Briehl Foundation in Los Angeles).

Concurrently, or sometimes predating these developments in Europe and North America, services were provided within countries where torture was taking place, often clandestinely. The main impetus for these efforts was often the individual physician and psychologist, a professional association such as the National Medical and Dental Association in South Africa, or the Church. In South America, Roman Catholics and Protestants often joined forces in a spirit of practical ecumenism to establish social ministries or human rights organizations such as the Vicariate of Solidarity in Chile, or centers like the Christian Churches' Social Assistance Foundation of Chile, which has been operational since 1977. These agencies serve victims of repression, families of the disappeared, and people accused of political crimes. According to the World Council of Churches' delegation to Chile, members of these groups currently suffer severe harassment from the military and are accused of "protecting terrorists" (World Council of Churches, 1986).

Medical and psychological services were and are provided to survivors of political repression in Argentina, Bolivia, Chile, Paraguay, the Philippines, South Africa, and Uruguay—often at great risk to the service provider. Dr. Pedro Castillo Yañez, one of the first to provide medical care to victims of torture in Chile, was detained and held in solitary confinement for three weeks. Joelito Filartiga, the 19-year-old son of Dr. Joel Filartiga, was detained, tortured, and murdered for his father's alleged medical treatment of "terrorists." Dr. Filartiga continues to suffer harassment for his work in Paraguay.

In January 1986, a coalition of physicians and attorneys formally established a center under the direction of the Philippine Action Concerning Torture (PACT). PACT is a program for the treatment and rehabilitation of survivors working under the auspices of the Medical Action Group. According to psychiatrist June Lopez, director of PACT, preparations for the launching of a center entailed two years. A debate over creating a physical center for what had been, by "force of circumstances," a decentralized and clandestine organization, was long and involved. Proponents of centralized service argued that public exposure and international support would provide protection for staff and clients. Others feared retaliation should the decentralized, clandestine network of volunteer health professionals be abandoned. Recently, this center has again faced the necessity to decentralize in the face of continuing human rights abuses (Lopez, 1988). The Children's Rehabilitation Center (CRC), also established in the Philippines, provides services to children who are victims of militarization. The staff of CRC works with children who are (or whose parents have been) disappeared, salvaged (extra-judicial execution), hamletted (forcibly relocated), and massacred (Marcellino, 1986).

QUESTIONS PERTAINING TO TREATMENT PROGRAMS

Awareness of the need for treating torture victims has nurtured a number of different ideologies, creating a framework within which programs are designed and treatment delivered. These issues are complex and thought-provoking and to date have raised numerous questions that service providers in the newly emerging field of torture treatment are discussing for purposes of program design and evaluation (Amnesty International, 1985). Five of these questions are described in detail.

1. What are the relative merits of providing treatment within the context of an identified and specialized center as opposed to treatment provided in a more generalized setting? The concept of a center for treating survivors of torture and their families is based upon the practical and moral assumption that they both need and deserve healing care. Creating an environment in which survivors can identify themselves and receive treatment is of critical importance. There is both a therapeutic and symbolic significance in the existence of a specified center created solely for the purpose of treating torture victims. The local, national, and international communities need to validate the reality of torture. Torture exists and has an impact on us all despite our immediate feelings of insulation. A center for victims of torture is an important acknowledgment of this fact.

Among the pervasive long-term effects of torture is a chronic sense of deep and profound shame. This shame has a variety of sources, depending on the culture and context of the torture experience itself. For some people, the extremely degrading and subhuman nature of the conditions under which they lived during detention, torture, and imprisonment is a source of shame. For example, an African client at the Center for Victims of Torture had been forced to bathe daily in his own urine and feces. Another had been forced to witness the rape, murder, and mutilation of his girlfriend. Many women and men suffered various forms of sexual assault and abuse as part of the torture experience. For some people, survival itself is an issue of shame, especially when family members and others have not survived. A client from Ethiopia sustained himself on a rigidly restricted, semi-starvation diet, unable to eat because friends and relatives at home were living under conditions of severe deprivation.

Receiving treatment in a center that is labeled and specified as a center for torture victims has sometimes been criticized as a source of further stigmatization for people who have already undergone intensely shameful experiences. On the other hand, it has been demonstrated by groups like Amnesty International that torture, like other forms of victimization, thrives on secrecy. When asked about this issue, one client commented that torture is an extremely ugly reality, one that must be recognized, admitted, and handled in a straightforward manner. He believed that sweeping the issue under the rug of generality only exacerbates the shame of the victims and the unwillingness of the population at large to deal with the realities of the issue. The creation of a specified center destroys the secrecy of the abuse, and with it, the shame involved in maintaining that secret.

Furthermore, people who have survived torture often believe themselves to be in need of very specific services. Like survivors of domestic violence, sexual assault, or other cases of extreme trauma, many people who have survived torture feel out of place in more generalized clinical settings. The specificity of the act of torture itself, which in essence seeks to dismantle the personality, crush the spirit, and destroy the mind, would appear to generate a need for specialized treatment that is multidisciplinary and designed to help the individual and family remake their world and transform hopelessness and victimization into survival (Scarry, 1985). Centralization of services allows for trust to develop with an entire treatment team. It also provides for easier coordination of services, client confidentiality, maximal accountability and supervision of staff, and concentration of expertise. Decentralized community service models can provide treatment when centralization is hazardous, client populations are high, and treatment resources are at a minimum.

Ultimately, the issue of treatment within the context of a center versus a generalized or more diffuse treatment strategy can and must be guided by a number of factors, including informed choice on the part of the survivor—a choice made within an environment that promotes safety and respect. Torture, as a phenomenon, reflects the narrowing of choices within a society and the unwillingness to respect the existence of alternatives. As treatment professionals, we must not mirror this process.

2. What is the appropriate role for treatment professionals in an admittedly political issue? How can we (or should we) avoid involvement with the political complexities and ramifications involved with the issue of torture? How can we (or should we) interface with administrative and legal systems on the local, national, and international level? Unlike other forms of victimization, which are often handled within the criminal or civil codes of states, cities, or counties, torture is viewed as a crime of international magnitude, and it is condemned at the level of international politics. More recently, however, some countries, such as Canada and Greece, and numerous organizations, like the International Service for Human Rights, are calling for the recognition that torture is a crime in which the individual perpetrator also bears responsibility. (See, for example, the landmark Joelita Filartiga case in the United States [*Filartiga v. Pena-Irala*, 1980]. The father of the victim was permitted to sue the individual perpetrator for damages, and the suit was brought by a third country.)

The impact of suffering experienced by torture victims is both personal and communal. Countries and cultures vary greatly in terms of how much an individual's personal identity is, in essence, his or her political identity. In its extreme form, this notion may lead us to understand the concept of the torture of entire communities and groups. Some practitioners and political analysts consider the deliberate and systematic destruction of the culture, rituals, and traditions of certain groups a newly recognized, emerging form of torture. The government of South Africa, for example, in denying Black South Africans the right of public funerals, is actually violating a very deeply held and sacred need for public ritual in the healing process of grief. Although the South African government rationalizes the banning of public funerals as a security precaution, many Black South Africans view this as an attempt to destroy a profoundly meaningful tradition and cultural bond. This destruction of social tradition has its counterpart in apartheid, which, among other consequences, destroyed the economic base of tribal culture (V. Mplumlwana, personal communication, 1987).

Dr. Norberto Liwski of Argentina (1983) defined the purpose of torture as "severing the links of solidarity." Dr. Elizabeth Lira of Chile stated that torture and oppression transforms a phenomenon that happens on a social and political level into a very personal and private event. In order to do this, "silence is imposed over the world of pain, poverty, injustice and persecution." Torture "does not originate in a private event and therefore is not completely resolved in that space" (Lira, Becker, & Castillo, 1988).

A client at the Center for Victims of Torture recounted what he termed the daily torture experienced by his entire town, living in an atmosphere of total helplessness because of the lack of logic, consistency, and predictability associated with the actions of a new military government. The notion that the deliberate and systematic infliction of severe psychological pain in order to repress and oppress can occur at the community, societal, or individual level, is one that clearly needs to be addressed by treatment professionals seeking to define their appropriate role vis-à-vis political systems. This issue is clearly elucidated in the dilemma of remembering and forgetting, the individual need to remember and the societal need to forget. As Lira stated, "on a social [political] level desires to forget are generated in the name of putting an end to the horror and these inevitably contradict the necessity of not forgetting which, on a therapeutic level, is a condition for mental [health]" (Lira et al., 1988, p. 20).

3. How do we define torture, an essentially legal concept, in terms that are appropriate for a treatment context? What role does culture play in people's own understanding of what happened to them? A Laotian woman came to a local clinic seeking symptomatic medical relief from painful headaches and insomnia. The people of her village had been sent to a reeducation camp where beatings, mock executions, and sexual abuse were common. Her father had been beaten and mutilated in front of her, and her infant daughter died when the woman tried to hide her from security police. This woman ascribed her present symptoms, not to these experiences, but to the fact that she became pregnant and caught a chill during her escape from Laos. According to village beliefs, catching a chill during pregnancy leads to dire consequences later in life. She does not view herself as a torture victim.

Dr. Richard Mollica, of the Indo-Chinese Psychiatry Clinic, proposed that differing cultural interpretations of torture and trauma need to play a key role in assessment and treatment. He has pointed out that the English derivation of the term has consistently been associated with legal procedures: indeed, the definitions that we use today are often associated with conventions, treaties, and other political statements. Other societies, such as some of the Southeast Asian groups, associate torture with the idea of karma, or the notion that actions or thoughts practiced in a previous existence can produce subsequent effects in present time. This mindset has tremendous treatment implications in that, to the victims, suffering is often seen to be deserved, or at least represents an action of fate over which one has no control (Mollica, 1988).

During the course of an afternoon meeting at the Center for Victims of Torture with bilingual workers from Cambodia, Laos, and Vietnam, the question was asked, "By what criteria do we know to send people to your center?" After explaining the United Nations resolution, the key notions of torture as psychological as well as physical, and the systematic and oppressive nature of it, there were still many puzzled expressions. One man, a Cambodian, raised his hand and started to tell his story in detail. For the next two or three hours, people told stories, their own or others'—all chilling narratives. One woman spoke of a family who, while fleeing the Khmer Rouge, hid their child in a water tower after seeing enemy soldiers approach their vicinity. The man of the family was beheaded in front of his wife. She was told that were she to cry or react in any way, she would be executed in the same manner. When they had gone, she slowly walked to the water tower only to discover that her child had drowned. The woman turned to me and asked, "Is that what you mean by torture?"

Our assumptions and beliefs about treatment cannot ignore the social or cultural context in which the trauma took place. More than a minimal understanding of culture is required, which would include recognizing the many subcultures within the client population's country of origin. This is particularly the case when heavy emphasis is placed on psychotherapy and counseling. Psychotherapy is clearly a Western concept and practice. As Dr. Zigfrids Stelmachers pointed out, "Even the highest level of expertise is useless if the victim finds it unsuitable" (Stelmachers, 1987, p. 7). It is important to reframe legal definitions to more adequately describe an experiential process that is heavily influenced by culture and context.

4. How much exposure should we give to our work? Can we raise awareness of the issue without being exploitative of our clients? When Governor Perpich of Minnesota first proposed the creation of a center to treat victims of torture by foreign governments who now reside in this region, local newspapers were rife with cynical letters and snide comments, usually making remarks about torture by politicians and legislators. Such scenarios are often faced by visionaries seeking to implement a new idea or create a new consciousness. This public resistance is exacerbated when the need involves fostering awareness of an issue that is so ugly and horrible that people would prefer not to think about it anyway. Once such an idea does establish itself, however, and the need has been documented, professional communicators and representatives of the media are then attracted to the issue, especially if it is both new and compelling.

Organizations such as Amnesty International, whose focus is the documentation and revelation of torture, are thoroughly within their mandates by providing speakers who have experienced torture. For those of us in the treatment professions, the issues become much more of a conflict. Most well-trained professional journalists realize that for their story to have much of an impact, there is a need for the human factor to be revealed in a way that touches an audience that is often inundated by sensationalistic stories. The human impact is delivered most compellingly through the auspices of one who has personally experienced torture. The complexities of working with clients who have a story to tell have been well documented in other areas (rape, crisis counseling, domestic violence, etc.). With the issue of torture, the dilemma becomes more extreme. For most treatment providers, the ethics of our professions require adherence to principles that include confidentiality. In addition, many of the people who use the center's services have a very real fear for their own safety, as well as fear for family members who are still living in countries where torture and political oppression are practiced. This victimization also imparts, as one of its consequences, a sense of alienation so profound that the development of trust is a key and most difficult clinical issue. The assurance of confidentiality may seem illusory for both present and potential clients viewing the live, detailed testimony of a person receiving services at a center.

In addition, as Mollica has eloquently expressed, it is not unusual for a torture or trauma victim to get "stuck" in their story. If a person's world has been so unmade, and the "loss of the world" becomes so complete, then the story, in essence, becomes his or her identity (Mollica & Lavelle, in press). One role of a center for the treatment of torture victims is certainly to help a person to move from the persona of victim to one of survivor. The firm establishment of one's identity as a victim through media attention is difficult to overcome. Many clients also feel such an overwhelming sense of obligation to service providers that they agree to publicly reveal stories that are very personal, and sometimes, very shameful. A client seen at a program working with domestic violence agreed to a media interview after a murder–suicide attempt. Months later, this interview became a source of deep shame, and many sessions of intensive therapy were required in order to rectify this issue.

The need to communicate the enormous extent of the problem of torture, and to give this awareness all of the supremely human form that it deserves through the testimony of others, is a difficult dilemma. Its resolution often depends on the philosophy of the program in question. Ultimately for the therapist, both the question and the answer must be framed in terms of professional ethics, therapeutic goals, and clinical outcomes.

5. *What differences arise when treatment occurs within countries of repression as opposed to treatment that occurs within countries of refuge?* Torture must be viewed as a process. This process begins when violence becomes normalized, communication censored, all systems politicized, and grief privatized. The process often ends with disappearance, death, or exile. Treatment practitioners are faced with the consequences of this process, consequences that are expressed differently in countries of repression and countries of refuge. Treatment practitioners in countries of repression often work under conditions that provoke an "external reality of danger and emotional disequilibrium" (Lopez, oral presentation, 1988). Also, therapeutic goals and assumptions are often perverted by the system itself. In addition, both therapist and client may be politically polarized. Both are facing the actual or potential destruction of their own families, communities, and life vision.

Treatment efforts in countries under repression are often directed to the families of the detained and disappeared. Groups such as the psychological team of Centro de Estudios Legales y Sociales in Argentina often work closely with groups such as the Abuelas (Grandmothers) de Plaza de Mayo, whose primary focus is the identification and recuperation of children lost during the period of repression. Another group, the Madres (Mothers) de Plaza de Mayo, works with a team of approximately 12 psychiatrists and psychologists. Both the Abeulas and the Madres are groups whose integrity, warmth, courage, and organizational ability represent the lengths to which solidarity, community, and commitment can provide results in the face of extreme oppression.

Recently, ideological issues have caused controversy among and between groups. For example, the Abuelas support the exhumation of the bodies of the disappeared, and the Madres are opposed. The Madres have themselves divided into two organizations because of differing viewpoints about how the fate of the disappeared should be handled clinically and politically. These reactions may well represent responses to different needs or may also reflect further consequences of politization and the resulting impact to society when everything becomes divided by ideology (D. A. Johnson, personal communication, 1988).

Maintaining professional standards and ethics becomes extraordinarily difficult in countries under repression. Therapeutic assumptions regarding confidentiality, client safety, and trust are often subverted. A South African client related the story of his medical treatment after months of detention. He was too afraid to tell his physician the conditions under which he received his very severe wounds, which included lacerations, broken bones, and destroyed muscle and ligament tissue. His physician, faced also with the realistic fear of reprisal, recorded the cause of injury as an accidental fall. Even clinical goals, such as the role of the therapist to re-frame the experience, can be subverted. During a visit to Argentina, Douglas Johnson, the executive director of the Center for Victims of Torture was told about a man who visited a therapist in order to receive treatment for severe physical and psychological abuse suffered in detention. The therapist responded by focusing treatment on the man's relationship with his father.

In countries of refuge, organizations confront other issues. These programs work with a heterogeneous rather than a homogeneous population. Also, because of the gap in time between torture and treatment, it is often more difficult to establish a link between the trauma and the social context, as well as between the trauma and the emerging symptoms. In addition, European and North American centers must always connect with the client through their new identity of refugee and exile. Dr. Laura Bonaparte, an Argentinian psychologist, said that "exile (itself) is a form of torture . . . each of us comes with a knapsack of pain, guilt and incorporated values. Each of us comes apart; our internal world is in pieces. . . . We live psychologically mutilated" (Bonaparte, 1986, p. 105).

FOUR INSTITUTIONAL RESPONSES

The way in which individuals, programs, or centers take shape is influenced by how the foregoing questions are answered. Torture is the deliberate, systematic, and strategic destruction of human beings. Intervention for survivors and families must therefore be as deliberate, systematic, and transforming as the trauma itself. In general, treatment of torture victims has been organized around three concep-tual frameworks: the use of testimony, cognitive restructuring, and biological ap-proaches, the latter relying heavily on approaches to posttraumatic stress disorder (PTSD) and on research (G. Randall, personal communication, 1988). In addition, treatment approaches will be heavily influenced by the political climate, the avail-ability of resources, and the nature of the groups who organize to provide this treatment. The following discussion briefly outlines the work of four organiza-tions: the Rehabilitation Center For Torture Victims, Fundacion de Ayuda Social de las Iglesias Christianas, the Indo-Chinese Psychiatry Clinic, and the Center for Victims of Torture.

The Rehabilitation Center for Torture Victims

The work of the Rehabilitation Center for Torture Victims in Copenhagen, Denmark is heavily influenced by its origins through the Amnesty International medical professionals' groups. Amnesty International relies heavily on existing treaties and conventions for its work and views torture from the perspective of investigation and documentation. The governing bodies of this center and a similar center in Paris are heavily weighted with representatives of the medical, legal, and human rights communities. Emphasis is on the specificity of the torture experience itself. The lengthy assessment process at the Center involves the need for tremendous detail regarding this experience in order that the integrity of the program be maintained, but also (and more important) that no aspect of the torture experience be unwittingly repeated by the physicians, neurologists, counselors, or physiotherapists on staff.

Because the emphasis is on the experience of torture, key elements of which are similar in most countries, the pre-morbid characteristics of the person are not seen as critical elements in either assessment or in later intervention. The treatment program can be seen as one that is tailor-made to the experience, as opposed to the individual. The approach is one that is espoused in the Center's cornerstone philosophy: The torture victim is a normal individual who has undergone a very abnormal experience. Intervention is designed to restructure and rehabilitate the client through physical and cognitive techniques. The emphasis on the need for parallel treatment of mind and social functioning body is also a vital part of the treatment philosophy.

FASIC

One approach emphasized in the Southern Cone stems from the personal experience of the service providers. Politics permeates all aspects of life in countries where torture occurs. Indeed, this is one of the societal antecedents of torture: politicization of all systems within a society, such as education, religion, and health care (Amnesty International, 1984). In addition, many of the service providers themselves, their friends, and family members experienced detention, disappearance, and torture. Their work is viewed as part of a larger struggle against oppression. Because of this stance, programs in Europe and the United States are often viewed with suspicion. There are misgivings that these more mainstream agencies will undermine legitimate political protest by medicalizing the issue.

Service providers in South America often turn to the use of spoken or written testimony for therapeutic purposes. Fundacion de Ayuda Social de las Iglesias Christianas (FASIC), for example, serves victims of direct repression and their families, under the extraordinary circumstances of military dictatorship in Chile. Its clientele consists of victims of torture, obligatory exile, and relatives of disappeared and executed prisoners (FASIC, 1981). In a monograph produced by the staff, Ana Cienfuegos stated: "In order to understand the tremendous significance the crushing of a life project has on an individual . . . it is necessary to concentrate on the relationship between emotions and feelings, and political commitment" (Cienfuegos & Monelli, 1983). The therapeutic use of testimony is based on a psychoanalytic model of communication, internalization, and catharsis. Testimony is usually elicited during a series of sessions under the supervision of a therapist, during which everything related to the trauma is recorded and later transcribed into a written document. The patient's previous history "both social and ideological" is also a vital part of this exercise.

Philosophically, the FASIC staff view mental health as a "resource for social and political transformation" (Cienfuegos & Monelli, 1983). They divide their work into three "tasks": the therapeutic task, the preventive-educational task, and the task of denunciation, study, and publication (FASIC, 1981). In light of changing conditions in Uruguay and the recent elections in Chile, practitioners such as Dr. Elizabeth Lira of the Latin American Institute of Mental Health and Human Rights recognize the additional task of preparing the community for the work of reparation in a global and social sense.

The Indo-Chinese Psychiatry Clinic

The Indo-Chinese Psychiatry Clinic (ICPC) in Boston views itself as a grass-roots motivated organization with strong input from refugees, especially Cambodians. Clients come from cultures that view Western mental health treatment as a method of last resort, and consequently they tend to have severe problems by the time they seek intervention. The Clinic is located in a primary care setting. Clients are given a medical examination, mental status examination, social history, and assessment of social welfare status. ICPC has developed three Indo-Chinese versions of the Hopkins Symptom Checklist-25. Importance is placed on issues such as a client's self-esteem and social position, and the "margination" of clients within their own communities as well as in the larger population. Richard Mollica, the Clinical Director of ICPC, stresses the need for service providers to be knowledgeable in the areas of major affective disorders, organic brain syndromes, schizophrenia, and PTSD (Mollica, 1988).

The categorization of PTSD in the DSM-III-R was an attempt to organize and classify the constellations of symptoms noted in survivors of events that are "outside the range of usual human experience." This can include stresses such as

serious threat to one's life or physical integrity; serious threat or harm to one's children, spouse or other close relatives and friends; sudden destruction of one's home or community; or seeing another person who has recently been or is being seriously injured or killed as the result of an accident or physical violence. (American Psychiatric Association, 1987, pp. 247-248)

This constellation of symptoms, including a reexperiencing of the traumatic event, numbing of responsiveness to the physical and social environment, and increased arousal, has been found in survivors of military combat, natural disasters, sexual assault, and other human-made and natural calamities. In a six-month outcome study of 52 Indo-Chinese patients Mollica and Lavelle (in press) found that half of these people met the DSM-III diagnostic criteria for PTSD. In comparison, 70% of the 58 clients at the Center for Victims of Torture who received complete psychological and psychiatric assessments during the Center's first two years of full operation received a diagnosis of PTSD. In addition, many of the symptoms noted by Eitinger (1971) and Allodi et al. (1985) suggest the common theme of both depression and PTSD in survivors of trauma and torture.

Although there are as many approaches to intervention with PTSD symptoms as there are to mental health treatment in general, biological approaches to symptom relief, such as the use of psychotropic drugs, are sometimes used in conjunction with long-term psychotherapy or support counseling (Butcher et al., 1988). The diagnosis of PTSD has also led to creating interesting and useful models that focus on how people might reenact the trauma on physical and intrapsychic levels (e.g., Ochberg, 1988; Van Der Kolk, 1984). However, both the lack of specificity and the overspecificity of PTSD as a diagnosis have been critized, particularly as it may be applied to torture victims (Lira et al., 1988).

This debate has also been directed to the concept of a "torture syndrome." Many practitioners believe that such a notion will medicalize the issue of torture or exclude from treatment those who do not exhibit a specific constellation of symptoms. In addition, the existence of such a syndrome can lead to a situation in which the trauma itself becomes removed from the social and political context in which it occurs. "Trauma always implies the breakdown of the structure of the self and its representations of reality. For this reason, the concept of trauma cannot be used as a synonym for severe distress and suffering" (Lira et al., 1988).

The Center for Victims of Torture

The Center for Victims of Torture in Minneapolis views building trust and the provision of objective and subjective feelings of safety and control as important ingredients in successful intervention. As with other forms of victimization, a safe environment is essential if trust is to be established with people whose boundaries have been so profoundly violated. Toward this end, the Center provides a variety of services to client survivors and family members, including medical, legal, psychotherapy, social work, support counseling, and advocacy. Services are typically provided on-site at the Center's out-patient facility, a small house near the University of Minnesota. The house is decorated with the artwork of many of the refugee communities, giving it an atmosphere of comfort and familiarity. Clients present treatment issues reflecting three distinct dynamics: (a) normal developmental issues, (b) psychological components of abuse and victimization, and (c) trauma associated with the long-term strategic destruction of the individual's physical, mental, and spiritual capacity. It is the addition of this third dynamic that makes torture victims unique among refugee populations or other victims of abuse.

The Center typically has clients from two different populations of survivors, populations distinguishable both by culture and experience. One group contains those people who have a fairly well-articulated set of political or religious values and have been outspoken about these values. Exercising their right to express these beliefs in the face of an oppressive regime has led to their arrest and subsequent torture. They clearly see themselves and are seen as victims of oppression, both needing and deserving of ameliorative health care. Because their experiences fit existing legal definitions of torture closely, other groups support and validate this experience as well as the person's right to service. Clients from South Africa or South America tend to fit this description, especially those who have been members of organized groups opposed to policies such as apartheid.

A second group of people come from areas in which torture and death occurred at such high frequencies as to be ethnocidal. This situation, reminiscent of the Holocaust in World War II, involves large numbers of people from areas such as Ethiopia and Southeast Asia. Some of these cultures do not have a specific word for torture with which to label and identify their experiences. This fact, as well as a karmic or fatalistic belief system also characteristic of some of these cultures, often leads to a lack of community support and unwillingness (or inability) of individuals to define themselves as survivors in need of or deserving of treatment services. The community also tends to isolate rather than to support them or may also be suspicious of them. Salvadoreans, for example, who survive detention and torture are often ostracized by their communities because of the fear that they have been turned into informants.

The therapeutic model used at the Center combines elements of cognitive re-structuring, which has also been employed by Genefke in Denmark and Danieli with Holocaust survivors; behavioral techniques such as pain management and discrimination; and the treatment model of PTSD developed by Horowitz (1976). In addition, approximately 30% of clients receive antidepressant medication. Regardless of the particular theoretical orientation, the staff of the Center works strategically, and applies certain common elements in their work. Of primary importance are the assessment procedures. Presently, the Center uses assessment procedures based on multiple input from team members. This includes a formal medical and psychiatric examination, and a six-page intake interview that assesses symptoms, pre- and posttrauma stressors (i.e., migration stressors), family history of mental illness and chemical dependency, significant medical history, and current problems the client is facing in the area of adjustment and functioning. The client is also assessed by objective measures including the Minnesota Multiphasic Personality Inventory (MMPI), a Mini-Mental Status Exam, the SCL-90, the Beck Depression Inventory, an Impact of Life Events Scale, and the Global Assessment Functioning Scale.

The individual clinician will assess the client's developmental stage, pre-trauma personality (as far as is possible), presenting issues, client expectations, and therapeutic goals. In addition, a neuropsychology test battery is given when indicated. When the assessment is complete, the clinical team meets to staff the potential client and to formulate a treatment plan. This plan includes referral if the client is not appropriate for the Center's services, a brief psychotherapy model, or a longer term, more intensive model that will address issues such as affect, dissociation, violation and intrusion, loss, guilt, and interpersonal relationships. Treatment at the Center involves the whole person. In addition, everything is considered part of the therapeutic process, from the way in which the first call is handled until the follow-up process is completed.

CONCLUSION

The provision of meaningful and effective intervention with survivors of torture and their families will be a mosaic shaped by the culture, history, and background experience of the client and the service provider. The center in Denmark received the first exiles from the Greek junta of 1967–1974 and, later, many people from South America and the Middle East; the center in Paris sees many refugees and political asylees from former French colonies such as French Guinea. Toronto has a large Central and South American population, which is reflected in the client profile of the Canadian centers, and the center in Minnesota sees numbers of Central Americans, Ethiopians, South Africans, and Southeast Asians. Willingness of people to seek medical and mental health services and conditions under which people from various cultures and subcultures request these services will to a large extent determine the type of care that is both provided and accepted.

Conclusions will ultimately be reflected in daily living. The mirror image of the mediocrity of evil is the ability to triumph in the mundane aspects of ordinary life—to laugh at a joke, to write a grocery list, to enjoy a quiet evening at home—in short, to feel oneself a piece of the fabric of humankind. A young man from Ethiopia considered seriously for several months the important and frightening step of treatment at the center. Imprisoned for almost nine years at the age of 16, he arrived in Minneapolis to the intense and almost smothering emotional greetings of his aunt and sister. This long dreamed-of reunion produced no euphoria, gladness, or feeling of any kind in his heart. Finally, during a holiday celebration, the young man found in himself numb in the midst of joy and laughter. The funeral of a childhood friend several weeks later produced no sorrow, no tears. During a recent therapy session, this same person spoke about a recent visit from his father who now lives in the Middle East. "I felt so very sad to see him go," he said, "and so very happy that he could be here."

In William Faulkner's beautiful story, "Delta Autumn," the question is asked, "Have you lived so long and forgotten so much that you don't remember anything you ever knew or felt or even heard about love?" (1942). Ultimately, the process of healing, whether it be on the part of the client, the family, community, or civilization, is a work dedicated to the necessity of remembering.

REFERENCES

Allodi, F. (1982). Psychiatric sequelae of torture and implications for treatment. *World Medical Journal*, pp. 29, 71, 74, 75.

Allodi, F., & Cowgill, G. (1982). Ethical and psychiatric aspects of torture: A Canadian study. *Canadian Journal of Psychiatry, 27*, 98–102.

Allodi, F., Randall, G., Lutz, E. L., Quiroga, J., Zunzunegui, M. V., Kolff, C. A., Deutsch, A., & Doan, R. (1985). Physical and psychiatric effects of torture: Two medical studies. In E. Stover & E. O. Nightingale (Eds.), *The breaking of minds and bodies: Torture, psychiatric abuse, and the health professions* (pp. 58–78). New York: Freeman.

American Psychiatric Association. *Diagnostic and statistical manual of mental disorders* (3rd ed. rev.). Washington, DC: Author.

Amnesty International. (1984). *Torture in the eighties*. New York: Author.

Amnesty International Danish Medical Group. (1980). Seminar on sequelae and rehabilitation of concentration camp victims, sailors from the Second World War, hostages and torture victims. Copenhagen, Denmark 1979. *Danish Medical Bulletin, 27*, 213–250.

Amnesty International. (1985, December). *Amnesty International and the Provision of Health Care to Victims of Torture: A discussion paper* (AI index Pol 03/04/87). Distr: CS/PG.

Association pour les Victimes de la Repression en Exile (AVRE). (1986). *Rapport de la mission de l'AVRE en Republique de Guinee Janvier–Novembre 1985*. Paris: Author.

Bonaparte, L. (1986, June). Sanctuary in Exile. In J. Corbett (Ed.), *Borders and crossings, some sanctuary papers 1981–1986* (Vol. 1, pp. 105–109). Trsg 739. Tucson AZ.

Butcher, J., Egli, E. A., et al. (1988, March 22). *Psychological interventions with refugees* (Report No. NIMH #278-85-0024 "CH"). Washington, DC: National Institute of Mental Health.

Cienfuegos, A. J., & Monelli, C. (1983). The testimony of political repression as a therapeutic instrument. *American Journal of Orthopsychiatry, 53*, 43–51.

Committee on Foreign Affairs and Subcommittee on Human Rights and International Organizations. (1984). *The Phenomenon of Torture*. (Report of the U.S. House of Representatives, 98th Congress, Second Session on H. J. Resolution 605, May 15, 16 and September 1984). Washington, DC: U.S. Government Printing Office.

Eitinger, L. (1971). Organic and psychosomatic after effects of concentration camp imprisonment. *International Journal of Psychiatric Clinics, 8*, 205–215.

FASIC. (1981, June). *Our work: A proposal in social psychology*. Santiago, Chile.

Faulkner, W. (1942). *Go down Moses and other stories*. New York: Random House.

Filartiga v. Pena-Irala, 630 F.2d 876 (2d Cir. 1980).

Genefke, I. K., & Aalund, O. (1983). Rehabilitation of torture victims: Perspectives for research. *Manedsskrift fur Praktisk Laegegerning, 61*, 31–38.

Horowitz, M. J. (1976). *Stress response syndromes*. Northvale, NJ: Aronson.

Levi, P. (1988). *The drowned and the saved* (R. Rosenthal, Trans.). New York: Simon & Schuster. (Original work published 1986)

Liwski, N. (1983). *Torture and threats*. Roundtable discussion. Montevideo, Uruguay.

Lira, E., Becker, D., & Castillo, M. I. (1988). *Psychotherapy with victims of political repression in*

Chile: A therapeutic and political challenge. Paper presented at the meeting of the Latin American Institute of Mental Health and Human Rights, Santiago, Chile.

Lopez, J. (1988, January 16). *Therapeutic assistance to survivors of torture in the Philippines*. Paper presented at the meeting of the American Association for the Advancement of Science, San Francisco, CA.

Marcellino, A. B. (1986, June). *Summary of a situational study and analysis on children caught in the political-armed conflict in the Philippines conducted by the Children's Rehabilitation Center last June, 1986*.

Marcussen, H., Rasmussen, O., & Pedersen, E. K. (1983). Medical work within the framework of Amnesty International. *Manedsskrift fur Praktisk Laegegerning, 61*(2), 77–89.

Minnesota Lawyers International Human Rights Committee. (1986). *The Minnesota Protocol: Preventing arbitrary killing through adequate death investigation and autopsy*. Minneapolis: Author.

Mollica, R. F. (1988). The trauma story: The psychiatric care of refugee survivors of violence and torture. In F. M. Ochberg (Ed.), *Post-traumatic therapy and victims of violence*. New York: Brunner/Mazel.

Mollica, R. F., & Lavelle, J. (in press). The trauma of mass violence and torture: An overview of the psychiatric care of the Southeast Asian refugee. In L. Comas-Diaz & E. E. H. Griffith (Eds.), *Clinical practice in cross-cultural mental health*. New York: Wiley.

Ochberg, F. M. (Ed.). (1988). *Post-traumatic therapy and victims of violence*. New York: Brunner/Mazel.

Petersen, H. D., Abilgaard, U., Daugaard, G., Jess, P., Marcussen, H., & Wallach, M. (1985). Psychological and physical long-term effects of torture: A follow-up examination of 22 Greek persons exposed to torture 1967–1974. *Scandinavian Journal of Social Medicine, 13*, 89–93.

Scarry, E. (1985). *The body in pain*. Oxford, England: Oxford University Press.

Stelmachers, Z. T. (1987). *Some reflections on the assessment and treatment of psychological reactions to victimization*. Manuscript submitted for publication.

Stover, E. (1987, July). *The open secret: Torture and the medical profession in Chile*. Washington, DC: American Association for the Advancement of Science.

Timerman, J. (1987, November 2). Reflections: Life under the dictator. *The New Yorker*, pp. 47–135.

United Nations General Assembly. (1984, December 10). *Convention against torture and other cruel, inhuman, or degrading treatment or punishment*. New York: United Nations.

Van Der Kolk, B. A. (1984). *Post-traumatic stress disorder: Psychological and biological sequelae*. Washington, DC: American Psychiatric Press.

World Council of Churches. (1986, October 28–November 2). *Report on the delegation to Chile*.

World Medical Association. (1985). *Declaration of Tokyo*.

APPENDIX: SERVICES FOR VICTIMS OF TORTURE

The following represents a partial list of services available to torture victims. For further information, contact these groups or any local chapter of Amnesty International.

Argentina:
 Centro de Estudios Legales y Sociales
 Rodriguez Pena 286
 1 piso
 1020 Buenos Aires
 Argentina
 Contact: Laura Conte, Ph.D.

Australia:
Service for the Treatment and Rehabilitation of Torture
and Trauma Survivors
69 Harris Street
Fairfield NSW 2165
Australia
Contact: Margaret Cunningham

Belgium:
Colectivo Latinoamericano de Trabajo Psicosocial (COLAT)
Rue du Gouvernement Provisoire 32
100 Bruxelles
Belgium

Chile:
Fundacion de Ayuda Social de las Iglesias Christiana (FASIC)
Manuel Montt 25011
Santiago, Chile

Canada:
Canadian Center for Victims of Torture
10 Major Street
M532L1
Toronto, Canada M5T 1S4
Contact: F. A. Allodi, M.D.

Survivors International, Inc.
Two Bloor Street West
Suite 100
Toronto, Canada M4W 3E2
Contact: Genevieve Cowgill, Ph.D.

Vancouver Association for Survivors of Torture
1599 West 71st Avenue, #307
Vancouver, B. C. V6P 3C3
Canada
Contact: Yaya DeAndrade

Denmark:
Center for Psycho-social Assistance for Refugees (CEPAS)
Stro damvej 28, 2nd fl.
DK-2100 Copenhagen
Denmark

International Rehabilitation and Research Centre for Torture Victims
Juliane Maries Vej 26
DK-2100 Copenhagen 0
Contact: Inge Kemp Genefke, M.D.

France:
Association pour les Victimes de la Repression en Exile (AVRE)
Fondation de France
125, rue d'Avron
75020 Paris
France
Contact: Helene Jaffe, M.D.

Comite Medical pour les Exiles (COMEDE)
78 Rue du General Leclerc
94270 Kremlin–Bicetre
France

West Germany:
Caritas-Asylberatung Koln e.V.
Psychosoziales Zentrum für ausl. Fluchtlinge
Norbertstr. 27
D-5000 Koln 1
Federal Republic of Germany
Contact: Dr. Brigitte Brand

Psychosoziale Hilfen für Politisch Verfolgte e.V.
Postfach 12 74 73
D-1000 Berlin 12
Federal Republic of Germany
Contact: Dr. Carolyn Landry

Norway:
Psychosocial Team for Refugees in Norway
University of Oslo Department of Psychiatry
Blindernvei 85 (2nd Floor)
P.O. Box 85, Vinderen
0319 Oslo 3
Norway
Contact: Dr. Edvard Hauff

The Netherlands:
   Regional Institute for Out-Patient Mental Health Care in the
   Netherlands
   Social Psychiatric Service for Latin-American Refugees
   Keizersgracht 477
   1017 DL Amsterdam
   The Netherlands

Philippines:
   Children's Rehabilitation Center
   5-B Escaler Street
   Loyola Heights
   Quezon City
   Philippines
   Contact: Elizabeth P. Marcelino, M.D.

   Philippine Action Concerning Torture (PACT)
   Medical Action Group, Inc.
   1344 Taft Avenue
   Room 707
   Ermita–Manila
   The Philippines
   Contact: June Lopez, M.D.

Pakistan:
   Psychiatry Center for Afghans
   Shaneen Town
   University Road
   P.O. Box 1131 G.P.O.
   Peshawar
   Pakistan
   Contact: M. Azam Dadfar, M.D.

South Africa:
   National Medical and Dental Association of South Africa
   P.O. Box 17160
   Congella 4013
   South Africa

Sweden:
   The Red Cross Rehabilitation Center for Tortured Refugees
   Brinellvagen 2
   114 28 Stockholm
   Sweden

United Kingdom:
  Medical Foundation for the Care of Victims of Torture
  2nd Floor, Insull Wing
  National Temperance Hospital
  110-114 Hampstead Road
  London NW1 2LT
  United Kingdom
  Contact: Helen Bamber

United States:
  Center for Rehabilitation of Torture Victims
  268 Dr. Martin Luther King Jr. Blvd.
  Saint Michael's Medical Center
  Newark, NJ 07102
  Contact: Randall Krakaver, M.D.

  Center for Victims of Torture
  722 Fulton Street SE
  Minneaplis, MN 55414
  Contact: Douglas Johnson, Executive Director
  Barbara Chester, Ph.D., Clinical Director

  The Group Project for Holocaust Survivors and Their Children
  345 East 80th Street #31J
  New York, NY 10021
  Contact: Yael Danieli, Ph.D.

  Indo-Chinese Psychiatry Clinic
  Department of Psychiatry
  Brighton Marine Public Health Center
  77 Warren Street
  Brighton, MA 02135
  Contact: Richard Mollica, M.D.

  The Marjorie Kovler Center for the Treatment of Torture Victims
  4750 N. Sheridan, Suite 300
  Chicago, IL 60640
  Contact: Antonio Martinez, Ph.D.

  Program for the Rehabilitation of Victims of Torture
  604 Rose Avenue
  Venice, CA 90291
  Contact: Ana Deustch, Ph.D.
           Jose Quiroga, M.D.

  Survivors International of Northern California
  P. O. Box 6313
  Albany, CA 94706
  Contact: Gerald Grey, MSW

12

Psychology's Role in the Campaign to Abolish Torture: Can Individuals and Organizations Make a Difference?

Stephen V. Faraone

Torture is an international phenomenon not unique to any political system or at any point in history. Despite the existence of a growing body of international law forbidding it, systematic state-inflicted cruelty has been documented in more than 60 countries around the globe. Torture is defined in the United Nations Declaration Against Torture as

> *any act by which severe pain or suffering, whether physical or mental, is intentionally inflicted by or at the instigation of a public official or a person for such purposes as obtaining from him or a third person information or confession, punishing him for an act he has committed, or intimidating him or other persons. (Amnesty International, 1984b, p. 13)*

Although it is clear that the abolition of torture is necessary for the establishment and maintenance of just and humane societies, the solution to the problem is certainly not straightforward. In this chapter I address one aspect of the solution by asking whether psychologists at the individual or organizational level can play a role in eradicating the current epidemic of torture. I pursue the answer to this question by examining the rationale for professional involvement, the development of relevant institutional infrastructures, and organizational activities in countries where torture is routinely practiced.

THE RATIONALE FOR PROFESSIONAL INVOLVEMENT

It has been argued that the abolition of torture is a political, not a professional issue. Human rights activitists have not infrequently heard the response "why should we get involved?" The justification for professional involvement has been succinctly stated by van Geuns:

> *If we accept the thesis that the systematic use of torture affects public mental health, then we have thus automatically established the responsibility of the medical profession to refuse to accept any form of torture. Quite apart from the question of direct involvement of individual doctors in torture practices, this constitutes a collective responsibility, which especially calls for*

professional organizations to assume this responsibility and give it adequate expression. (1984, p. 14)

These considerations can of course be extended to other health professionals and scientific organizations.

The epidemic of torture is especially relevant to the profession of psychology given the multiple role of psychological factors in this regrettable international phenomenon. Other chapters in this volume clearly indicate that psychological knowledge can facilitate a more comprehensive understanding of various stages of the torture enterprise. Staub (chapter 4) has described the social psychological preconditions that lead societies to use torture and allow individuals to become torturers. His work assets that the use of torture results in a maladaptive course of societal evolution. In addition to providing a succinct and powerful argument against the utilitarian defense of torture, Staub's work may lead to the ability to identify psychological preconditions, and milestones along the path, to torture. This raises the hope that early identification of torture prone nations may be possible, thereby facilitating the prevention of torture. Such an approach is consistent with current attempts to eliminate legal and administrative preconditions to torture such as incommunicado detention, the existence of secret detention centers, and the lack of specific safeguards during interrogation and custody (Amnesty International, 1984a).

Melamed, Melamed, and Bouhoutsos (chapter 2, this volume) have noted the increasing use of psychological forms of torture. The techniques currently in use have not been based on methods, theories, or empirical results from the psychological literature; nor have they required special psychological training for their implementation (Suedfeld, chapter 7, this volume). Nevertheless, the potential for the systematic abuse of psychological knowledge is a serious issue that must be carefully monitored by organized psychology. Consider, for example, the systematic psychological torture that had been implemented in the Libertad Prison of Uruguay (Amnesty International, 1981, 1983; Breslin, Goldstein, & Kennedy, 1984). Although this was not the work of a recognized psychologist, it provides an instructive example of the systematic manipulation of psychological factors in the service of a repressive regime.

At Libertad prison, four specific techniques have been identified by independent observers from a variety of organizations (e.g., Amnesty International, the Red Cross, the National Academy of Sciences, and the American Psychological Association). These include the disruption of human relationships, the constant fear of torture, the creation of a constantly changing and unpredictable environment, and the inadequate treatment of the mentally ill. Human relationships were disrupted by censoring mail, not allowing prisoners to smile or glance at one another, and constantly changing cellmates. Conversations with visitors were taped, allowing authorities to use personal information (e.g., the death of a loved one) to tailor the times and means of interrogations to the prisoner's psychological state. The fear of torture was underscored by using known torturers as prison guards. The unpredictability in the prison was magnified by the almost daily changing of prison rules without notification of the changes, the use of senseless rules (e.g., one day prisoners are required to clean cell bars, the next day they are not), and violent, destructive searches of cells for no apparent reason. The inadequate treatment of the mentally ill included excessive use of neuroleptic medication for behavioral control and the withholding of needed treatment.

Psychological knowledge can play a positive role in the areas of diagnosis and treatment. As chapter 2 indicates, there is no torture without scars. Although it is possible to torture without leaving physical scars, the psychological sequelae of the torture experience are enduring. Therefore, in many cases, accounts of torture can be psychologically verified years after the torture occurred. From a forensic perspective, this should facilitate the prosecution of torturers. More psychological research is needed to provide a clearer understanding of posttraumatic stress disorder (PTSD) and other syndromes (e.g., major depression) that afflict survivors of torture. The treatment of torture survivors is an area in which psychological factors have already played a major role. Because psychological disability is perhaps the most common and enduring sequela of torture (Goldfeld, Mollica, Pesavento, & Faraone, 1988), psychological treatment has been prominent in the growing literature on the rehabilitation of torture survivors (e.g., Mollica & Lavelle, in press). More research is needed to (a) isolate therapy components that may be especially useful with this population, (b) develop methods that may be particularly useful within countries where torture is practiced, and (c) integrate available psychological research about the treatment of PTSD into the treatment of the torture survivor.

In summary, the rationale for the organizational involvement of psychology in the campaign to abolish torture is unassailable. Psychologists have a special concern for the abolition of torture. As human beings we are shocked and dismayed at the seemingly chronic brutality of the human race. As health professionals, we abhor the complicity of other health professionals in the process of torture, such as the use of physicians to certify prisoners as fit for torture. As scientists we are concerned about the potential misuse of some scientific principles to develop a technology of psychological torture and hope that the use of others will facilitate the campaign to abolish torture and improve the diagnosis and treatment of torture survivors.

The necessity for professional involvement was poignantly argued for by Anatoly Koryagin, MD, who had been incarcerated in a labor camp because of his active opposition to the political use of psychiatry in the Soviet Union (Faraone, 1982). In an open letter to the world psychiatric community smuggled from his cell in a Soviet labor camp he wrote:

> Our professional duty demands of us that we care for others. I appeal to you, my colleagues, not for a moment to forget those who have stood up for the rights and freedoms which people need, and now are condemned to spend years in the nightmarish (for a healthy person) world of psychiatric wards, exhausting themselves in a debilitating struggle to preserve their psyches, a struggle against torturers armed with drugs. To remember them and to do every thing possible for their release is our obligation. Their fate is a reproach to our conscience, a challenge to our honour, a test of our commitment to compassion. We must brand, brand with shame, those who out of self-interest or anti-humanitarian motives trample on the ideals of justice and on the doctor's sacred oath. (Koryagin, 1981, p. 3)

Koryagin was subsequently released from prison and allowed to emigrate after an international outcry on his behalf by health professional and scientific organizations, including the American Psychological Association.

DEVELOPING AN INFRASTRUCTURE

The most basic element of an organization's commitment to addressing national and international human rights problems is the presence of a palpable infrastructure that expresses the organization's position and provides resources toward their resolution. Most organizations express their basic values through a code of ethics. For example, the opening statement of the American Psychological Association's (1981) *Ethical Principles of Psychologists* states: "Psychologists respect the dignity and worth of the individual and strive for the preservation and protection of fundamental human rights" (p. 1). The code goes on to state that psychologists use their skills and knowledge only "for the promotion of human welfare." They have a responsibility "to attempt to prevent distortion, misuse or suppression of psychological findings" and to "avoid any action that will violate or diminish the legal and civil rights of clients or of others who may be affected by their actions" (p. 1). Thus, the ethical codes of American psychologists, like those of other professional organizations, clearly forbid the involvement of members in the practice or facilitation of torture. This position was stated more explicitly in the Joint Resolution Against Torture of the American Psychological Association and the American Psychiatric Association (see Preface, Table 1) approved by the American Psychological Association's Council of Representatives in February 1986. The resolution "condemn[s] torture wherever it occurs," and supports the United Nations' *Principles of Medical Ethics* (1982) and *Convention Against Torture* (1984). A similar resolution had been approved by the International Union of Psychological Science a decade earlier.

The transition of human rights related ethical codes from a generalized expression of values to explicit statements regarding the role of professionals in human rights situations is a welcome phenomenon. The endorsement of specific United Nations documents provides a means of placing organizational commitment in an international context. An examination of the *Principles of Medical Ethics* is instructive. It speaks directly to the issue of protecting prisoners and detainees against torture and ill treatment. This document, adopted in 1982, emphasizes six basic principles:

1. Health care standards should not differ for prisoners and nonprisoners.
2. Health professionals should not actively or passively facilitate torture or ill treatment.
3. Activities of health professionals with prisoners are limited to the evaluation, protection, or improvement of health.
4. Certification for, or involvement in, interrogation or punishment that may have adverse health consequences is forbidden.
5. It is forbidden to participate in the physical restraint of prisoners unless necessary for the protection of the prisoner or others.
6. There may be no grounds for violating the above principles, including public emergency.

These principles are unequivocal in requiring health care personnel to maintain a professional relationship with prisoners or detainees that is unaffected by the political or criminal reasons for their incarceration. That is, the health professionals' goal is to maximize the health of prisoners, not to pursue the goals of administrators, politicians, police, or military personnel. These principles clearly forbid even the most remote involvement in the torture process. Principle 4 specifically takes an unambiguous stand on the role of health care personnel in the evaluation of tortured individuals. Medical personnel in countries where torture is routinely practiced have been asked by authorities to determine whether the prisoners are physically fit enough to withstand torture and to determine whether a tortured individual is too close to death for torture to continue. Although some might have construed these activities as consistent with a commitment to preserve the prisoner's health, such activities only serve to further institutionalize the torture process.

In discussing codes of ethics, one must heed the admonishment of McEwan (1974) "that there is more talk and less effect about medical ethics . . . than any other subject excepting war itself" (p. 307). This point has been appreciated by Heijter (1984), who suggested three criteria for judging the potential effectiveness of a code of ethics. First, the code should be more than a declaration of good intentions; it should clearly establish detailed norms of conduct. Second, the code should provide mechanisms for implementation and enforcement. Finally, information about the code, reports of infractions, and efforts at enforcement should be available to the public. Implicit in these suggestions is the requirement that professional organizations provide adequate resources for the implementation and enforcement of codes of ethics. One tangible demonstration of resource commitment is the presence, within an organization, of an administrative department or committee the function of which is fully, or in part, to deal with international human rights issues. A partial list of professional organizations that provide resources committed to human rights activities follows.

- American Association for the Advancement of Science
- American Mathematical Society
- American Psychiatric Association
- American Psychological Association
- American Physical Society
- American Public Health Association
- American Statistical Association
- Association for Computing Machinery
- National Academy of Sciences
- Society for Industrial and Applied Mathematics

The American Psychological Association has demonstrated its commitment to human rights issues by forming the Joint Subcommittee on Human Rights consisting of members from the Committee on International Relations in Psychology and the Board of Social and Ethical Responsibility for Psychology. The statement by the American Psychological Association's Joint Subcommittee on Human Rights (1984) clearly indicates that American psychology has a role in working toward the elimination of human rights abuses relevant to psychology (i.e., the systematic abuse of psychological knowledge, abuses by individual psychologists, and abuses against psychologists) in other countries. The Joint Subcommittee also recommended specific actions to aid implementation and enforcement. These actions range from information gathering and sending letters of concern to instituting legal action in international forums and making site visits to countries of abuse.

An excellent example of organizational effectiveness is the Clearinghouse on Science and Human Rights of the American Association for the Advancement of Science (AAAS). The Clearinghouse is mandated by the AAAS's Committee on Scientific Freedom and Responsibility to respond to alleged human rights violations or restrictions on international scientific communication involving scientists, engineers, and students in other countries. The Clearinghouse has been involved in many human rights related activities including the following:

- the validation of reports about individual cases of alleged human rights violations,
- the dissemination of information about substantiated cases to other organizations to coordinate efforts on the behalf of prisoners,
- the formulation of statements of concern or recommendations for use by AAAS officials,
- the publication of reports (e.g., Stover, 1987; Stover & Nightingale, 1985) to educate the scientific community,
- the organization of workshops and symposia on scientific human rights issues,
- the preparation of testimony for the U.S. Congress and international human rights groups, and
- the organization of missions to countries where human rights violations are occurring.

ACTIVITIES OF ORGANIZATIONS IN COUNTRIES WHERE ABUSE EXISTS

When an organization must deal with human rights abuses in its own country, the rationale for involvement is strengthened but actions to be taken become more dangerous. Thus, colleagues in countries where abuse exists need external support, and organizations in other countries need to be prepared for the potential emergence of human rights violations in their own countries. The development of a relevant institutional infrastructure provides one means of preparation. Another is to learn from (and be inspired by) the activities of our less fortunate colleagues who must deal with extensive human rights violations in their own countries.

An instructive example from Chile is the role of physicians as facilitators of torture and the response of the Chilean Medical Association (CMA). Details are provided in *The Open Secret: Torture and the Medical Profession in Chile* (Stover, 1987), which documents the development of human rights violations in Chile under the Pinochet regime, the participation of physicians in government-sponsored torture, and the efforts of the CMA to bring these activities to an end. Since 1973, human rights organizations had suspected, and subsequently validated, the involvement of physicians in Chilean state torture. Substantiated areas of involvement include (a) the performance of medical examinations before and during torture to certify prisoners as fit for continued torture, (b) attendance during torture sessions in order to intervene if the victim's life is at risk, (c) the administration of nontherapeutic drugs or hypnotic induction, and (d) the preparation of false certificates of good health before victims leave torture centers.

Between 1973 and 1982, professional Chilean organizations were not allowed to democratically elect their leadership. In 1982, when new CMA leaders were elected democratically, allegations of physicians' complicity in torture were investigated. Concrete actions taken by the CMA include suspension or expulsion of members for their involvement in torture, testimony before the U.S. Congress to provide evidence for state-sponsored torture in Chile, and the education of physicians and the public about the CMA's knowledge of, and opposition to, torture in Chile. The CMA also provides financial and legal assistance to the families of physicians imprisoned for their political or human rights activities.

In their 1986 report, *The Participation of Physicians in Torture* (cited in Stover, 1987), the CMA is unequivocal about the ethics of even the most remote involvement in torture:

> *It is our opinion that the work of a physician and that of a torturer or an accomplice are incompatible. The Department of Ethics believes this so strongly that proof of the mere presence of a physician in a place of torture is sufficient grounds for his expulsion from the association.* (p. 67)

Justifying involvement in torture as being necessary to comply with legal requirements or orders from superiors in the armed forces is considered unacceptable by the CMA because "from a moral point of view responsibility is not transferable, but always personal" (p. 69). For those of us who live in the nonrepressive societies where torture does not exist, it is notable that the CMA opens their report with the following: "We never thought that we would be writing about this subject. This shows us once again how life exceeds the imagination" (p. 65).

CONCLUSION

Professionals and their organizations can be actively involved in human rights issues, but are they effective? Will codes of ethics, organizational infrastructures, and the other modes of involvement discussed in this chapter lead to the prevention and abolition of torture? The experience of British physicians in Northern Ireland suggests the answer to be "yes." In 1976, the European Commission on Human Rights concluded that the British government had been responsible for the maltreatment of detainees in Northern Ireland. It is notable that the British excesses in Northern Ireland had been reported by the police physicians working with the prisoners. That is, the strong ethical code of the British physicians resulted not only in a passive refusal to participate but also in an active, and ultimately successful, attempt to eliminate systematic torture in Northern Ireland. Organizations in North America and Western Europe have successfully worked for the release of colleagues imprisoned by repressive regimes and have given their efforts international recognition and support. In some countries where human rights are systematically violated, professional associations are educating the public and taking concrete steps toward the restoration of these rights and the punishment of colleagues who aggravate the situation. Professional responses to international human rights issues are not only possible, they are effective.

International human rights organizations have developed a sophisticated network of individuals and organizations that provide valid and timely data about human rights violations. Amnesty International, a worldwide movement independent of any government, political ideology, or religious belief, has developed a 12-point program for the prevention and abolition of torture (Amnesty International, 1984a, 1984b). The goal of the program is to encourage governments to implement safeguards that will effectively eliminate preconditions that facilitate or encourage torture. The existence of legislation giving security forces broad powers of arrest and detention places many citizens at risk for torture. The use of incommunicado detention and the suspension of habeas corpus protects the torturer and provides time for many of the physical sequelae of torture to disappear. Other preconditions are trial procedures that accept as evidence information extracted under torture, governmental refusals to investigate allegations of torture, the censorship of information about torture, and the immunity from prosecution given to alleged torturers. The removal of administrative and legal preconditions to torture provides a solid foundation for those trying to build a world without such abuses.

The work of Amnesty International provides several effective avenues of involvement for psychologists concerned about torture and the systematic violation of civil and political rights. Those who wish to write letters or send telegrams on behalf of individuals at imminent risk for being tortured can join the Urgent Action Network. Involvement can be increased by joining an Amnesty International Health Professional Group (HPG). These groups include a variety of individuals ranging from clinical practitioners to basic research scientists. Members receive information about torture and are involved in letter writing actions relevant to health professionals such as supporting foreign colleagues who work to oppose torture in their countries. The HPGs also encourage members to educate their colleagues by giving or sponsoring talks, writing articles or letters for professional publications, placing information about the campaign to abolish torture in professional newsletters, and increasing the awareness of other health professionals about the specific needs of torture victims. This latter education is especially needed for clinicians working with refugee populations.

Psychologists involved in certain areas of research can stimulate the development and dissemination of torture-related research. Behavioral scientists examining the effects of stress can work toward an understanding of the long-term stress response syndrome that would enable investigators to document the psychological sequelae of torture more precisely. Clinical researchers can work toward improved treatment of PTSD, a common disability of torture survivors. Researchers in social, personality, and clinical psychology can continue their investigations into human aggression, brainwashing, and obedience to authority. This should deepen our understanding of the psychological development of torturers and lead to the formulation of guidelines that will limit the existence of situations that allow humans to become torturers.

REFERENCES

American Psychological Association. (1981). *Ethical principles of psychologists*. Washington, DC: Author.

American Psychological Association, Joint Subcommittee on Human Rights. (1984). Statement by the Joint Subcommittee on Human Rights. *American Psychologist, 39*(6), 676–678.

Amnesty International. (1981). *Libertad Prison, Uruguay: A report by a recently released prisoner of conscience*. (Index #52/40/81). London: Author.

Amnesty International. (1983). *Mental health aspects of political imprisonment in Uruguay*. (Index #52/40/81). London: Author.

Amnesty International. (1984a). *Against torture*. London: Author.

Amnesty International. (1984b). *Torture in the eighties*. London: Author.

Breslin, P., Goldstein, R., & Kennedy, D. (1984). *Report on a mission to Uruguay*. New York: New York Academy of Science.

Faraone, S. V. (1982). Psychiatry and political repression in the Soviet Union. *American Psychologist, 37*, 1105-1112.

Goldfeld, A. Mollica, R. F., Pesavento, B., & Faraone, S. V. (1988). The physical and psychological sequelae of torture: Symptomatology and diagnosis. *Journal of the American Medical Association, 259*, 2725-2729.

Heijter, D. (1984). Codes of professional ethics against torture. In Amnesty International (Ed.), *Codes of professional ethics* (pp. 3-11). New York: Amnesty International.

Koryagin, A. (1981). Open letter to world psychiatrists. *International Association on Political Use of Psychiatry Information Bulletin, 2*, 1-3.

McEwan, P. J. M. (1974). The role of scientists in the protection of human rights. In World Health Organization (Ed.), *Protection of human rights in the light of scientific and technological progress in biology and medicine* (pp. 307-319). Geneva: World Health Organization.

Mollica, R. F., & Lavelle, J. (in press). The trauma of mass violence and torture: An overview of the psychiatric care of the Southeast Asian refugee. In L. Comas-Diaz & E. E. H. Griffith (Eds.), *Clinical practice in cross-cultural mental health*. New York: Wiley.

Stover, E. (1987, July). *The open secret: Torture and the medical profession in Chile*. Washington, DC: American Association for the Advancement of Science.

Stover, E., & Nightingale, E. O. (1985). *The breaking of minds and bodies*. New York: Freeman.

United Nations General Assembly. (1984). *Convention against torture and other cruel, inhuman, or degrading treatment or punishment*. New York: United Nations.

United Nations General Assembly. (1982). *Principles of Medical Ethics*. New York: United Nations.

van Geuns, J. P. (1984). The responsibilities of the medical profession in connection with torture. In Amnesty International (Ed.), *Codes of professional ethics* (pp. 12-18). New York: Amnesty International.

Name Index

Subject Index